Cognitive Studies in Literature and Performance

Series Editors
Bruce McConachie
Department of Theatre Arts
University of Pittsburgh
Pittsburgh, PA, USA

Blakey Vermeule
Department of English
Stanford University
Stanford, CA, USA

This series offers cognitive approaches to understanding perception, emotions, imagination, meaning-making, and the many other activities that constitute both the production and reception of literary texts and embodied performances.

Freya Vass

William Forsythe's Postdramatic Dance Theater

Unsettling Perception

palgrave
macmillan

Freya Vass
Drama and Theatre
University of Kent
Canterbury, UK

ISSN 2945-7297 ISSN 2945-7300 (electronic)
Cognitive Studies in Literature and Performance
ISBN 978-3-031-26657-7 ISBN 978-3-031-26658-4 (eBook)
https://doi.org/10.1007/978-3-031-26658-4

This Palgrave Macmillan imprint is published by the registered company Springer Nature Switzerland AG.
The registered company address is: Gewerbestrasse 11, 6330 Cham, Switzerland

O! daß der Sinnen doch so viele sind!
Verwirrung bringen sie in's Glück herein.
Wenn ich dich sehe wünsch' ich taub zu seyn,
Wenn ich dich höre blind.
Johann Wolfgang von Goethe, *Book of Suleika,*
West-östlicher Divan, 1819

PREFACE

In March 2003, I somewhat timidly entered the ballet studio in Frankfurt's Städtische Bühne for an invited visit to the Ballett Frankfurt. William Forsythe greeted me with a warm hug and a cup of green tea, immediately asking me to introduce myself to the dancers. Feeling more than a bit put on the spot, I told them that I was researching for a PhD dissertation on the company's work, that my focus was on the intersection of dance and cognitive science, and that I was interested in the role of perception in the ensemble's choreographic practices and performance. "Oh, I don't know how much perceiving we're going to be doing in here," Forsythe chortled, I thought perhaps somewhat uncomfortably.

I was a bit uncomfortable myself, as it was not the first time I had been in that studio. As a company hopeful between 1988 and 1992, I had frequently visited Frankfurt to watch the company's performances, take class, and laugh and learn along with the dancers as I watched rehearsals, participating in the back of the studio if I dared. And I seldom did dare: the company's popularity was at a zenith, dancers from around the world were visiting like me, and I was afraid that I might be judged inadequate and discouraged from returning. Bill—I'll call him Bill for the time being—had learned of my back-story when I had participated in a weeklong interdisciplinary workshop at UCLA two years prior, and the invitation he had extended then to become the company's on-call at-large "research consultant" had led to this visit. But I was made welcome that day, and our discussion ranged from cross-lateral coordination to Stroop tests to linguistic syntax and across numerous other topics. When it was over, though, Bill gently told me that I would not be able to visit the studio over the next few days—the company was in the first week of developing a new work, and beginnings are always delicate moments—but I would be permitted to return as soon as possible. Banished to the video room, my discomfort returned.

Thankfully my exile was brief, I was able to return to watch the early stages of what would become *Decreation*, and my short visit was a productive one. I was invited to Frankfurt again in 2006, this time to watch the newly formed Forsythe Company develop a new work. Shortly after my arrival, Bill unexpectedly offered me a contract as dramaturg, and my planned three-month stay turned into seven years. During this time, I watched countless rehearsals and also took on the task of inputting process notes into the *Piecemaker* software in development by dancer David Kern—a sneaky way to take field notes while also letting them do double-duty as reference documentation for the ensemble. Taking on the added role of production assistant a short time later, I would participate in the development of a dozen new works, writing and updating the nightly script used to navigate performances and serving as Bill's *aide memoire*, note-taker, and clock-watcher during performances. Beyond this, I had access to an extensive video archive, toured with and gave public talks for the company, and had many discussions with current and past company members, composers, technicians, and other affiliates.

The dissertation I finished in 2011 gave visual perception rather limited consideration in favor of three arguments: for increased recognition of dance as a *visuosonic* art form, for greater attention to the way sensory apprehension of dance is both performed and performative, and for cognitive studies, understood as a broad plurality of approaches, as a productive means to undertake these analytic shifts. By expanding on the narrower sonic focus, which resonated with the then current "acoustic turn," this volume's inclusion of close visual analysis aligns it with more recent critical interest in scenography.

I explored the idea of expanding this volume to include other choreographers in a series of conference papers presented between 2015 and 2017. After presenting a paper in Hamburg that compared instances in Forsythe works with sometimes fleeting "noisy" physical and musical moments in works by George Balanchine, Merce Cunningham, Yvonne Rainer, Twyla Tharp, Karole Armitage, and Michael Clark, I ultimately chose to keep the volume focused on Forsythe. This is, however, not a book "about" Forsythe in the sense of tracing a history of the choreographer or his companies, or a narrow analysis of his choreographic aesthetics. Anecdotes like the one above are also few. Though I retain Forsythe's oeuvre and choreographic methods as a lens, I isolate scenographic and choreographic conditions that recur within the performance environments that Forsythe, together with his dancers, composers, and technicians, has composed over the past four and a half decades. In particular, I focus on conditions that unsettle the performance of perception by problematizing visual, aural, and intermodal sensing. I consider such conditions to be perceptual experiments, set up by the choreographer within the unique laboratory of post-dramatic performance-making and including not only audiences and performers but also Forsythe himself as research subjects.

The unsettling conditions considered here reflect those found in many other postdramatic dance and theatre works, as well as in works that pre-date this theatrical style. It is my hope that this will make the volume reso-nate with an audience beyond those interested in Forsythe and late twentieth-/early twenty-first-century dance.

Canterbury, UK   Freya Vass

Acknowledgments

My deepest gratitude and respect goes to William Forsythe, whose works, support, encouragement, and friendship have meant so much over the years. Thanks, Bill, for letting me step inside. Alex Scott of Forsythe Productions has also been instrumental and a wonderful friend, and further thanks are due to Rebecca Groves and Dorsey Bushnell.

So many members of the Ballett Frankfurt and Forsythe Company have offered their rich knowledge and support, and all have inspired with their courageous artistry. Special thanks to Antony Rizzi, Andrea Tallis, Nora Kimball, Ana Catalina Roman, Iris Tenge, Mayra Rodriguez de Matthews, Kathryn Bennetts, Laura Graham, Thierry Guiderdoni, Stephen Galloway, Kate Strong, Ayman Harper, Jodie Gates, Derrick Brown, Michael Schumacher, Georg Reischl, Jone San Martin, Yoko Ando, Ander Zabala, David Kern, Fabrice Mazliah, Amancio Gonzalez, Brigel Gjoka, Dana Caspersen, and Esther Balfe.

Tanja Rühl has fielded countless technical questions, as have Niels Lanz, Dietrich Krüger, David Morrow, and Thom Willems. Thank you all for sharing your art and craft with me. Special thanks to Dietrich and to Nicholas Champion for assistance with video archives, without which the scope of this project would not have been possible. Added and grateful thanks to Alex Scott and David Morrow, as well as to Dana Caspersen, David Kern, and William Forsythe for assistance with this volume's appendix, which has its roots in Gerald Siegmund's original curation.

I am grateful for the Forsythe scholarship of Steven Spier, Gerald Siegmund, Roslyn Sulcas, Prue Lang, Thomas McManus, Tony Rizzi,

Dana Caspersen, Nik Haffner, Chris Salter, Heidi Gilpin and Patricia Baudoin, Marinella Guatterini, Ann Nugent, Mark Franko, Christiane Berger, Sabine Huschka, Gabriele Brandstetter, and many others. Early discussions with Wolf Singer and Ivar Hagendoorn also informed my initial ideas.

Bruce McConachie has shown exemplary patience and support while I navigated the turbulent cross-currents of industry and academia—thanks so very much for waiting. Thanks also to the editorial staff at Palgrave Macmillan, and to the photographers who have delved through their archives for this volume's images: Julieta Cervantes, Foteini Christofilopoulou, Wilfried Hösl, and especially Dominik Mentzos.

I would like to express my gratitude to Taylor & Francis for granting me permission to elaborate on my previously published work in 'Dancing Music: The Intermodality of The Forsythe Company', in Steven Spier's edited volume *William Forsythe and the Practice of Choreography: It Starts From Any Point* (Routledge, 2011) and 'Auditory Turn: William Forsythe's Vocal Choreography' (*Dance Chronicle*, 2010).

Past and present colleagues at the University of Kent have offered support and encouragement. Thanks to Nicola Shaughnessy, Rosie Klich, Helen Brooks, Paul Allain, David Roesner, Oliver Double, Sophie Quirk, Margrethe Bruun Vaage, Murray Smith, and Ruth Herbert. Beyond Kent, I am grateful to Sally Ness for being a wonderful *Doktormutter*, to Gabriele Klein for her vote of confidence for a Forsythe-focused interdisciplinary monograph, to Rhonda Blair and Tamara Tomić-Vajagić for support and camaraderie, to Norah Zuniga Shaw, and especially to friend and inspiration Pil Hansen. Thanks also to the Dance Engaging Science community, especially Scott deLahunta, Bettina Bläsing, Maaike Bleeker, Emily Cross, James Leach, Kate Stevens, Guido Orgs, David Rittershaus, and Letizia Gioia Monda.

Lastly, endless thanks to my beloved sprout, who grew up with this book.

CONTENTS

LIST OF FIGURES

CHAPTER 1

Introduction

The first work I saw by William Forsythe—*Say Bye Bye*, performed in New York by the Nederlands Dans Theater in 1982—left me baffled. On a walled stage with a burning red horizon and an oversized, abstract cardboard car inching inexorably forward toward the audience, black-gloved men in trousers, shirts, and ties partnered women in little black dresses Apache-style, diving, flailing, and screaming to a collage of Little Richard, Elvis Presley, and Roberto Delgado's version of "The Peanut Vendor." It would be five years before I saw more of Forsythe's work, a mixed program including the now widely performed *In the Middle, Somewhat Elevated* and the shadowy *The Vile Parody of Address*, with dancers speaking almost inaudibly behind scrawled-on transparencies as they moved to faint tones of Bach's *The Well-Tempered Clavier*. Over the years that followed, I noted the continuing diversity of Forsythe's repertoire as he created chamber-length works like *Behind the China Dogs*, *Herman Schmerman, the second detail*, and *The Vertiginous Thrill of Exactitude*, which he would later refer to as "ballet ballets,"[1] but also highly theatrical works like *Slingerland, Limb's Theorem, The Loss of Small Detail*, and *Eidos:Telos*. In these full-length works, wide, deep proscenium stages were populated with moving set pieces and objects framed in darkness or swift shifts of often dappled lighting, while dancers moved and sometimes vocalized in counterpoint to soundscores that whispered or roared. After the transformation of the Ballett Frankfurt (1984–2004) into the smaller,

© The Author(s), under exclusive license to Springer Nature Switzerland AG 2023
F. Vass, *William Forsythe's Postdramatic Dance Theater*, Cognitive Studies in Literature and Performance,
https://doi.org/10.1007/978-3-031-26658-4_1

more autonomous Forsythe Company (2005–2015), Forsythe continued making both shorter and full-length works in non-proscenium venues like Frankfurt's Bockenheimer Depot and Dresden's Festspielhaus Hellerau. As Dramaturg and Production Assistant for the Forsythe Company ensemble from 2006 to 2013, I continually noted Forsythe's in-the-moment responsiveness to spaces, acoustics, venues, and chance events.

Over the nearly 50 years since Forsythe produced his first ballets for the Stuttgart Ballet, Nederlands Dans Theater, Joffrey Ballet, Ballet de l'Opéra de Paris, and the Frankfurt Ballet, where he became director in 1984, critics and scholars have largely highlighted his innovative choreographic engagement with (or as some view it, his deconstruction of) classical ballet. Comments on Forsythe's scenographies—his stagings, lighting, and sound-score choices—have been quite rare and often superficial. I find this an egregious oversight as, like many choreographers of the past century, Forsythe has been more than simply a stepsmith. "Choreography is about organizing bodies in space," he has said, "or you're organizing bodies with other bodies, or a body with other bodies in an environment that is organized."[2] In accord with his extension of the definition of choreography to include the composition of both movement and the performance environment, this volume offers Forsythe a promotion from choreographer to *choreo-scenographer*. In doing so, it recognizes the linkages between movement aesthetics and *mises-en-scène*. Like theatre directors, choreographers envision the performances they create holistically, whether in responsive collaboration with set and costume designers, lighting designers, and composers or sound designers, making more autonomous visual and sonic design decisions, or even devising scenography as part of ensemble process. In tandem, it also recognizes that the experience of dance, by both its audience and its performers, involves the visual and auditory perceptual systems functioning in concert, taking in not just bodies but whole scenic worlds and understanding both movement and theatrical spaces as rhythmic and dynamic. The inherently visuosonic nature of dance performance, particularly when it is situated within agile and sensorially complex scenic environments, implicates perception in ways that can affect the experience of attending.

After taking up the role of director of the Ballett Frankfurt—and motivated by institutional pressure on the ensemble's budget, especially following the German reunification in 1989—Forsythe moved increasingly toward single-handed determination of his works' staging, lighting, and costuming choices. The extensive *oeuvre* of more than 120 works he developed in collaboration with the members of his Frankfurt ensembles and other companies is strikingly varied, not only in terms of movement aesthetics but also in terms of their overall scenographies, a term that Arnold Aronson succinctly defines as considering "the sum total of the visual, spatial, and aural components of a performance."[3] The term captures all interrelated aspects of performance design: sets, props, costuming, lighting, sound, bodies, movement, and use of stage and auditorium space. As Joslin McKinney and Scott Palmer point out, though, scenography has undergone a radical shift since the early twentieth century in which it has come to do more than just decoratively frame performance and establish narrative context. Instead, modern scenography became capable of being "a construction in its own right with its own inherent logic or meaning and capable of a dialogue or even a confrontation with other elements of the theatre."[4]

Forsythe's alignment with balletic tradition is indisputable and is best known through his widely renowned "ballet ballets." His catalogue of works, however, reveals that he has been highly prolific along the lines of what Hans-Thies Lehmann delineated as *postdramatic theatre* in 1999.[5] Notoriously difficult to define precisely as a style or paradigm of performance, postdramatic theatre is charted by Lehmann as a shift that emerged from the mid-1960s in dialogic tension with the Western tradition of text-driven, largely representational or mimetic dramatic theatre. This shift, however, has roots reaching back to the hybrid experimental theatre forms developed in the early twentieth century by Dadaists and Futurists, which explored the materiality of both matter and sound.[6] Discussing dance in postdramatic theatre, Lehmann signals a

> postdramatic exploration of a "choragraphie" in every direction—gesture and dance coming into play as silent commentary on and questioning of the spoken word; the word entering into new forms of dialogue with the space and the gesture of the present and dancing body.[7]

Further, in Lehmann's analysis, the relative autonomy of scenography requires audiences to engage not just with the performers but also with the multi-sensorial, dynamic performance of these worlds themselves.[8] Beyond this, though, the contours of performance and presentation become diffused in postdramatic theatre, and the distinction between dance and theatre is often blurred. Lehmann recognizes instances of postdramatic theatre based on the presence of "traits" that are common within the style but not necessarily present in all works. As such, a wide range of performance types and practices fall within the rubric, including works not only by Forsythe but also by numerous choreographers typically aligned with other genres (postmodern dance, *Tanztheater*, contemporary dance). Lehmann's traits of postdramatic theatre are woven throughout this volume, which focuses on movement and scenography across Forsythe's catalogue of works.

Rather than honing in on Forsythe's choreography or dramaturgies, this volume surveys Forsythe's works as holistically conceived ecologies, taking Elinor Fuchs' "middle distance" view of stage(d) worlds: their terrains and architectures, their affective "climates," mood and tone, and the "music" of each world's soundscape.[9] Forsythe's stage-worlds are varied and often volatile places: in some cases sparse but more often extremely complex, cool and dim or animated by unexpected shifts in lighting, whispering or gushing with sound, or complicated by the presence of objects, architectures, or media. Interestingly, several of his "ballet ballets" began as standalone works but motivated full-length productions shortly after their initial creation, more often than not offering contrastive aesthetics to the initial performances.[10] His dramaturgies, in tandem, are wide-ranging and firmly situated within their made environments, with eclectic blends of dance, text, and utterance informing and informed by the performance designs. By expanding my scope to survey Forsythe's works from a choreoscenographic perspective, I aim to provide models through which to explain our responses to the perceptual conditions offered by these and similar performance environments. I do this by using instances of Forsythe's choreo-scenographic practices that iterate across his oeuvre as a ground upon which to bring Lehmann's ideas on postdramatic theatre into dialogue with a wide range of research on perception, from both cognitive psychology and cognitive-interdisciplinary fields. As such, analysis of Forsythe's choreographic aesthetics receives a differently articulated treatment here than might be expected: one that considers dancing bodies as an important but ultimately constituent factor in the perceptual equation of performance. Forsythe's extensive series of *choreographic objects*, interactive installation works that implicate attendees as performers, offers similar ground for analysis but is outside of the scope of this volume.[11]

Theatre unfolds within *made* worlds composed to engender affective valences that support and augment the affective power of performance. In McKinney and Palmer's view, spectatorial perception "highlights the experiential and embodied nature of scenographic experience and the dynamic interaction of bodies, environments, and materials that expanded scenography aims to generate."[12] Contemporary scenography, then, does more than suggest environment and produce mood; like choreography, it sets perception into action. Lighting, sound, sets, objects, performers, and audience attention interact to produce perspective, scale, and either real-world or perceived motion. Michael Simon, who collaborated on the visual and sonic designs of several of Forsythe's early works, ratifies the activating power of choreo-scenography in his recollection of the altered perspectives created by *Gänge*'s (1983) opening and closing walls and *LDC*'s (1985) shifting light sources and enormous turbine and five-meter cube on the Frankfurt Opera's huge stage revolve. As he notes, space in *LDC* was

> never a static hollow form, a frame in which the dancers were placed, but instead a dynamic principle that emerges from targeted interaction with light and changes through movement. They are always pulsating, living spaces that breathe with the dancers.[13]

As a cognitive dance researcher, I become most interested when performances trouble or unsettle perception: when amalgamations of movement, staging, lighting, sound, and event structure produce conditions that are counterintuitive, counterproductive, or contraindicated, troubling tacit understandings of theatre as designed to be well seen, well heard, and well understood. The term "experimental theatre" has a specific historical remit that stretches back to avant-garde theatre of the late nineteenth century, but I consider all theatre, and indeed all art, to be experimental in a cognitive sense. Theatre makers think about how other minds think; in turn, theatregoers think about the thinking of those performing, those who make the worlds they present, and—potentially—also their own thinking. Creative practices provide not only unique physical and social conditions for this cognitive research but also permit relaxation of the constraints that limit scientific investigation. To this end, I not only promote Forsythe to choreo-scenographer in this volume but also grant him the mantle of cognitive researcher, taking him at his word when he says

> Every good dance is, in a certain sense, a well-designed experiment. You're not quite sure, but you think 'probably' and 'if,' or you're hoping 'if.' So it's not so dissimilar [to science] in some respects, in its function — maybe not the outcome.[14]

In this I align with several cognitive researchers whose interest lies at the crux of art and science. Semir Zeki, who pioneered the subdiscipline he named *neuroesthetics,* holds "the somewhat unusual view that artists are in some sense neurologists, studying the brain with techniques that are unique to them, but studying unknowingly the brain and its organisation nevertheless."[15] Richard Latto, a cognitive psychologist specialized in vision and the arts, preceded Zeki's contention in his descriptions of how visual artists, by exploiting the ways in which the visual system works through their techniques and forms, have preceded vision scientists in discoveries of how the visual brain functions.[16] Jonah Lehrer further extends Latto's perspective in his volume *Proust Was a Neuroscientist* by finding "results" in the works not only of painters but also of composers, novelists, and chefs that presage later findings by cognitive scientists, sometimes by many decades.[17]

Ultimately, I want to understand how not only Forsythe's works but also other theatre works affect the *performance of perception* and how they reveal tacit understanding about how perception and minds work. I am not trying to explain aesthetic choices, but instead to better comprehend their perceptual ramifications and their resonances within the theatre-historical and cultural moment of their creation. Theatre worlds are distinct from our everyday ones, particularly since technological advances in the latter part of the twentieth century led to the stage becoming an increasingly agile, mutable, and choreographable environment that in turn permits perception itself to be more choreographable. Discussing Jan Fabre's work as an example, Lehmann highlights how the "dramatic centre" of conventional Western theatre has been replaced by a perceptual one in postdramatic theatre:

> In a frame of meaning that has become porous, the concrete, sensuously intensified *perceptibility* comes to the fore…While mimesis in Aristotle's sense produces the pleasure of recognition and thus virtually always achieves a result, here the sense data always refer to answers that are sensed as possible but not (yet) graspable; what one sees and hears remains in a state of potentiality, its appropriation postponed. It is in this sense that we are talking about a *theatre of perceptibility.* Postdramatic theatre emphasizes what is incomplete and incompletable about it, so much so that it realizes its own 'phenomenology of perception' marked by an overcoming of the principles of mimesis and fiction. The play(ing) as a concrete event produced in the moment fundamentally changes the logic of perception and the status of the

subject of perception, who can no longer find support in a representative order.[18]

Postdramatic theatre, then, is theatre of and for the senses in which presentation arrests signification and thwarts sense-making. Neither eyes nor minds stand still in the performance of perception. When attendees are offered *events* to perceive as such instead of dramatic narrative to follow, structures of sights, sounds, objects, and ongoing action delay the appropriative act of interpretation by virtue of their multisensory richness.

For Lehmann, though, this "empty" formalism carries a threat of absence. Is there no tale at all being told, no meaning to be pieced together? Faced with this saturated "surface," spectators may be left with the question asked by Thomas Mann's blasé Venetian stranger, which was paraphrased in song for Peggy Lee: Is that all there is?[19] I hold that it is not. In the works of Forsythe and many other choreo-scenographers, visual, aural, and spatial choices actively unsettle perception in ways that I frame as *perceptually performative*, in that they afford and evoke reflective recognition of our own performance of perception: its capabilities, proclivities, and limits. In my analysis, this reflexive awareness of the performance of spectating is what occurs when, as Lehmann, notes, the concrete theatre of not-necessarily-referential signs results in attendees being "thrown back onto the perception of structures."[20]

For audience members anticipating the assuring roadmap that narrative provides, whether through a story or through more abstract themes or relationships,[21] postdramatic theatre can be very unsettling indeed. Forsythe is fond of recounting a story about an encounter with woman in the theater foyer before one of his performances early in his career. Clearly keen to engage with his work, she told him that she was unsure how to approach his ballets and asked for advice. Smiling, Forsythe replied: "Just watch." His characteristically polyglot language in a more recent public talk reframes the same view, signaling that the audience's self-aware performance of perception is of central interest:

> The only product – regardless of theatre piece, mine or anyone else's – the only valuable thing that is produced is the attention of the audience. The End. [Audience laughter] That's all. Ja? That's it. So the interest of the spectator, the curiosity, what happens next and ok, thinking back, thinking forward, guessing what might happen, and also the feeling of desire, ja?…And this attention is…Your sense of attention, I want to *steer* it. [Audience

laughter] Yes, I do, I really do...No, I want you to be like that, really, I want you to stop thinking in a way, ja? I want you to start feeling. Just to experience, stop thinking and just experience it.[22]

When audiences "just watch" both performances and their own attentive performance, a deepened engagement with both choreo-sceongraphic craft and with oneself as a perceiver and thinker becomes possible. My analysis aims to show how Forsythe's works afford this engagement by unsettling perception, which, as Alva Noë emphasizes, is action rather than "something that happens to us, or in us."[23] When we apprehend the potentials, tendencies, and limits our own perception, we are better able to understand our place, and that of performance, in the world.

ABOUT THIS BOOK

My primary interest in focusing on Forsythe is the way that his works and working methods reflect a sustained though—not entirely naïve[24]—interest in perception and how, to adopt Zeki's idea above, choreo-scenographic conditions in these works can be read as perceptual research within the "laboratory" of theatre. Paradoxically, cognitive scientists often explore how minds work by studying conditions when minds *don't* work—in other words, by observing subjects' performance at the limits of perceptual or cognitive functioning or in situations of extraordinary perception ranging from common sensory illusions to cognitive disorders. Analyzing conditions in Forsythe's works that take spectators, and sometimes also performers, to the limits of their perception affords *re-cognition* of these limits. In the sections that follow, I first highlight an array of scenographic conditions that unsettle seeing and hearing before discussing cases in which the senses are merged in visuosonic choreographic practice.

A factor that complicates any consideration of Forsythe is the diversity of his repertoire. Much has been written about his "algorithmic" or "deconstructive" improvisational explorations of the ballet codex during the Ballett Frankfurt's first decade. Over the years, however, the trajectory of Forsythe's investigation of ballet's generative and performative potentials led to an effacement of the connection to ballet's visual aesthetics, to the point where they became nearly indiscernible. With reference to the 1993 work *Quintett*, Roslyn Sulcas observed,

[D]ancers move on unsteady, buckling limbs, their movements dissolving into and collapsing upon one another in a poignant series of encounters and solos...here, balletic form is visible but the steps themselves are not, as if their dynamics have been erased, leaving mere vestiges of their shapes.[25]

Steven Spier clarifies that

In earlier works...the tension between academic forms and those forms pushed to their extremes is explicit. In more recent pieces...the slippery, dislocated, densely coordinated movement style may initially appear to have little to do with ballet's formal positions and clear lines, but his dancers' classically trained bodies hold that clarity and articulation within the movement, keeping ballet as a shimmering, elusive physical presence reference point [sic] to which he constantly returns.[26]

Dramaturgically, some of Forsythe's works have been motivated by explicit themes or narratives or have used literature as referents, while others have a more hermetic focus on the experience of dancing, the ensemble as collaborative community, or the place of the dance profession in contemporary knowledge economies. Interestingly, though, a number of Forsythe's earlier work titles refer directly to perceptual phenomena, including *Mental Model* (1983), *Audio-Visual Stress* (Forsythe's first mixed program in 1984), and *Parallax* (a 1989 mixed program), while numerous others reference perception more obliquely. Over time, Forsythe provided less and less guidance in program booklets, preferring to permit audiences to "just watch." However, he is somewhat more forthcoming in rehearsals and public talks. He has, for example, explained that the "small detail" that is lost in *The Loss of Small Detail* is the dancer's normative sense of balance as they move in a mode the ensemble referred to as *disfocus*,[27] while the title *I don't believe in outer space* reflects an inverse statement: dancers "do believe" in their highly developed understanding of the "inner space" of physical sensation and embodied thought that constitutes lived experience.[28]

Together, these more and less straightforward references point to perception as a key interest of Forsythe's. At the same time, they also highlight the multiple senses of the term. Many writers have commented that Forsythe's work alters or makes us question our "perceptions"—our elaboration of thoughts or maintenance of concepts—of ballet or of dance more generally. However, others highlight how Forsythe's works trouble the processes of sensing, as well as of "making sense" of what is sensed. Writing in 1987 about *Artifact* (1984), critic Anna Kisselgoff commented somewhat ambiguously, "One doubts one's ability to perceive,"[29] while Sulcas called *Limb's Theorem* (1990) "a dark and thrilling poem about vision and perception, form and chaos."[30] Alice Bains covers both bases, commenting that *Impressing the Czar* (1988) "floats ideas and visual stimuli as fast as blowing bubbles, our senses multitasking just to keep up with what is going on, never mind analyse it."[31]

Sensory perception is of course not isolated from cognitive perception, though we tend to think of them as distinct faculties. Gestalt psychologist Rudolf Arnheim observed in 1969 that sensory perception had long been considered a "lower" subordinate component of "higher" cognition. For Arnheim, the reason the arts are neglected in education and in society is because they are based on sensory perception, which is assumed to not involve thought.[32] Computationally based theories of cognition commonly use terms like "bottom-up" and "top-down" to distinguish between cognitive processes that begin with the stimulus and proceed through successive, more complex stages, and those that rely on prior knowledge and past experience in memory. Even linguistically, the verb *perceive* (from *per-* denoting throughness and *-cipere* denoting taking; compare *Wahrnehmung*) is constituted as a full *grasp* or complete understanding—a wishful expression of a phenomenon that is now better understood as partial, subjective, and fallible, and that is increasingly analyzed from perspectives involving the body and its dynamic relationship with the environment. Many current lines of cognitive research that fall under the broad "4E" cognition rubric (embodied, embedded, enacted, extended) both reject the reductionist tendencies of representationalism and implicate the world beyond the perceiver as a crucial factor when considering perception. Ecological perspectives first indicated by Jakob von Uexküll[33] in 1934 and later elaborated by Roger Barker, James J. Gibson, and other ecological psychologists insist that behavior and thought must be considered in reference not only to social contexts but crucially also to physical ones. The physical and social contingencies of environments are also the key concern addressed by cognitive theories of situativity—so termed by James Greeno and Joyce Moore to emphasize their view that there is no cognition that is not situated and reflective of the physical environment and sociocultural context within which it occurs.[34]

The persistent devaluation of sensory perception warrants critical attention, particularly where contemporary performance is concerned. By acknowledging the enhanced role of perception in postdramatic theatre more generally, and by viewing Forsythe's works and working methods specifically through a choreo-scenographic lens, this volume aligns both with situated approaches and with Fuchs' advice—a clear early instance of scenographic thinking—to first seek to understand the made worlds of theatre from a holistic "middle distance" before progressing to interpretation. Rather than moving past the "surface" manifestations of performances to then focus on interpretive analysis, though, this volume seeks to naturalize postdramatic theatre by explaining the perceptual mechanisms that underpin the aesthetics and impact of performances.[35] To do this, I focus on specific visual, sonic, and intermodal compositional conditions that recur across Forsythe's larger oeuvre. The conditions I examine, however, are neither unique to Forsythe nor to the postdramatic genre or style. Vision is blurred and illusion and drama enhanced in nineteenth-century Romantic ballet "white scenes" and in numerous contemporary dance works by means that I consider in Part 1 of this volume. Postmodern choreographers have experimented with the "independent auditory semiotics" signaled by Lehmann and termed "dramaturgy of sound" by Mladen Ovadija in ways that I isolate in Part 2, while non-linguistic orality and language-like vocalizations are found in early twentieth-century avant-garde theatre as well as more recent sound art compositions. My analysis brings not only Forsythe's works, Lehmann's ideas, and cognitive research into dialogue but also draws on commentaries by Forsythe and other choreographers, along with both positive and negative assessments by dance critics. Works from other choreographers and theatre makers provide further comparative examples.

NATURALIZING POSTDRAMATIC THEATRE

Naturalizing theatre by bringing it into dialogue with scientific research is by no means an uncomplicated matter, and looking at theatre through a cognitive lens necessarily involves an array of choices. Cognitive psychology considers a vast range of factors applicable to the study of dance, including attention, perception, language and gesture processing, cognitive development, and consciousness. As Rhonda Blair and Amy Cook discuss in the introduction to their volume *Theatre, Performance, and Cognition: Languages, bodies and ecologies*, cognitive science is also not a monolithic discipline but is instead a broad field with numerous theoretical approaches, many of which are at odds with each other.[36] Deciding *how* to study it is thus problematic in two ways: cognition can be analyzed at the level of the sensory-perceptual, the behavioral, or the neuronal, and within these analytic levels different cognitive research paradigms—representational, computational, ecological, neurophysiological, 4E perspectives, and others—are represented to greater or lesser degrees in the literature. Beyond this, there is a highly productive body of interdisciplinary cognitive research from humanistic disciplines including linguistics, embodied philosophy, musicology, art history, environmental psychology, comparative literature, film studies, and performance studies. Aligning with Blair and Cook, I have chosen to embrace cognitive studies as a broad plurality of approaches rather than applying a single cognitive research perspective, and accordingly I apply an eclectic range of paradigms, cross-disciplinary contexts, and levels of analysis to speculatively address how perceptual performance is choreographed through Forsythe's works and compositional methods, and to do so as rigorously as is feasible. These include computationalist, ecological, social, situated, and embodied perspectives, along with research methodologies including behavioral studies, neurological studies, and purely theoretical analyses. This volume, however, intentionally avoids neuroscientific research for pragmatic reasons. Though many outstanding neuroscientific studies of dance have been carried out over the last 30 years, I find its granularity less productive, as well as less user-friendly, than the array of others included here.

Getting from the science to the stage is not a straightforward disciplinary mapping: stimuli and conditions used in scientific experiments are usually vastly different from the real-world phenomena that studies seek to investigate. I agree with Blair and Cook, who highlight the reductive tendencies that limit much empirical research practice, that approaching theatre from a cognitive perspective is also necessarily reductive. Further, I too highlight scientific research as an endeavor to approach potential truths using the best means possible at any given moment, rather than as the final representation of any "truth" about perception and cognition.[37] Scientific conclusions are by definition works in progress: it is not simply a matter of tallying up how many papers argue for which one at a given point in time, and it is healthy to be suspicious when science maps too neatly onto performance phenomena.

Blair and Cook also aptly signal that a cognitive perspective can never be purely scientific, as cultures are in play. Again, though, the question becomes one of analytical level:

A cognitive analysis of the phenomenon of spectating – what it means to take in information in a theatrical setting – does universalize the experience insofar as the biologies of the agents are more similar than they are different; but *that* an Elizabethan man and a twenty-first-century Korean-American woman both understand an experience is different from thinking about *how* or *what* they understand. In the same way, a cognitive analysis of how any dancer or actor works is likely to find significant similarities in neural, cognitive and kinaesthetic operations, though these operations are understood and applied differently across cultures and 'ecologies.'[38]

Constructing a collective identity of perceivers as such is therefore also not a straightforward matter. However, given this volume's postdramatic-driven focus on perception as sensing, differences of culture as well as differences in perceptual and cognitive ability will be side-stepped for the sake of an analysis that admittedly and apologetically falls short of truly universal application. There is of course more work that can and should be done here.

Naturalizing approaches to theatre are not intended to supplant other analytic approaches, but rather to join and potentially augment or interrogate them. I echo cognitive film theorist David Bordwell's view that while cognitive research is not necessarily a superior analytical lens to other arts-analytic paradigms, it is "*at least* as enlightening" as others that can be applied.[39] In considering instances of specific choreo-scenographic conditions found within postdramatic dance pieces, I am working in a mode that film, art, dance, and aesthetics philosopher Noël Carroll, who partnered with Bordwell on their pro-cognitivist (and anti-psychoanalytic) volume *Post-Theory: Reconstructing Film Studies*, refers to as a "piecemeal" theorizing. This asking of "middle-level" questions aims to generate explanatory theories which, though tied to specific instances within works, might potentially but must not necessarily be unified into larger theoretical constructs:

> The approach I advocate is piecemeal inasmuch as it recommends initially considering [filmic] devices...one at a time, developing explanations of their operation without trying to fit those explanations into a totalizing theory of film. Of course, this does not mean that theorizing must remain atomic. Once we have the various piecemeal analyses of film structures in front of us, we may then proceed to see whether they can be assembled into larger theoretical constellations – i.e., whether there are generalizations that can coordinate our piecemeal analyses into larger frameworks. Yet even here I suggest

that we should resist the expectation that all our small-scale theories will fit into one unified, overarching theory of film.[40]

In addition to advocating the building of "local theories," Carroll also stresses the multidisciplinary diversity that such theory-building entails. As he notes, different approaches and levels of inquiry will send researchers toward different disciplinary frameworks at the outset, including perceptual psychology, sociology, economics, anthropology, linguistics, or theories of narrativity.[41] This posing of "hard-nosed questions about humbler topics"[42] motivates the chapters in this volume, which cover conditions of lighting, sound, stage design, choreography, and vocal performance. Following Bordwell and Carroll, I also refrain from attempting to produce a "Big Theory of Everything," seeking instead to theorize unsettling choreo-scenograpic conditions in Forsythe's works by bringing them into dialogue with experimental methods and findings from perceptual research.

Perceptual Performativity

This book, however, is not without a "local" theory. Beyond understanding the sensory dynamics of Forsythe's works and compositional methods, I am interested in how these highlight a performativity that is based explicitly on perception. In work after work, Forsythe has crafted conditions that complicate vision, audition, and comprehension in ways that invite *re-cognition* of perception as an active and reflective performance, either by attendees, performers, or both. Instances in the works I consider here highlight the fallibilities that inhere in the performance of perception, providing opportunities for viewer-auditors to become aware of and reflect on the experience of perceiving. The term *performativity* is of course not new, having first been coined by linguistic philosopher John L. Austin in the 1950s to refer to the way that utterances can effect change in the world under certain conditions.[43] For example, the phrase "The court finds the defendant guilty" alters the legal status of the individual identified as the defendant, provided it is uttered by the right person in the right circumstances. Refinements to Austin's theory by Émile Benveniste, a linguist associated with Jacques Lacan, catalyzed the poststructuralist "textual" theory of subjectivity developed by members of the Tel Quel group in the late 1960s, while sociologist Pierre Bourdieu argued for more attention to the social, cultural, and political conditions of utterances than afforded by

Austin's purely linguistic analysis.[44] Post-Marxist theorists including Marcuse, Lyotard, Foucault, and Žižek, have applied the term performativity in various ways to the social and knowledge dynamics of the postmodern capitalist society, while critical theorists hold that the habitual practice of encultured actions is a performance through which identity itself is constructed and evaluated in terms of society's reception. Judith Butler's concept of gender performativity, which subsequently drew on ideas above, motivated critical analysis of the performativities of class, race, and queerness,[45] and a further social dimension of performativity is explored within the field of economic sociology, through the work of authors including Michel Callon and Donald MacKenzie.[46] The term is also more loosely used to indicate qualities of theatricality.

Poststructuralist theorists of performativity view bodies, narratives, stagings, and actions as texts out of which either iterative reinforcement or subversive interrogations of prior practices can be deconstructively "read." While semiotic studies of performance have also found substantial traction with deconstructively oriented approaches, recent writings by Erika Fischer-Lichte return to a more Austinian direction by shifting the focus from interpretation to affect and highlighting how performance has the power to transform the spectator. Noting that performances have both a subject-constructive and a semiotic dimension, she points out that "While the semiotic approach asks 'What do performance processes *mean*,' the performative approach instead raises the question 'What do they *do*?'"[47] Her delineation of a perceptual "order" of presence remains at the conceptual level of recognizing bodies, things, and space for what they are, while a second "order" of representation imbues actions with potentially symbolic meaning. Performances commonly oscillate between these two orders, she claims, with shifts between them creating an instability that transfers perceiving subjects into a liminal state. When this happens with frequency, Fischer-Lichte holds that subjects

increasingly become aware of their inability to cause, steer, and control the shifts. They may consciously try to adjust their perception anew – to the border of presence or to the order of representation. Very soon, however, they will become aware that the shift takes place even if they do not intend it, that it simply happens, befalls them, that they are moved between the two orders without wanting or being able to prevent it. At that moment, the spectators experience their own perception as emergent, as withdrawn from their will and control, and yet as an action performed consciously. That is to say that the shift draws the attention of the preceding subject to the process of perception itself as well as to its particular dynamics. At the moment of shift, the process of perception itself becomes conspicuous, thereby self-conscious, and in itself the object of perception. The preceding subject begins to receive itself as proceeding subject. That is a performative as well as semiotic process in itself and produces new meanings which, in turn, generate other meanings and so forth.[48]

Though her comment above references a performativity that relies on perception-as-apprehension, Fischer-Lichte et al. have also read the history of theatre as a history of the staging of perception, noting that in contemporary theatre,

dramatic techniques of focusing and prioritizing attention give way...In the egalitarian juxtaposition of utterly different types of sensory impressions and information, the spectator is left with the task of selection and valuation and requires them to formulate and justify the criteria for the choices made. Through this, the spectator's attention is steered from the object back to him or herself, reminding them that at the origin of every description stands a reflection of one's own perception [translation mine].[49]

This performative awareness of the self as perceiver had previously been signaled by others in direct relation to Forsythe's choreographic work. Sabine Huschka describes Forsythe's choreographic practices as "perceptual technologies," recognizing the role of perception in his working methods by commenting that

ballet operates with a technical-geometric movement corpus which not only medially effaces all irregularities and inconsistencies of its execution but also hypothetically establishes and presupposes the perfect embodiment of its ideal figures. Forsythe subtends this aesthetic idealism with a perceptual aesthetic of physical performativity and shifts ballet's premise – the correct execution of figures – into the unpredictable territory of corporeal perceptual processes.[50]

Kirsten Marr instead reflects on the performer-audience relationship, indicating the role played in spectatorial experience by his combining of the balletic rule system with improvisational modalities as

a matter of the exploration, the sounding of…marginal zones, e.g. of the
kinesthetic sense up to the boundary of vertigo, of disequilibrium, the desta-
bilization of balance…Of habitual relations becoming insecure, of situations
of delirium in which for a short time no quality of difference, no discretion
functions, but instead overload in which there are no pauses or separations,
and of the loss of positionality (…) Only through this sounding of marginal
zones is it possible to maneuver the spectator also into a similar condition of
insecurity, of not knowing, in which accustomed patterns of judgment can
no longer be implemented and others must be developed.[51]

Lastly, in a comparative examination of Forsythe's and Saburo Teshigawara's
choreographic practices, Christiane Berger similarly cites the performative
effect of Forsythe's choreography as an "irritation of expectancy and
habit" due to semiotic reading of the choreography being problematized
by the illegibility of the movement and its extreme dynamic contrasts and
ongoing flow. As a result of these conditions,

It is not the constitution of meaning that is decisive, but rather how the
dance event affects the spectator as the performance of the action
occurs…The quality of movement that can be experienced with the senses
becomes the focus of attention, in comparison to the meaning-bearing spatial form.[52]

It is worth noting that Huschka, Marr, and Berger describe Forsythe's
choreographic performativity as a function of various cognitive mechanisms, including kinesthetic recall, attention, expectation, and embodied
experience. These processes, along with many others regularly invoked in
analytic dance studies, are subjects of programs of empirical research
within the broad field of cognitive psychology as well as cognitive-
interdisciplinary studies within arts and humanities disciplines. It is to this
literature that I turn in the following chapters as I highlight the perceptual
performativity of differing registers of Forsythe's choreography in the scenographic environments within which they are situated.

I hope that this book will be informative to those interested in how
dance, theatre, and scenography "work" as well as those interested in
human sciences and arts/sciences interdisciplinarity. Bruce McConachie
emphasizes the potential for cognitive theatre studies to engender interdisciplinary exchange by informing not only performance studies but also
the discipline of cognitive science itself, by viewing performance as offering "a rich body of evidence with which to test and elaborate their

theories."[53] Political and social philosopher Brian Massumi, who is both an advocate and practitioner of "shameless poaching" of scientific concepts, maintains that optimally, borrowing should take place in a way that does not leave the scientific concepts "tamed, a metaphorical exhibit in someone else's menagerie." For Massumi, the aim of such "poaching" should not be to make the humanities scientific, but rather to cause the humanities to differ from the sciences in unaccustomed ways. This offers the humanistic disciplines opportunities to define their uniqueness as well as to renegotiate their relations to the sciences. As he maintains, such borrowing is a positive, additive occurrence in that scientific concepts, while being "naturalized into the humanities," also maintain their function within the source discipline.[54]

In turn, approaching perception as performative offers a means through which other discourses on performativity, particularly those grounded in sensory metaphors, might be questioned and potentially refined. My conclusion, which re-views Forsythe's performativity within and as part of a choreo-scenographic ecology, is guided in part by Chris Salter's comment that

> Forsythe's deployment of stage languages like sound, lighting, video, and scenography have developed in parallel with his relentless questioning of the perceptual-political frameworks by which we come to experience the dancing body as a medium of expression and way of knowing the world.[55]

As the physical environment, social context, and cultural-political economies of theatre all figure in the generation of performativity, a perceptual-performative view offers dialogic potential with ecological, social, and political discourses on theatre, which I explore in my final chapter.

Notes

1. For an interesting recent analysis of Forsythe's "ballet ballets," see Adeline Chevrier-Bosseau, "Renewing the Discipline: William Forsythe's *Blake Works I.*"
2. Quoted in Spier, "Dancing and drawing." Original source: "A Conversation between Dana Caspersen, William Forsythe and the architect Daniel Libeskind" at the Royal Geographical Society, London, March 7, 1997.
3. Arnold Aronson, Foreword, xiii.
4. Joslin McKinney and Scott Palmer, "Introducing 'Expanded' Scenography," 4–5.
5. Hans-Thies Lehmann, *Postdramatic Theatre.*

6. See Mladen Ovadija's outstanding history of these developments in *Dramaturgy of Sound in the Avant Garde and Postdramatic Theatre.*
7. Hans-Thies Lehmann, "'Postdramatic Theatre,' a decade later," 38.
8. McKinney and Palmer, "Introducing 'Expanded' Scenography," 5.
9. Elinor Fuchs, "EF's Visit to a Small Planet," 6–7.
10. These include *In the Middle, Somewhat Elevated* (Part 2 of *Impressing the Czar*), *Enemy in the Figure* (Part 2 of *Limb's Theorem*), *the second detail* (Part 1 of the 1991 version of *The Loss of Small Detail*), *Self Meant to Govern* (Part 1 of *Eidos:Telos*), and *Duo* (part of *A Quiet Evening of Dance*, as *Dialogue (DUO2015)*). Most recently, however, Forsythe has created a work titled *Défilé* (2022) as a prequel to sections of *Artifact* (1984) that are performed as *Artifact Suite*.
11. Forsythe's installation works are catalogued at https://www.williamforsythe.com/installations.html. See also his 2008 essay "Choreographic Objects."
12. McKinney and Palmer, "Introducing 'Expanded' Scenography," 8.
13. Michael Simon, Clair-obscure: Licht, Raum und Körper im Dialog. See also "Bühne-Bild: Interview 2006 mit Eva-Elisabeth Fischer," "Michael Simon – FERTIG gibt's nicht," and "Conversation with the choreographer William Forsythe."
14. USC Glorya Kaufman School of Dance, "Little Lectures: William Forsythe on Connection through Curiosity."
15. Semir Zeki, *Inner Vision: An Exploration of Art and the Brain*, 10.
16. Richard Latto, "The Brain of the Beholder," 68.
17. Jonah Lehrer, *Proust Was a Neuroscientist.*
18. Lehmann, *Postdramatic Theatre*, 99.
19. Thomas Mann, "Disillusionment" (*Enttäuschung*); Jerry Leiber and Mike Stoller. *Is that all there is?*
20. Lehmann, *Postdramatic Theatre*, 98.
21. George Balanchine famously quipped, "You put a man and woman onstage together, and already it's a story." See also Tamara Tomić-Vajagić, "The Balanchine Dilemma: 'So-Called Abstraction,' and the Rhetoric of Circumvention in Black-and-White Ballets."
22. William Forsythe, *Decreation* post-performance talk, Haus der Berliner Festspiele, Berlin, January 21, 2009. German text sections translated by the author. I am grateful to the Haus der Berliner Festspiele for the German transcription of this talk.
23. Alva Noë, *Action in perception*, 1.
24. Since early in his Frankfurt career, Forsythe sustained a friendship with Prof. Wolf Singer, director of Neurophysiology at the Max Planck Institute for Brain Research in Frankfurt, who recalled their frequent discussions (interview, October 2006). Forsythe also frequently invited cognitive researchers and philosophers to visit him in the studio, including Ivar

Hagendoorn, Alva Noë, Brian Massumi, and Erin Manning, and as Elizabeth Waterhouse points out, myself (*Processing Choreography*, 156). Forsythe also included a dance-science research component in his Motion Bank project (2010–2013). See the *Dance Engaging Science* page at http://motionbank.org/en/content/dance-engaging-science.html.

25. Roslyn Sulcas, "Using Forms Ingrained in Ballet to Help the Body Move Beyond It."
26. Spier, *William Forsythe and the Practice of Choreography: It Starts From Any Point*, 5.
27. For a detailed description of this modality, which was used in some works in the 1990s, see Dana Caspersen, "The Body is Thinking."
28. Freya Vass-Rhee, "William Forsythe's I don't believe in outer space: dramaturg's note."
29. Anna Kisselgoff, "The Sound and the Flurry of William Forsythe."
30. Roslyn Sulcas, "Both a New World and the Old Made Explicit."
31. Alice Bains, review of the Royal Ballet of Flanders.
32. Rudolf Arnheim, *Visual Thinking*.
33. J. von Uexküll and G. Kriszat, *Streifzüge durch die Umwelten von Tieren und Menschen* (a stroll through the environments of animals and humans).
34. J. Greeno and J. Moore, "Situativity and Symbols: Response to Vera and Simon," 50. These perspectives are sometimes collectively referred to as *grounded* or *situated cognition*; for an overview, see S.J. Durning and A.R. Artino, "Situativity theory: a perspective on how participants and the environment can interact."
35. Like the "naturalized epistemologies" elaborated by Quine, Kornblith, Kim, and others, naturalizing approaches seek to render phenomena compatible with explanations offered by the natural sciences. Rather than extrapolating from overarching theoretical doctrines to posit inhering structures of meaning and exemplify their presence and constitution, naturalizing approaches aim to understand and explain "how things work" in and of themselves through a grounding in highly specified and duplicable research.
36. Rhonda Blair and Amy Cook, *Theatre, Performance, and Cognition: Languages, bodies and ecologies*, 10.
37. Blair & Cook, 2, 11.
38. Blair and Cook (2016, 3).
39. David Bordwell, "A Case for Cognitivism."
40. Noël Carroll, N., *Theorizing the Moving Image*, 75. Carroll borrows the concept of piecemeal theorizing from Bertrand Russell's 1914 essay that recommends the development of a philosophy which is "...piecemeal and tentative like other sciences; above all, it will be able to invent hypotheses which, even if they are not wholly true, will yet remain fruitful after the

necessary corrections have been made." "On Scientific Method in Philosophy," 113.
41. Noël Carroll, "Prospects for Film Theory," 39–40.
42. Deborah Knight, review of *Post-Theory*.
43. James Austin, *How to do Things with Words*.
44. See, for example, Émile Benveniste, *Problems in General Linguistics*; Jacques Derrida, "Signature Event Context"; and Pierre Bourdieu, *Language & Symbolic Power*.
45. Judith Butler, *Gender Trouble: Feminism and the Subversion of Identity*.
46. Michel Callon, "The embeddedness of economic markets in economics"; and Donald MacKenzie, "Is economics performative? Option theory and the construction of derivatives markets."
47. Erika Fischer-Lichte, "Sense and Sensation: Exploring the Interplay Between the Semiotic and Performative Dimensions of Theatre." See Fischer-Lichte, *The Transformative Power of Performance: A new aesthetics*.
48. Fischer-Lichte, *The Transformative Power of Performance*, 78.
49. Erika Fischer-Lichte et al., "Einleitung," 10.
50. Sabine Huschka, "Verlöschen als ästhetiscer Fluchtpunkt oder 'Du musst dich selbst wahrnehmend machen,'" 96. Translation by the author.
51. Kirsten Marr, "Forsythes Konzepte des imaginären Raums," 109. Translation by the author.
52. Christiane Berger, *Körper denken in Bewegung: Zur Wahrnehung tänzerischen Sinns bei William Forsythe und Saburo Teshigawara*, 49. Translation by the author.
53. McConachie B. & Hart, F.E. (2006). *Performance and Cognition: Theatre studies and the cognitive turn* (London &New York: Routledge, 2006), p. xiv.
54. Massumi, *Parables for the Virtual: Movement, affect, sensation* (Durham and London, Duke University Press, 2002), 20–21.
55. Chris Salter, "Timbral architectures, aurality's force," 55.

BIBLIOGRAPHY

Arnheim, Rudolf. 2004 (1969). *Visual Thinking*. Berkeley: University of California Press.
Aronson, Arnold. 2017. Foreword. In *Scenography Expanded: An Introduction to Contemporary Performance Design*, ed. Joslin McKinney and Scott Palmer, xiii–xvi. London and New York: Bloomsbury Publishing.
Austin, James L. 1962. *How to Do Things with Words: The William James Lectures Delivered at Harvard University in 1955*. Edited by J.O. Urmson. Oxford: Clarendon.

Bains, Alice. 2007. Review of the Royal Ballet of Flanders. *The Guardian*, 21 August. https://www.theguardian.com/stage/2007/aug/21/dance.edinburghfestival2007. Accessed 31 October 2007.

Benveniste, Émile. 1971. *Problems in General Linguistics*. Translated by Mary Meek. Coral Gables: University of Miami Press.

Berger, Christiane. 2006. *Körper denken in Bewegung: Zur Wahrnehung tänzerischen Sinns bei William Forsythe und Saburo Teshigawara*. Bielefeld: transcript Verlag.

Blair, Rhonda, and Amy Cook. 2016. *Theatre, Performance, and Cognition: Languages, Bodies and Ecologies*. Oxon and New York: Bloomsbury.

Bordwell, David. 1989. A Case for Cognitivism. *Iris* 9: 11–16.

Bordwell, David, and Noël Carroll, eds. 1996. *Post-Theory: Reconstructing Film Studies*. Madison: University of Wisconsin Press.

Bourdieu, Pierre. 1991. In *Language & Symbolic Power, transl*, ed. Gino Raymond and Matthew Adamson. Cambridge: Polity Press/Blackwell.

Butler, Judith. 1990. *Gender Trouble: Feminism and the Subversion of Identity*. New York: Routledge.

Callon, Michel. 1998. The Embeddedness of Economic Markets in Economics. In *The Laws of the Markets*, 1–57. Oxford: Blackwell Publishers and The Sociological Review.

Carroll, Noël. 1996a. *Theorizing the Moving Image*. Cambridge: Cambridge University Press.

———. 1996b. Prospects for Film Theory: A Personal Assessment. In *Post-Theory: Reconstructing Film Studies*, ed. David Bordwell and Noël Carroll, 37–68. Madison: University of Wisconsin Press.

Caspersen, Dana. 2007. The Body Is Thinking. Walker Art Center. http://blogs.walkerart.org/performingarts/2007/03/09/the-body-is-thinking-the-body-is-thinking-by-dana-caspersen/. Accessed 13 May 2008. Earlier version: 2004. Der Körper denkt: Form, Sehen, Disziplin und Tanzen. In *William Forsythe: Denken in Bewegung*, ed. Gerald Siegmund, 107–116. Berlin: Henschel Verlag.

Chevrier-Bosseau, Adeline. 2020. Renewing the Discipline: William Forsythe's *Blake Works I*. *Revue francaise d'etudes americaines* 165 (4): 82–97.

Derrida, Jacques. 1972. Signature Event Context. In 1982. *Margins of Philosophy*, trans. Alan Bass. Chicago: University of Chicago Press.

Durning, S.J., and A.R. Artino. 2011. Situativity Theory: A Perspective on How Participants and the Environment Can Interact: AMEE Guide no. 52. *Medical Teacher* 33 (3): 188–199.

Fischer-Lichte, Erika. 2008a. *The Transformative Power of Performance: A New Aesthetics*. Translated by Saskya Iris Jain. Oxon and New York: Routledge. Original: 2004. *Ästhetik des Pereformativen*. Frankfurt am Main: Suhrkamp.

———. 2008b. Sense and Sensation: Exploring the Interplay Between the Semiotic and Performative Dimensions of Theatre. *Journal of Dramatic Theory and Criticism* 22 (2): 69–81.

Fischer-Lichte, Erika, Barbara Gronau, Sabine Schouten, and Christel Weiler, eds. 2006. Einleitung. In *Wege der Wahrnehmung: Authentizität, Reflexivität, und Aufmerksamkeit im Zeitgenössischen Theater*, Recherchen 33. Berlin: Theater der Zeit.

Forsythe, William. 2008. Choreographic Objects. In *William Forsythe: Suspense*. Geneva: Jrp Ringier Kunstverlag Ag. https://www.williamforsythe.com/essay.html.

Fuchs, Elinor. 2004. EF's Visit to a Small Planet: Some Questions to Ask a Play. *Theater* 34 (2): 4–9.

Greeno, J., and J. Moore. 1993. Situativity and Symbols: Response to Vera and Simon. *Cognitive Science* 17: 49–59.

Huschka, Sabine. 2004. Verlöschen als ästhetiscer Fluchtpunkt oder 'Du musst dich selbst wahrnehmend machen'. In *William Forsythe: Denken in Bewegung*, ed. Gerald Siegmond, 95–106. Berlin: Henschel Verlag.

Kim, Jaegwon. 1988. What Is Naturalized Epistemology? *Philosophical Perspectives* 2: 381–405.

Kisselgoff, Anna. 1987. The Sound and the Flurry of William Forsythe. *The New York Times*, 19 July.

Knight, Deborah. 1998. Review of Post-Theory: Reconstructing Film Studies. David Bordwell and Noël Carroll, eds. *Journal of Aesthetic Education* 32 (2): 109–112.

Kornblith, Hilary, ed. 1985. *Naturalizing Epistemology*. Cambridge, MA: MIT Press.

Latto, Richard. 1995. The Brain of the Beholder. In *The Artful Eye*, ed. R.L. Gregory, J. Harris, P. Heard, and D. Rose, 66–94. New York: Oxford University Press.

Lehmann, Hans-Thies. 2006. *Postdramatic Theatre*. Translated by Karen-Jürs-Munby. Abingdon and New York: Routledge. Original version: Lehmann, Hans-Thies. 1999. *Postdramatisches Theater*. Frankfurt am Main: Verlag der Autoren.

———. 2011. 'Postdramatic Theatre,' a Decade Later. In *Dramatic and Postdramatic Theater Ten Years After: Conference Proceedings*, 31–46. Belgrade: Faculty of Dramatic Arts.

Lehrer, Jonah. 2007. *Proust Was a Neuroscientist*. Boston: Houghton Mifflin.

Leiber, Jerry, and Mike Stoller. 1969. Is That All There Is? Leiber-Stoller Music, Australia.

MacKenzie, Donald. 2006. Is Economics Performative? Option Theory and the Construction of Derivatives Markets. *Journal of the History of Economic Thought* 28 (1): 29–55.

Mann, Thomas. 1896. Disillusionment (*Enttäuschung*), trans. H.T. Lowe-Porter. In 1994. *The McGraw-Hill Book of Fiction*, ed. R. DiYanni and K. Rompf, 737–740. New York: McGraw-Hill

Marr, Kirsten. 2005. Forsythes Konzepte des imaginären Raums. In *Tanz im Kopf: Dance and cognition*, ed. Johannes Birringer and Josephine Fenger, 99–112. Münster: LIT Verlag.

McKinney, Joslin, and Scott Palmer. 2017. Introducing 'Expanded' Scenography. In *Scenography Expanded: An Introduction to Contemporary Performance Design*, 1–19. London and New York: Bloomsbury Publishing.

Noë, Alva. 2004. *Action in Perception*. Cambridge, MA: MIT Press.

Ovadija, Mladen. 2013. *Dramaturgy of Sound in the Avant-Garde and Postdramatic Theatre*. Montreal: McGill-Queen's University Press.

Quine, W.V. 1969. Epistemology Naturalized. In *Ontological Relativity and Other Essays*. New York: Columbia University Press.

Russell, Bertrand. 1918. On Scientific Method in Philosophy. In *Mysticism and Logic and Other Essays*. New York: Longmans, Green and Co.

Salter, Chris. 2011. Timbral Architectures, Aurality's Force. In *William Forsythe and the Practice of Choreography: It Starts from Any Point*, ed. Steven Spier, 54–72. Abingdon and New York: Routledge.

Simon, Michael. 2006. Bühne-Bild: Interview 2006 mit Eva-Elisabeth Fischer. *Der Theaterverlag*. https://michaelsimon.ch/text/buehne-bild/. Accessed 10 February 2022.

———. 2012. Clair-Obscure: Licht, Raum und Körper im Dialog. Presentation for colloquium *Le metteur en scène et ses doubles*, 30–31 March, Theater Grütli, Geneva. http://www.michaelsimon.de/homeMichaelSimon/buhne-tanz/. Accessed 13 August 2019.

———. 2022a. "Conversation with the choreographer William Forsythe, 10.4.2022" https://michaelsimon.ch/book/bonus-tracks/ (accessed 2 Feb 2023).

———. 2022b. Michael Simon – FERTIG gibt's nicht. Bühnenbild. Prozesse, ed. Tilman Neuffer and Stephan Wetzel. Berlin: Theater der Zeit.

Spier, Steven. 2005. Dancing and Drawing, Choreography and Architecture. *The Journal of Architecture* 10 (4): 349–364.

———, ed. 2011. *William Forsythe and the Practice of Choreography: It Starts from Any Point*. Edited by Steven Spier. Abingdon and New York: Routledge.

Sulcas, Roslyn. 2000. Both a New World and the Old Made Explicit. Booklet Accompanying. In *William Forsythe: Improvisation Technologies*, ed. William Forsythe and ZKM, 29–46. Ostfildern: Hatje Cantz Verlag.

———. 2001. Using Forms Ingrained in Ballet to Help the Body Move Beyond It. *The New York Times*, 9 December.

Tomić-Vajagić, Tamara. 2020. The Balanchine Dilemma: 'So-Called Abstraction' and the Rhetoric of Circumvention in Black-and-White Ballets. *Arts* 9 (4): 119.

University of Southern California Glorya Kaufman School of Dance. 2017. Little Lectures: William Forsythe on Connection Through Curiosity. https://kaufman.usc.edu/9962-2/. Accessed 27 October 2017.

Vass-Rhee, Freya. 2012. *William Forsythe's I don't believe in outer space: dramaturg's note.* The Forsythe Company.

Von Uexküll, J., and G. Kriszat. 1934. *Streifzüge durch die Umwelten von Tieren und Menschen. Bedeutungslehre.* Frankfurt am Main: Fischer Wissenschaft.

Waterhouse, Elizabeth. 2022. *Processing Choreography: Thinking with William Forsythe's Duo.* Bielefeld: Transcript Verlag.

Zeki, Semir. 1999. *Inner Vision: An Exploration of Art and the Brain.* Oxford: Oxford University Press.

PART I

Unsettling Seeing: Obscuration

I could agree that light is there to illuminate, but what is fascinating is its ability to actually obscure.[1]

When the curtain raises on a typical classical ballet or modern dance performance, the world onstage is usually a wide, uncluttered space framed by illustrative set pieces or a plain backdrop. Any necessary furnishings are arranged at the periphery of the stage or encroach only temporarily. Giselle canoodles with Albrecht on a bench placed by a pulled-back house, while tables and chairs for Bathilde and her hunting party's brief respite are swiftly brought out and tucked away again; *The Nutcracker*'s Christmas tree and grandfather clock rest against the backdrop, and the performers themselves carry Kurt Jooss' long table quickly into the backstage during the blackout that ends *The Green Table*'s opening scene and return it for the closing scene. Props like cups, crossbows, and spinning wheels appear and disappear almost magically as well.

Ballet and modern dance worlds are also flooded with light. Sets and costumes glow with it, as do dancers' bodies and their made-up faces. Careful lighting design keeps performers visible over auditorium distances, making them stand out clearly in stage space as they move even when plots call for night or gloom. Lighting can also enhance illusions of ethereality and proximity, bringing the dancers closer or making them seem farther away. Much as the 14-year-old Louis XIV dazzled against a dark background in 1653 as *Le roi soleil* in the *Ballet de la nuit* thanks to Giacomo Torelli's pioneering lighting techniques,[2] modern lighting bathes dancers in otherworldly light, while their broad gestures and movements also ensure that action and emotion are clear to see. The worlds of postmodern dance performance have often been more intimate or everyday environments. Yvonne Rainer's "no" to spectacle, which captured the postmodern ethos of rejecting artificiality and contrivance in favor of a more quotidian aesthetic, was not only a choreographic "no" but also a scenographic one.[3] Experimenting with distance and perspective in empty church buildings, industrial halls, and outdoor spaces, postmodern choreographers have also tended to keep their performers clearly visible, sometimes augmenting existing light with a few additional and often unhidden instruments.

For Laura Gröndahl, contemporary lighting has become "a performance of its own, a scene machine that endlessly reproduces images and meanings."[4] Katherine Graham agrees, referencing Lehmann's idea of parataxis (non-hierarchical relation of performance elements), to describe the emergence of a new illuminative aesthetics. In her view, light is a generative dramaturgical agent that engages in a "conversant autonomy" with other elements, most notably but not exclusively texts, to contribute to the emergence of meaning.[5] Writing about the 2015 performance <<*both, and*>>, choreographed by Russell Maliphant in collaboration with lighting designer Michael Hulls, Graham comments productively on lighting's ability to generate perceptual instability. Following visual themes in Maliphant and Hulls' work, she discusses how the work's lighting creates illusory presences through the creation of differently scaled and sometimes multiple shadows, creating "drama of appearance and disappearance" through generated interplay of light and darkness.[6] Her account hints at how attention and apprehension are changed when an altered visual reality is created in which lighting might more aptly be described as "darking". Dance staged in this different light projects choreographic thinking about what these conditions enable, but how does it also reflect the perceptual performativity afforded by this register?

Dance and theatre photographers favor brightly lit subjects that cameras can capture clearly. As such, though, images of dark postdramatic works, including Forsythe's, do a limited job of capturing their aesthetics. Roslyn Sulcas offers more in her description of Forsythe's lighting as

as much part of the choreographic structure as the physical movements of the dancers. Using shadow and reflection, blackness and phosphorescence, subtle shade and the glare of a photographic shoot in equal measure, the extraordinary manipulation of light carves the stage into areas of mystery, obscurity or clarification cutting the spectator off from the dance by delimiting the space, and then revealing it afresh amidst new shapes and perspectives. Often the dancers disappear, swallowed up by darkness, or are only dimly visible, emphasising what Forsythe has called "the illusory unity of the dancing body" and forcing the spectator to choose between concentrating upon retaining the dancing image, or relinquishing it to the play of light and space—"I like to hide, to make uncertain that which takes place on stage," Forsythe has said, "and to extend that which I call the poetry of disappearance. People are always frightened that things will disappear. But life without death, light without obscurity, would be terrifying. Shadow is that which permits imagination."[7]

The dim lighting in many Forsythe works from the 1980s and 1990s has had a profound influence on contemporary dance scenography, and this in turn has broadly impacted on choreographic aesthetics. However, the change has not always been well received. Critics complain of contemporary dance lighting that is "too dark" as it causes difficulties with seeing choreographic detail, or describe the impact of such lighting with limiting terms like "moody" or "foreboding." Something else is produced, though, when these atmospheres of obscurity frame the dynamics of contemporary dance: coolly energetic worlds where the desire to see is performatively called to attention through simultaneous scaling up of movement and problematizing of viewing. This is not a staging of absence but instead a "poetry of disappearance" in which vision—and by extension apperception—is challenged, rewarded, and thwarted.

To consider how lighting factors into the perceptual performativity of these obscure postdramatic dance works, an understanding of vision in darkness is needed, along with a recognition that darkness comes in different varieties. Pitch blackness, gloom, and vision-obscuring optics have recently become the defining conditions of the genre that Adam Alston and Martin Welton refer to as "theatre in the dark."[8] Most commonly though, when we speak of theatrical darkness we mean dim lighting, which I refer to as *gloaming* in order to avoid the predetermined valences of terms like *twilight* or *gloom*.[9] Beyond blackness and dimming, though, choreography can also be obscured by other means. Just as events can be highlighted onstage, they can also be hidden—either concretely obstructed by barriers or attentionally obstructed through the concurrent staging of competing events of interest.

How is our experience of performance affected when vision is unsettled? In essence, the staging practices described in the following chapters effect periodic and changing complications of vision that provide conditions for the performance of vision, with its drives and limitations, to be apprehended as such. As Forsythe comments in a 2001 interview,

> if you're looking at something very hard, if you're trying to watch very carefully because it's somewhat obscured, you tend to be a more careful viewer, to ask 'what are we doing there?' Are we teaching people the aesthetics at hand? No, we're teaching them about watching, about being a viewer. I'm not trying to refine someone's taste, I would like to make people who watch dancing better dance viewers.[10]

The language used by Forsythe here is notable as it indicates a specific focus on the action of perception—watching, viewing—rather than on processes of interpretation. Forsythe specifically foregrounds the experience of perceptual limitation as a means to reveal the experience of perception to spectators, and to thereby prompt them toward deeper, more fully aware spectatorship. Such stagings are not "easy on the eyes," but instead challenge viewing in a context in which facilitative lighting would be expected. In following I consider four obscuring strategies, noting how each affects vision and in turn, by problematizing seeing, makes a performative engagement with vision possible.

Notes

1. Forsythe in Senta Driver, "A Conversation with William Forsythe," 93.
2. Craig Koslofsky, "Princes of Darkness: The Night at Court, 1650–1750," 239.
3. Yvonne Rainer, "Some Retrospective Notes on a Dance," 178.
4. Laura Gröndahl, "From Candle Light to Contemporary Lighting Systems: How Lighting Technology Shapes Scenographic Practices," 30.
5. Katherine Graham, "The Play of Light: Rethinking Mood Lighting in Performance," 14.
6. Katherine Graham, "In the Shadow of a Dancer: Light as Dramaturgy in Contemporary Performance," 201.
7. Roslyn Sulcas, "William Forsythe: The Poetry of Disappearance and the Great Tradition." Quote translated from Gilles Anquetil, "L'archéologue du mouvement. Un entretien avec William Forsythe."

8. Adam Alston and Martin Welton, *Theatre in the Dark: Shadow, Gloom, and Blackout in Contemporary Theatre.* See also Andrew Sofer, *Dark Matter: Invisibility in Drama, Theater, and Performance.*
9. Compare for example Tim Edensor, *From Light to Dark: Daylight, Illumination, and Gloom.*
10. Forsythe in Julie Copeland, "William Forsythe In the Middle."

Bibliography

Alston, Adam, and Mark Welton. 2017. *Theatre in the Dark: Shadow, Gloom, and Blackout in Contemporary Theatre.* London and New York: Bloomsbury.

Anquetil, Gilles. 1990. L'archéologue du mouvement. Un entretien avec William Forsythe. *Le Nouvel Observateur,* October: 25–31.

Copeland, Julie. 2001. William Forsythe in the Middle—Interview. Radio National, Australian Broadcasting Corporation, December 3. http://www.abc.net.au/arts/default.htm. Accessed 27 May 2005.

Driver, Senta. 1990. A Conversation with William Forsythe. *Ballet Review* 18 (1): 86–97.

Edensor, Tim. 2017. *From Light to Dark: Daylight, Illumination, and Gloom.* Minneapolis: University of Minnesota Press.

Graham, Katherine. 2018. In the Shadow of a Dancer: Light as Dramaturgy in Contemporary Performance. *Contemporary Theatre Review* 28 (2): 196–209.

———. 2020. The Play of Light: Rethinking Mood Lighting in Performance. *Studies in Theatre and Performance* 40 (3): 1–17.

Gröndahl, Laura. 2015. From Candle Light to Contemporary Lighting Systems: How Lighting Technology Shapes Scenographic Practices. *Nordic Theatre Studies* 26 (2): 21–32.

Koslofsky, Craig. 2007. Princes of Darkness: The Night at Court, 1650–1750. *Journal of Modern History* 79 (2): 235–273.

Rainer, Yvonne. 1965. Some Retrospective Notes on a Dance for 10 People and 12 Mattresses Called 'Parts of Some Sextets,' Performed at the Wadsworth Atheneum, Hartford, Connecticut, and Judson Memorial Church, New York, in March, 1965. *Tulane Drama Review* 10 (2): 168–178.

Sofer, Andrew. 2013. *Dark Matter: Invisibility in Drama, Theater, and Performance.* Ann Arbor: University of Michigan Press.

Sulcas, Roslyn. 1991. William Forsythe: The Poetry of Disappearance and the Great Tradition. *Dance Theatre Journal* 9 (1): 4–7 and 32–33.

CHAPTER 2

Tenebrism: Seeing (in) the Dark

As we sit outside in the evening watching children play, our eyes smoothly adjust to the steady reduction of light as dusk sets in. If we remain long enough, we may eventually notice that they are becoming harder to see and call the shadowy figures inside. What we won't have noticed is the gradual process of visual adaptation that the lowering light evokes—that as darkness sets in, our vision has optimized along certain lines. There is a limit to this improvement, though: like all organisms, we are unable to see objects in total darkness due to the complete absence of retinal stimulation by photons.

This does not, however, mean that we cease to see anything in pitch darkness. Despite visual experience being largely contingent on neural firing in response to visible light, what we see in the dark is darkness itself, as philosopher Roy Sorensen explains.[1] Our experience of the dark, in other words, is not an absence of perception but the apprehension of darkness. Simultaneously an absence of light and an active presence in its own right, darkness affects us by heightening the sensitivity of our other senses. Darkness is not just seen; it is also heard and felt, even tasted. Contingent on the environments and contexts in which they occur, darknesses have tangible atmospheres of their own: an almost cottony density on a mild moonless summer night, a hard, pressing closeness in a sealed stairwell. Set and lighting designers, who know that the spaces, fittings, and acoustics of stages and auditoriums permit theatrical darknesses to afford

© The Author(s), under exclusive license to Springer Nature Switzerland AG 2023
F. Vass, *William Forsythe's Postdramatic Dance Theater*, Cognitive Studies in Literature and Performance,
https://doi.org/10.1007/978-3-031-26658-4_2

33

hiding, revelation, and uncanniness, engineer them with varying nuances and an acute awareness of their potentials for influencing mood and tension.

Like light, darkness also performs. Writing on "theatre in the dark," or works performed either in complete darkness or in deep shadow, Liam Jarvis makes this assertion in response to Robert Wilson's view that light functions as "an actor" in his works.[2] Other authors, though, point out how darkness is often relegated to a secondary role. Martin Welton, for example, comments that theatrical darkness "most often seems an effect, rather than a state—a signaling of something else, rather than a medium or condition to be appreciated for properties all its own. Darkness is illumination's relief."[3] Noting that theatrical darkness is seldom absolute due to light spillage and safety regulations, Stanton Garner highlights how the theatre's not-fully-real darkness nonetheless evokes our phenomenological responses to the "real" thing: a displacement of experience and an unmooring of perception.[4]

In his works, Forsythe carefully imbricates the performance of light and darkness by balancing their potentials against those of the moving dancers. In an early interview with lighting designer Jennifer Tipton, who collaborated on the lighting design for the Joffrey Ballet's premiere of *Square Deal* (1983), he comments on the visual effects of low light and the irritation they can cause:

> Lighting cannot dominate; you're lighting a dance. You've got to make the dance visible or invisible…I noticed over the years working that lighting, given *little* enough of it, *obscures.* I mean it doesn't only illuminate; after a certain point, it obscures. But [the piece] *is still lit*. And people are infuriated by that. Or the critics are, usually, for some reason or other…But it is obviously on purpose. I really want the scene to look that way. You want something to be disappearing, or to be obscure.[5]

Forsythe's larger oeuvre reveals an interest not only in conditions of extremely low light but also in the performative power of complete darkness as well. In following I consider pitch-black and exceptionally bright conditions in Forsythe's works, addressing the threshold of visibility by first stepping to vision's two poles. From these extremes I move to a discussion of dramaturgies of darkness in the section that follows.

BLACKOUTS AND BUMPS

The candles, Argand burners, and gas lamps used in seventeenth-century European theaters required significant manpower and time to extinguish, lift, lower, or cover the numerous units needed to light the stage,[6] while relighting obviously required the same. Gaslights, limelights, and carbon-arc lights developed later also required numerous attendants to dim or block them. Following the development of incandescent lighting in the late nineteenth century, theatrical blackout effects were achieved in the 1920s through techniques of phantom load, or offstage doubling to balance circuits.[7] The development of SCR (silicon-controlled rectifier) technologies in the 1950s finally made blackout conditions more easily producible, though filaments within these instruments do continue to glow for some time as they cool.

Full-stage blackouts are conventionally used to effect instantaneous shifts in onstage time, place, or both. However, blackouts can also be localized to affect only part of the stage space. Though typically (and pragmatically) associated with stoppage of action, both global and localized blackouts also permit figures—and voices—to emerge from or disappear into them. With the exception of "theatre in the dark," though, blackout conditions are seldom sustained for long in practice and are even less frequently seen during dance performances. Occasionally, blackouts serve practical purposes: in Kurt Jooss' *The Green Table* (1932), for example, sudden blackouts frame the opening and closing "table" scenes, as previously described, while the work's middle six scenes depicting consequences of war are more conventionally separated by evocative fades to black or, in the case of sudden flight of "the Profiteer," an instantaneous blackout that causes him to disappear in mid-air.

Though Forsythe has occasionally separated scenes with blackouts in the conventional manner, extremely frequent blackouts included in a number of his works function like the jumpy editing of postwar European films.[8] *Square Deal* (1983) prompted one critic to declare that

> We are made uncomfortable from the start. A great deal of the action takes place in obscurity. The senses are assaulted by extremes of dark and light, fragmented pieces of speech, dance and acting in cinematic blackouts. The sound score by Thomas Jahn and Mr. Forsythe rumbles out in loud staccato blocks; silhouettes and body parts are isolated by onstage projections of light.[9]

Gänge (1983, subtitled *Ein Stück über Ballett*), Forsythe's first full-length production as for the Frankfurt State Theater, offered a similar aesthetic over the course of its first 30 minutes, while *Pizza Girl* (1986), which was co-choreographed by Forsythe and 12 associates,[10] used blackouts to separate the "ninety one-minute ballets" of the work's subtitle. The repeatedly falling fire curtain in part 2 of *Artifact* (1984), which Forsythe disavows as a form of postmodern disruption,[11] casts audiences into six musically determined but unanticipated blackouts over the work's 14-minute span, while Bach's *Chaconne in D minor* continues to play throughout. In *Angoloscuro*, a non-proscenium work from 2007 with an extremely rudimentary light plot, blackouts delineated over 30 separate scenes in just over 1 hour, including a series of 11 rapid-fire blackouts within 2 minutes.[12] By comparison, Spencer Finch's hanging "light object" of tubular trusses pulses slow visual rhythms throughout most of the first half hour of *Sider* (2011), fading slowly to black and snapping on again or snapping to black and then slowly fading up.[13]

How does vision react to blackouts and afterward when light returns? Transitions between darkness and light set off adaptive processes that are mitigated by the entire visual system, from photoreceptor cells in the retina to the neuronal pathways that connect the eyes to the brain's visual processing areas. Rod and cone cells, the two types of photoreceptors at the surface of the retina, are differently distributed, with color-sensitive cones tightly packed in the tiny area called the fovea, which is responsible for sharp detailed vision, and rods covering most of the retinal periphery. More sensitive than cone cells (but not to color), rods fire selectively in response to highly localized contrasts between light and dark. Individual photoreceptor cell impulses are locally summed via a network of bipolar cells, while excitatory and inhibitory processes occur at the level of ganglion cells, which ultimately send signals to the brain via the optic nerve. This results in the detection of edges.

The component responsible for neural firing in rods is a chromoprotein pigment called rhodopsin, or visual purple. When exposed to light, its molecules change configuration: the pigmented retinal element, which the body synthesizes from beta-carotene (Vitamin A), separates from the colorless opsin protein. Once this photobleaching occurs, darkness is required for rhodopsin to regenerate through a process of recycling. At sudden exposure to intense light, for example, when the curtain rises on a bright stage or during a zero-second "bump" (snap cue in zero seconds) to bright light, our pupils quickly constrict to reduce light flooding into the eyes, with additional adaptive responses occurring further along the neural pathway. Not only do our visual systems respond to sudden light changes, they also anticipate them; even thinking about seeing light or dark objects or scenarios has been shown to trigger pupil dilation or constriction.[14] However, the latency of pupillary response (200–350 milliseconds, depending on light intensity) nonetheless results in a depletion of rhodopsin. Recovery from photobleaching is slow, with approximately half an hour needed to restore maximum sensitivity to light. It is a good deal faster, though, if we are instead plunged from well-lit conditions into relative darkness, because bright-active cone cells adapt faster to reduced light than rod cells. It still takes around 10 minutes for our eyes to fully adapt to sudden darkness.

Regardless of the transition, both blackouts and bumps to full light have a dazzling effect that temporarily stuns our vision. In our distant evolutionary past, we were less frequently plunged into sudden darkness or bright light; in the age of candles and light switches, trains and tunnels, and blackouts and bumps, these alterations affect both how we see and our phenomenological experience. Given this, it is clear that sudden light shifts impact us differently than more stably illuminated scenographies. Stephen Di Benedetto analyzes the sensory impact of lighting by focusing on how Robert Wilson's flooding and blending of color and gradual changes in works like *Einstein on the Beach* (1976) and *Maladie de la Mort* (1991) shape scenic space, rhythm, focus, and mood while creating a sense of the surreal.[15] While designers and directors have long recognized that motion and change attract and maintain audience focus, Di Benedetto highlights how Wilson's technique of contrasting stasis with distinctively slowed movement makes visual change all the more perceptually significant.[16] But Wilson also clearly understands the perceptual impact of abrupt light changes as well, as evidenced by his works' climactic moments: the flickering chiaroscuro finale of the "spaceship" scene in *Einstein on the Beach* (lighting by Beverly Emmons) or the moment that Lucinda Childs, far down a ramp projecting into the audience, turns in a sudden silence to face an intense flare from the wall of glowing onstage lights in *Adam's Passion* (2015, scenography by Serge von Arx). The plunge from darkness to light or vice versa compromises visual perception in a way that we are only aware of at the most extreme of transitions; however, the arresting optical effect of dazzle, however subliminal, renders our visual world temporarily spectacular.

The standard presentational protocols of European theatrical performance set up conditions that can be used to unsettle vision through a process of dishabituation. As bells ring five minutes before curtain time, attendees move from brightly lit foyers into dimmer auditoriums, their eyes adjusting as they settle into their seats. Houselights slowly dim to a twilight that signals for conversations to end, cell phones to be switched off, and attention to be directed to the stage. A few seconds later house-lights dim to full darkness, and audiences quieten in anticipation. This is a moment of choice for theatre makers: to open the curtain onto static or changing illumination, or to reveal a matching darkness and then increase lighting. In his perhaps most frequently staged work, *In the Middle, Somewhat Elevated* (1987), Forsythe opts for the latter strategy, shocking the audience with brightness. At the explosive crash that launches Thom Willems' rhythmic metal-edged score, the lighting of the bare black stage snaps "in zero" from blackout to high illumination. The jarring, sonically emphasized transition heightens arousal but at the same time momentarily handicaps vision. No choreography is lost to rhodopsin depletion, though, as the harsh, rehearsal-like lighting reveals two women casually standing at the center of the stage, warily sizing each other up as each waits for the other to leave.[17] One eventually walks off after 30 seconds, and a man joins the remaining woman to start the work's high-powered opening duet. At the work's closing musical crash some 27 minutes later, one of the women vanishes mid-air in a *soubresaut* as the lights snap off again as abruptly as they came on.

In other works, Forsythe's lighting design produces localized blackouts that demarcate shifting architectures of full and partial visibility but also invisibility. For *New Sleep*, created a few months prior to *In the Middle, Somewhat Elevated*, a uniformly black floor is marked out with an X of black lines extending from corner to corner and dividing the space into four triangles. At times one diagonal swath or the other is completely blacked out; at other junctures, only a single triangle of space is illumi-nated or the four areas appear to have three distinct hues. Tanja Rühl, who has collaborated with Forsythe since 2002 as lighting technician, designer, and consultant for stagings of Forsythe-licensed works, explains that the upstage wing flats "cut" high-intensity beams from profile lamps mounted in the wings, while the shutters of cross-focused top lights also "carve" sharp lighting delineations. In some scenes, spaces between the rows of wing flats are lit by vertically focused top lights positioned over the gaps, while the darkened stage is illuminated only by tightly focused follow spots or a Gobo projection.[18] Shifting blackout spaces compete for atten-tion with the black-clad, energetically moving dancers, whose pale shoes and bare calves, forearms, necks, and faces catch and reflect light as they move. Occasionally, dancers are silhouetted in the spill of light from the wings, and at one point an illuminated wing gap is occupied by one of three differently costumed "family" characters who come and go throughout the piece (Fig. 2.1).

At times, *New Sleep*'s choreo-scenography seems to offer ratifying commentary on fundamental visual processes through the interface of the lighting design and the staging. Visual focus is inherently drawn to the contrast provided by edges as they are fundamental for distinguishing objects from background and for vision in depth. Our attention, in other words, is attracted not just to fields of differing intensity but specifically to the junctures where these fields meet.[19] When *New Sleep*'s stage is divided diagonally into bright and blacked-out sectors, trains of dancers appear from the wings and move in repetitive step patterns along the contrast edge, sometimes on the illuminated side and sometimes on the darkened one. Their emergences and disappearances increase arousal, an instinctive response of the primitive or "reptilian" brain noted as well by Di Benedetto

Fig. 2.1 A moment in *New Sleep* showing the performers and the uniformly black floor differently illuminated. (Source: photo courtesy of Dominik Mentzos)

in his discussion of the opening lighting and sound in Mark Morris' *L'Allegro, il Penseroso, ed il Moderato* (1988).[20]

Additionally, the shifting patterns of *New Sleep*'s blackout and other light settings, together with the work's sleek black costumes and high-energy choreography, create an continuously changing array of atmospheres. Rühl explains that two different temperatures of light affect the appearance of both the floor and the dancing bodies: HMI (Hydrargyrum Medium-Arc Iodide) lamps provide a cool daylight feel, while tungsten lamps offer a warmer, more artificial one.[21] Lighting cues matched to percussive musical accents abruptly cast dancers into deep shadow or make them sprout shadows themselves, change the visual temperature of their skin, reduce their figures to a swarm of whirling calves, hands, faces, and bared women's backs, cause them to disappear entirely, or even make them appear to shift location while standing still. The mobile regions of light and blackout keep retinal cells in ongoing cycles of recovery, repetitively triggering responses to the changing conditions. With each new light cue, not only is attention spatially shifted but also perception is qualitatively altered. Within this visually unstable environment, the dancers appear and disappear, cascading and visually morphing before our busy and bedazzled eyes.

DARK DRAMATURGIES

Though our gaze is inherently drawn to performers in motion, even tracking them when they vanish as I discuss in a following chapter, darkness itself also performs its own attentional lure. We *mind* darkness: we keep an eye on it because its unyielding nature arouses our instinctive desire to know what it might harbor. Sensitizing our eyes, our ears, and our skin, darkness also frees our minds, for better or for worse. Architect and philosopher Juhani Pallasmaa emphasizes how darkness and deep shadows "dim the sharpness of vision, make depth and distance ambiguous, and invite unconscious peripheral vision and tactile fantasy."[22] Baroque artists like Caravaggio and those he influenced clearly recognized this, harnessing the influence of darkness in the tenebrism of their night scenes and candle-lit surrounds. Surrealist René Magritte also recognized the power of the obscure, commenting that

> Everything we see hides another thing. There is an interest in that which is hidden by what we see. There is an interest in that which is hidden and

which the visible does not show us. The interest can take the form of a quite intense feeling, a sort of conflict, one might say, between the visible that is hidden and the visible that is present.[23]

Magritte's 1928 painting *La voix du silence* deploys the visual and psychological pull of darkness in a similar manner to *New Sleep*. The right half of the canvas shows a sedate domestic dining-room with bare painted floorboards, mundane furniture, and a shelf of bric-a-brac, while the room on the left side of the canvas beyond the partitioning wall is a pitch-black void. Only a fading spill of light across the bottom of the canvas marks it as a continuation of the depicted space. Magritte's darkness seems to almost roll out of the picture like a heavy fog; its indeterminate presence troubles our attempts to focus on the small, well-lit salon, yet it offers us "nothing" to see except itself.

Darkness, by yielding no clues about what is occurring within it or what might emerge, casts the viewer into the unmoored, predictive mode of the future tense, or better put, the *tense future*. Far from being a neutral void, Magritte's static pictorial blackout is ominously pregnant; Forsythe's menacing blacknesses, on the other hand, magnify tension as they manifest and shift, altering our perception of moving bodies that are themselves in constant states of visual change. Here, the aesthetics of duration and repetition that Lehmann cites as having developed within postdramatic theatre are supplanted by an aesthetics of iterating appearances and disappearances, though similarly evoking an "attending to the little differences" that manifest as a result of the changing light that strikes them.[24]

Darkness also ruptures the vast, wintry paleness of Forsythe's hourlong 1991 version of *The Loss of Small Detail*, with nightmarish figures emerging and being swallowed again by a chaotic and thundering blackness during a four-and-a-half-minute section of the work.[25] As film projections on the back wall snap on and off, a strobing "door" at the edge of the stage frames the silhouette of a shouting, gesticulating nude man, while other dancers move within a speckled pool of blackness, making it seem to writhe. The light lifts to a thick powdery gray, revealing a tableau of broken frozen figures before plunging again into cacophonic darkness. Afterward, a pale, nude "primitive figure"[26] is left wandering in cross-lit snow. In Forsythe's rarely performed *Four Point Counter* (1995), the threat of darkness manifests as a morphing diamond-shaped blackout that is created by spinning an opaque square plate on a track in front of a top light. The elastic black shape lurks, unexpectedly engulfing four men as they move on a bright white rectangle of stage, while the work's irregular sonic collage of low, arcing rumbles and explosive, snapping metal clatter is eerily at odds with its smooth looming motion, rendering it a voiceless presence.

Unaccustomed to darkness, sighted individuals move differently when they cannot see, gingerly stepping and groping as they search with their skin and ears. Forsythe tapped these physical effects, together with the frightening disorientation that darkness can elicit, as dramaturgical resources for the 2008 work *I don't believe in outer space* On the first rehearsal day, he discussed his experience working with a blind performer in 2005 in the early stages of developing an installation work, before sending the ensemble home to blindfold themselves and navigate their own apartment spaces "in a dancerly fashion" part of each day for a week. Returning to the studio, some dancers spoke of how their perception of objects' spatial or tactile qualities had changed while sightless, while one recounted an instinctive terror when, having lost their orientation, they accidentally touched a bathrobe hanging on a door and mistook it for a person. Using the dancers' re-enacted movements as choreographic foundations, Forsythe developed a danced dramaturgy focused on the illusory quality but paradoxical depth of the lived experience of sensing, together with our fear of what is perhaps the ultimate darkness: death and the loss of bodied experience.

Pitch darkness, then, has been a versatile and dynamic performer in Forsythe's works, one that draws the viewer into a heightened and emotionally vibrant mode of anticipatory perception. Exploiting the responses of the visual system to sudden shifts of illumination, as well as the salience of the dark, mobile architectures of light and darkness serve as active and often ominous onstage partners and catalyze embodied dramaturgies. At the end of *Angoloscuro*, Jone San Martin draws slowly back in fading light toward the work's eponymous dark corner, speaking an unintelligible language that morphs from conversational to guttural and incantatory as she and the light recede from view. Lowering herself slowly to the ground and finally covering herself with her black cloth cape, her voice fades to a whisper and then even her shadow is gone, leaving a dark empty stage and faint, slowly fading music. One poetry of disappearance among many.

NOTES

1. Roy Sorensen, *Seeing Dark Things*, 237–241.
2. Liam Jarvis, "Creating in the Dark: Conceptualizing Different Darknesses in Contemporary Theatre Practice," 88–89.
3. Martin Welton, *Feeling Theatre*, 52.
4. Stanton B. Garner, *Bodied Spaces: Phenomenology and Performance in Contemporary Drama*, 40–41.
5. Driver, "William Forsythe and Jennifer Tipton: A Conversation About Lighting," 69–70.
6. Among the many inventions of pioneering stage designer and engineer Nicola Sabbattini (1574–1654) was a means of plunging the stage into darkness by lowering opaque cylinders over onstage lamps. See Chap. 12, "How to Darken the Whole Stage in a Moment," in Sabbattini's *Instructions for the Manufacture of Scenery and Stage Machines* (*Pratica di fabricar scene e macchine ne' teatri*), Pesaro, 1638.
7. See Theodore Fuchs, *Stage Lighting*.
8. For a deeper consideration of cinematic aspects of Forsythe's work, see Roslyn Sulcas, "Forsythe and Film."
9. Anna Kisselgoff, "Ballet: Joffrey Premiere."
10. Other credited choreographers are Alida Chase, Stephen Galloway, Timothy Gordon, Dieter Heitkamp, Evan Jones, Amanda Miller, Vivienne Newport, Cara Perlman, Antony Rizzi, Ana Catalina Roman, Iris Tenge, Ron Thornhill, and Bernard Uithof.
11. Forsythe clarifies that the falling fire curtain is "a musical caesura... It wasn't designed as a disturbance or anything. There is a change in the music each time, so it is giving you the structural chunks of the music." Quoted in Sarah Crompton, "William Forsythe interview: *Artifact* is an ode to ballet."
12. Version performed from 2009.
13. Finch's "light object" was created for use in Forsythe's 2005/6 work *Three Atmospheric Studies*.
14. B. Laeng and U. Sulutvedt, "The Eye Pupil Adjusts to Imaginary Light."
15. Stephen Di Benedetto, *The Provocation of the Senses in Contemporary Theatre*, 35–51.
16. Di Benedetto, 45.
17. Sulcas describes the competitive dramaturgy of *In the Middle, Somewhat Elevated* in "Watching Dancers Grow, as Cultivated by a Daredevil."
18. Tanja Rühl, email discussion with the author, February 2019.
19. Excitatory and inhibitory processes of ganglion cells in fact result not only in edge detection but also perceptually enhance edges, causing contrast to appear stronger than it actually is in the area immediately surrounding them.

20. Di Benedetto, *The Provocation of the Senses*, 65.
21. Tanja Rühl, email discussion with the author, February 2019.
22. Juhani Pallasmaa, *The Eyes of the Skin*, 46.
23. René Magritte, radio interview with Jean Neyens (1965), cited in Harry Torczyner, *Magritte, Ideas and Images*, trans. Richard Millen (New York: Harry N. Abrams), 172.
24. Hans-Thies Lehmann, Postdramatic Theatre, 156–157.
25. Part of this scene, which was nicknamed "bunraku" by the company, is documented in Mike Figgis' documentary film *Just Dancing Around?*
26. Forsythe's description of a scene from *The Loss of Small Detail* reads in part:
     it is snowing.
     apparently,
     it has been snowing
     for quite some time.
     The light that now increases reveals
     several figures that
     are watching a film
     of primitive people
     portrayed by contemporary
     performers. The figures
     are snow covered as
     are the primitive Performers in the
     film. The film watched
     is printed in negative.
     The snow is black. The
     primitive performance, white.
     (Ballett Frankfurt program booklet, *The Loss of Small Detail*)

BIBLIOGRAPHY

Crompton, Sarah. 2012. William Forsythe Interview: *Artifact* is an Ode to Ballet. *The Telegraph*, April 18. https://www.telegraph.co.uk/culture/theatre/dance/9211413/William-Forsythe-interview-Artifact-is-an-ode-to-ballet.html. Accessed 3 January 2015.

Di Benedetto, Stephen. 2011. *The Provocation of the Senses in Contemporary Theatre*. Abingdon and New York: Routledge.

Driver, Senta. 1990. A Conversation with William Forsythe. *Ballet Review* 18 (1): 86–97.

———. 2000. William Forsythe and Jennifer Tipton: A Conversation About Lighting. In *William Forsythe (Choreography and Dance: An International Journal* 5 (3)), ed. Senta Driver, 41–78. Chur: Harwood Academic Publishers.

2 TENEBRISM: SEEING (IN) THE DARK   45

Figgis, Mike, director. *Just Dancing Around?* 1996; *Channel Four* version, Euphoria Films, 50′59″. Aired 27 December 1996.

Fuchs, Theodore. 1929. *Stage Lighting*. Boston: Little, Brown and Company.

Garner, Stanton B. 1994. *Bodied Spaces: Phenomenology and Performance in Contemporary Drama*. Ithaca: Cornell University Press.

Jarvis, Liam. 2017. Creating in the Dark: Conceptualising Different Darknesses in Contemporary Theatre Practice. In *Theatre in the Dark: Shadow, Gloom and Blackout in Contemporary Theatre*, ed. Adam Alston and Martin Welton, 88–112. London and New York: Bloomsbury Publishing.

Kisselgoff, Anna. 1983. Ballet: Joffrey Premiere. *The New York Times*, November 4. https://www.nytimes.com/1983/11/04/arts/ballet-joffrey-premiere.html. Accessed 25 June 2010.

Laeng, B., and U. Sulutvedt. 2014. The Eye Pupil Adjusts to Imaginary Light. *Psychological Science* 25 (1): 188–197.

Lehmann, Hans-Thies. 2006. *Postdramatic Theatre*. Translated by Karen-Jürs-Munby. Abingdon and New York: Routledge. Original version: Lehmann, Hans-Thies. 1999. *Postdramatisches Theater*. Frankfurt am Main: Verlag der Autoren.

Magritte, René. 1965. Radio Interview with Jean *Neyens*. In *Magritte: Ideas and Images*, ed. Harry Torczyner. 1977. Translated by Richard Miller. New York: Harry N. Abrams.

Pallasmaa, Juhani. 2005. *The Eyes of the Skin: Architecture of the Senses*. Chichester: Wiley-Academy.

Sabbattini, Nicola. 1638. *Pratica di fabricar scene e macchine ne' teatri*. Ravenna: Pietro de' Paoli and Giovanni Battista Giovannelli.

Sorensen, Roy. 2008. *Seeing Dark Things: The Philosophy of Shadows*. Oxford: Oxford University Press.

Städtische Bühnen Frankfurt. 1991. Program for *The Loss of Small Detail*.

Sulcas, Roslyn. 2003. Forsythe and Film. In *Envisioning Dance on Film and Video: Dance for the Camera*, ed. Judy Mitoma, 96–102. Abingdon and New York: Routledge.

———. 2012. Watching Dancers Grow, as Cultivated by a Daredevil. *The New York Times*, December 28. https://www.nytimes.com/2012/12/29/arts/dance/william-forsythe-revival-at-paris-opera-ballet.html. Accessed 30 December 2012.

Welton, Martin. 2011. *Feeling Theatre*. Basingstoke and New York: Palgrave Macmillan.

CHAPTER 3

Gloaming: Dimming and Visions

Staging darkness and dim lighting might seem fundamentally at odds with the idea of the *theatron* as a "seeing place." Why problematize vision in an environment built to facilitate it? Reviewer Paul Ben-Itzak expresses displeasure at not being able to see the dancers clearly in a 2002 review of Forsythe's 1984 *Artifact*, commenting that the dancing

> appears mostly in shadow, producing the frustration born of wanting to watch something—this is William Forsythe choreographing, after all, on the extraordinary dancers of his home company!—and not being able to see it. (A problem compounded by the dark lighting, also designed by Forsythe. I know, I know, it's artistic, but if you have to strain to see the performance, what's the point?!)[1]

The postdramatic *theatron* does not so much make vision possible as it makes *visions* possible, harnessing architecture and technologies to generate a broad and sensuous spectrum of visual experience. Yaron Abulafia offers that "[t]he aesthetics of light is now used to *evoke a transcendental realm of emotions and atmospheres,* raising levels of physiological and/or neural activity and aiming at an emotional experience."[2] Anna Kisselgoff signals this power in a 2001 review of Forsythe's *Enemy in the Figure* (1989), exhorting audiences to

© The Author(s), under exclusive license to Springer Nature   47
Switzerland AG 2023
F. Vass, *William Forsythe's Postdramatic Dance Theater*, Cognitive
Studies in Literature and Performance,
https://doi.org/10.1007/978-3-031-26658-4_3

Forget the theories and watch the movement, especially when the dancers are dancing in the dark (...) A sequence with dancers performing in a brightly lighted section of the stage is often juxtaposed with dancers moving in darkness at the other side. These could be barely made out but their movement was sensed. One could regard them as images caught in the web of distant memory: present but not visible.[3]

There is more behind the evocative quasi-presence that Kisselgoff signals. Postdramatic theatre frequently engages with sensing on a level that is also perceptually *provocative*, thwarting expectations and opening avenues for transformative experiences of spectation. Lehmann addresses the ways in which presence, rhythm, gesture, language, music, and "the qualities of the visual beyond representation" have become compositional elements, noting that

the *theatrical* conditions of perception, namely the aesthetic qualities of the-atre...are precisely the point in many contemporary theatre works—by no means just the extreme ones—and are not employed as merely subservient means for the illustration of an action laden with suspense.[4]

Postdramatic theatre engages with qualities of light, space, sound, and situation to create unsettled and unsettling *atmospheres*. This concept, first elaborated by Gernot Böhme in 1993,[5] offers a phenomenological means of approaching the subjective experience of natural or composed environ-ments from cultural, material, and philosophical perspectives. Atmospheres, which are omnipresent but not always concretely apprehended, are both felt by us and evoke feelings within us, as Tonino Griffero asserts.[6] Böhme's description of atmospheres as "tuned spaces" (*gestimmte Räume*) reflects how they can be composed with a variety of goals in mind, among them the perturbation of experience through the creation of unexpected, "oth-erworldly" conditions. As Mikkel Bille and colleagues comment,

[R]ather than aiming at performing ideals or negotiating norms, staging atmosphere may also explicitly work towards creating discontinuities in our experience of the world. Such disruptions occur when we suddenly find our everyday perception disturbed, being forced to re-assemble our world from a new point. (...) We may argue then that staging atmosphere may not only be about obtaining social goals, but may also work as a way of encountering other cosmologies and repertoires beyond our common sense experience of the world.[7]

How do postdramatic theatre makers engage visual perception to create atmosphere? One way is through the presentation of dim conditions, which are never purely sinister or benevolent due to our two-sided history with the dark. Tim Edensor explains that

> Negative conceptions that emerge out of religious and modernist thought have always been accompanied by positive understandings about the promises that darkness offers. These different ideas have informed a host of practices through which darkness offers pleasure and transgression, mystic and religious expectation, nocturnal sublimity, aesthetic delight, sensory immersion, social intimacy, and political opposition. Alternatively, darkness provokes fear at perilous conditions, supernatural forces, immorality, and malign intent.[8]

The optics of postdramatic theatre are not necessarily defined by how much one sees or even necessarily by what one sees, but rather by *how many ways* one is enabled to see. The multiple registers of vision made possible by the modern *theatron* implicate the full spectrum of visual experience, and with it the wide range of affective atmospheres that can be generated. But within the genre, and perhaps surprisingly also within contemporary dance, certain visual registers have become increasingly commonplace, including what I refer to as *gloaming*.

ATMOSPHERIC STUDIES

Dim theatrical lighting was common long before blackouts were a viable option. The atmospheres of Renaissance, Baroque, and Romantic theatre performances were enhanced by lighting which, though cumbersome to operate, both created mood and facilitated illusion.[9] Pioneering theater architect and engineer Nicola Sabbatini (1574–1654), whose novel dimming techniques produced the first near-blackouts, also recognized that greater illusory depth could be created by lighting the downstage area more brightly than the upstage. The production of spatial, temporal, and rational illusion reached an apex in European theatre between the eighteenth and nineteenth centuries as new lighting technologies enabled presentation of increasingly phantasmagorical characters and themes. Romantic ballet choreo-scenographers responded by populating dusky or gloomy glens with ethereally glowing supernatural creatures: sylphs, wilis, fairies, and ghosts. The fluidity and *ballon* of Romantic ballet movement, together with the new fashion of long, layered skirts of muslin and gauze, further exploited the twilight optics and distancing proscenium architecture to produce dreamlike illusions of floating, blur and flight. Avant-garde theatre of the late nineteenth century, by contrast, began to interrogate these principles of presentation, using low light to instead turn action inward within what Michael Kirby calls a 'hermetic' model of detachment, distance, and relative stillness.[10]

Despite the emergence of this poetics of theatrical darkness, dance audiences retained an expectation of easy viewing. For this—and also for reasons of safety—choreographers have seldom kept dancers in darkness that is too profound or too long. Instead, gloaming usually occurs as a temporary contrasting register in which brighter illumination literally highlights specific performers or movements. Sometimes this can be overt, through the use of static or following spotlights. Maurice Bejart's *Bolero* (1961) tracks Ravel's famously extended musical buildup by first following only the solo performer's hands with tightly focused pin spots, then gradually illuminates the soloist's body before lifting general lighting to reveal the male corps de ballet in murky darkness around the glowing red table on which the soloist dances. Brightness in *Bolero* grows in subtle muscially congruent stages over the building crescendo, until a sudden ecstatic blackout marks the final musical flourish.[11] Palettes of contemporary stage lighting often shift with a subtlety that goes largely unnoticed by audiences. Writing in 1985, Peter Mumford described his work lighting dance stages as "painting the air" in a rhythmically orchestrated manner that relates to music and the composition of space and time, while also supporting, amplifying, and reinforcing the choreography.[12]

Crosslighting (lamps rigged on towers in the wings with beams pointed horizontally across the stage) is widely considered to be ideal for dance as it "models" the body, causing its surfaces to reflect light and rendering choreographic forms more distinct. Forsythe, however, prefers to work without it, which also eliminates the need for wings to hide the instruments. Instead, he prefers a blend of backlighting (lamps on upstage battens angled diagonally down) and toplighting from overhead lamps, with small amounts of additional light from the front to reduce shadows. Proper balancing of these elements ensures that the dancers stand out clearly as figures within the space. Forsythe also rarely uses overt color, relying by preference on the warmer or cooler illumination provided by differing types of bulbs.[13] Developed in collaboration with lighting designers since his earliest works, his light scores are characteristically "busy,"

with many subtle and barely perceptible changes of illumination intensify-
ing impact or altering spatial focus as dancers join scenes, form groups, or
change tasks. Detail is frequently effaced by dim lighting and other scenographic means: dark costuming frequently renders dancers as silhouettes
or makes them melt into gloomy regions or disappear altogether, while
dancers' faces, which are not heavily made up, are sometimes left in a
degree of shadow.

Forsythe calibrates lighting (or more aptly *darking*) with atmosphere
firmly in mind. His appreciation of the impact of low illumination developed over his early career, as shown in his 1997 comments about the ballet
Artifact that

> it's a *degree*, or *two* at the most, because at one point things stop. And
> there's a way that things glow in the dark. It has a lot to do with what you're
> wearing. In *Artifact*, [one] scene has gotten darker and darker over the
> years. [It] is just 20 women taking a simple step like this, moving across the
> stage on pointe, like a flock of birds, sort of evoking the Romantic period.
> The light is so low, so I can just see their arms moving, really flying in space.
> It's not about making a dark scene, it's that the scene looks best like that.
> It's amazing like that. But you turn it up two more degrees and it [only]
> looks like a bunch of girls, going across stage. That's not the point.[14]

The "point" is clearly the creation of a specific affective atmosphere
through the coupling of extremely reduced illumination with sweeping,
repetitive *port de bras* movements. For Forsythe, atmosphere is also clearly
a delicate phenomenon that requires real-time management. During many
of his stage works and performance installations, he orchestrates light in
real-time, making small, tactical changes in response to the unfolding performance atmosphere and energy both onstage and within the auditorium. Throughout his career, he has consistently refused confinement
behind the glass of the technical booth, instead requiring the technical
desk to be set up in the back rows of orchestra seating so that he can see,
hear, and feel the audience around him. At times he asks technicians to
"sneak in" a bit of additional light on a duet or slowly reduce the general
level by a small degree to focus the attention of an audience. He "pulls
down" crucial fades by hand like a conductor quieting an orchestra, his
eyes on the stage as he makes smooth rolling gestures with his hands
directed sideways toward the lighting operator, perhaps slowing or even
holding for a moment before darkening the stage with a final flourish.

Hard (sudden) blackouts are likewise cued live, with a sharp chopping gesture and a whispered "go."

Differing light conditions evoke one of three partially overlapping ranges and experiences of visual perception. In bright light, the *photopic* range enables us to see both color and contour clearly, as both rod and cone cells are highly active. Too much light, however, diminishes retinal cell function and we experience blinding glare. When conditions are dark enough, such as by faint starlight, cone cells—the eyes' color receptors—stop working and the world appears to us in shades of gray as colors at the red end of the spectrum shift toward blue-green before fading to grayscale, a phenomenon known as the Purkinje effect. In this range of rod-only activity and grayscale *scotopic* vision, our fovea are rendered functionally ineffective and fixation on visual targets is compromised. Above the scotopic threshold, we experience an intermediary range of *mesopic* vision in which both color-sensitive cones and the rods that mediate edge detection are active. Rod function is at its best in this range, while cone function is reduced.

Though grayscale vision is enhanced, we effectively see slower under mesopic visual conditions due to two factors. Since foveal cone cell function is compromised, we rely more on peripheral rod cells for visual search. Rods have slower functional response as well as longer integration times, because multiple rods converge on interneurons for integrative processing. Rods thus also register temporal change less accurately, for example, in response to quick-moving images or during fast motion of the eyes within the visual field. Further, despite their high degree of sensitivity to low illumination, rod cells are themselves not directionally selective and thus have lower spatial acuity. Because rod-reliant visual experience becomes increasingly extrafoveal (peripheral), we also apprehend visual space differently in lower light. These combined factors explain why figures become indistinct, blurry, or even glow or flicker in twilight and gloaming, as well as seeming less temporally and even existentially concrete.

Essentially, low light results in a loss of visual detail that leaves forms and motion visible but less accurately apprehended. In the dark, our daylight-attuned everyday vision compels us to look *harder* in order to determine whether threats might be present. Immersed in this state, we may have an increased awareness of the activity of "the mind's eye" as it interpolates what our eyes are incapable of conveying.

Low light is not the only scenographic tactic employed by Forsythe that effaces the forms of bodies. In a few works' scenes, extremely bright lighting "bleaches" the contours of white-clad dancers' bodies and faces from view. As he has noted, "Light does obliterate objects at some point. You can overlight something and have it equally invisible."[15] At the end of the second version of *The Loss of Small Detail* (1991), Forsythe stages an apocalyptic whiteout with a thick, pulsing snowfall and cool, diffused lighting that partially obscures dancers as they tumble and thrash on a pale stage in Issey Miyake's mica-colored costumes. In other non-proscenium works, a combination of distance and darkness provides the conditions for effacement. *The Defenders*, created in 2007, exploited the dimensions of the Zürich Schiffbauhalle to stage an "evolutionary allegory"[16] that passed before audiences seated along one long edge of an oppressive 34 × 17-meter rectangular ceiling suspended one meter above an orange-carpeted floor. Lit only by a small strip of floor lighting and spillage from downlighting around the periphery of the huge ceiling box, dancers seemed to materialize from dark mist and fade back into it again, while the sounds of their movement, vocalizations, and in one scene high-pitched pea whistles preceded their appearance and endured after they vanished. Four years later, in *Now This When Not That*, Forsythe shifted the long visual axis from x to z on a dark, 40-meter-deep stage in Bochum's massive Jahrhunderthalle, with a series of rising and falling black scrim curtains at various depths further exploiting the obscuring capacity of the stage's extreme depth. All of these conditions—semi-darkness, bleaching glare, heavy snow, scrims, and extreme distance—have obscuring and atmospheric effects that Forsythe performatively exploited through the choreography set within them. In the following section, I focus on a discussion of these choreo-scenographic dynamics within what is perhaps Forsythe's darkest work.

Dancing, in the Dark: *Limb's Theorem*

Limb's Theorem, a full-length ballet created in 1990, incorporates the stand-alone work *Enemy in the Figure* created the previous year as the second of its three parts.[17] The grounding of the ballet's choreography and scenography in Rudolf von Laban's physical geometries of the kinesphere and Daniel Libeskind's architectural drawings has been frequently detailed by others, as have its dark aesthetics, architectural set elements, and moving bodies.[18] Beyond this, though, the work activates shifting registers of vision not only through extremes of brightness and darkness but also through a murky, intermediate gloaming that evokes a performance of vision that is distinct from responses to high visibility and full darkness. The work's impact is enhanced by Thom Willems' immersive synthesized music, which ranges from the barely audible to palpable streams of sound.

Dance scholar Erika Fischer-Lichte's review saliently captures *Limb's Theorem*'s atmosphere and perceptual effects:

> *Limb's Theorem* is a black piece...The light confusedly seeks openings and slits, out from under the moving wall, from shafts, from a single mobilized flood-light (in *Enemy*), or it streams ice-cold from the flyspace as austere working light. Sometimes the stage is so dark that movements can only be hazily discerned. However, movement does not fade away with the light, but instead develops compulsively further in the mind of the observer...*Limb's Theorem* exposes the dancing in fragments that conglutinate the viewer's expectations into a seamless whole. The gaps are filled by the imagined ballet (hi)story.
>
> The dance just prior to extinguishment sharpens the senses, dilates the bounds of perception. And thereby one becomes frightfully cold. Because the abstraction has driven out the last remains of feeling. The intellectual kick sends impulses like electrical surges. Dance as metaphor is nerve impulse, albeit smeared with theatrical grease.[19]

Part 1 of *Limb's Theorem* begins with the sparse, airy ticking of Willems' score sensitizing the ear, as the curtain opens very slowly onto a completely darkened stage that similarly tunes the eye. As in *The Defenders*, dancers are heard before they are properly seen: with excruciating slowness, a small panel in the side wall slides open over the course of three minutes, letting in a faint shaft of light that illuminates a black-clad quartet in progress and a bright, shining diagonal in mid-air that signals a solid plane. The barely perceptible movement of dancers clad in black leotards and tights shimmers through the darkness for three more minutes as quiet chordal structures slowly emerge; then the panel begins slowly closing and opening again, faintly revealing and obscuring more dancers and the shining line in space. After eight of Part 1's 28 minutes, fuller illumination finally reveals the stage to be dominated by a huge, silvery-white suspended rectangle, which according to one critic "could easily pass as a photovoltaic panel,"[20] anchored at center stage by one corner and attended by a seated man in shirt and trousers. With the music now ticking and pulsing at fuller volume, this enormous "sail" casts shifting darkness onto the floor beneath it when lighting changes and as the man periodically pivots it to new positions, while its top or bottom surfaces both reflect light and create and displace mobile pools of black shadow on the stage. Dancers emerge from or are engulfed by

Fig. 3.1 Dancers, shadows, and the giant "sail" in *Limb's Theorem* Part 1. (Source: photo courtesy of Bridgeman Images)

the darkness, and black figures run across the downstage area in front of illuminated solos and duets. Meanwhile, the man waiting in his chair pulls faces so slowly as to be almost imperceptible before rising to turn the huge sail again (Fig. 3.1).

In *Enemy in the Figure*, which I discuss further in the following chapter, lighting is provided almost exclusively by a single adjustable 5 kW rolling floodlight that dancers re-position onstage throughout the performance.[21] Light spillage from the floodlight only partially illuminates large areas of the stage as it is placed in corners, behind a large, undulating wooden wall at center stage, or at one point has its beam bounced off of a reflective cloth hung in the wings. At other times, the fully illuminated 5 kW lamp throws a harsh glare onto nearby dancers clad in black or white leotards, shaggy, black-fringed pants, black jackets over bare chests, and an odd black shirt with white polka dots, while rendering other dancers into black silhouettes. Part 3 of *Limb's Theorem* is a darkly triumphant closing to the work, with a similar visual and sonic palette to Part 1. Now hung from cables, the 5 kW light swings gently back and forth like a soft searchlight as dancers fade in and out of its glow, while at other times they move in a pervasive dimness while the softest of spotlights frame solos and duets in faint pools of illumination. Bright white shirts, leotards, and socks, together with the mud-colored trousers worn by some of the men, catch more light and contrast with black costuming worn by others. The finale of *Limb's Theorem* is signaled by one entire side wall rising to let an intense, cold flood of HMI light pour in from the wings. As it closes again, the audience seated on the right side of the auditorium can glimpse a white-clad male dancer performing an angular solo as he is slowly obscured; then the evening ends as it began in deepest gloaming, with Willems' irregular ticks slowly fading against long elegiac tones.

Without opening a chicken-or-egg question regarding the origins of Forsythe's movement aesthetics and dark stagings, it is not surprising that movement in *Limb's Theorem* and other dark early works like *Gänge* (1982–1983) and *Artifact* (1984) is, as some have deemed it, "hyperkinetic." Dim lighting renders slower or small-scale dance movement less visible or even invisible, while broad, high-speed movement specifically activates and interfaces with the diffused, blurry perception of the mesopic register. The fringed and loose costume pieces worn in *Limb's Theorem* Parts 2 and 3 further contribute to the effects on vision by blurring the contours of the dancers' bodies, whether they are moving in the dark or in fuller light.

Over the longer term, though, dimness and blur are taxing to watch. As with any ongoing high-speed activity seen in shifting light, the swift, broad-scope dancing in *Limb's Theorem* and similar works pits our strategic and agentive performance of effortful focus against the more reflex-driven activity of peripheral vision. Objects that appear at the edges of our visual range trigger a *visual grasp reflex* in frontal areas of the brain, which shifts focus automatically to them.[22] Though we become more adept at voluntarily maintaining our desired visual focus throughout childhood and young adulthood,[23] this reflex remains intact in adulthood, barring damage to the cortical areas responsible for it.[24] With this in mind, it is noteworthy that the focally lit solos, duets, and group passages occurring throughout *Limb's Theorem* are set against a near constant substrate of other movement events in the gloaming: dancers unexpectedly appearing out of the black periphery or from the wings, and unpredictable shifts of light and shadow regions and set elements. Over the work's full duration, these competing regions of interest tax the eye and mind by engendering constant shifts between reflexive and voluntary visual tracking and refocusing. *Limb's Theorem* and similar works in gloaming thus choreograph a distinct—and difficult—performance of vision compared to works with brighter light.

Welcome to What You Think You See

Fischer-Lichte's reflection above also resonates with research by environmental and occupational psychologists that reveals how low-light environments lead us to actually *think* differently. Since the early 1990s, studies examining the effects of lighting on employee activity and output have shown that differing levels of illumination influence affective state. This in turn influences mental and social factors including categorization, judgments, cognitive flexibility, and cooperative behavior.[25] Given that these studies focus on office workspace environments, the range of light conditions in this body of research is very limited, typically ranging from lighting adequate for simple tasks (150 lux) to the extremely bright lighting required for work like technical drafting (1500 lux). Nonetheless, the effects measured within even this narrow everyday range are striking.

In several more recent studies investigating lighting's impact on "cognitive styles" in the workplace, social and organizational psychologists Anna Steidle, Lioba Werth, and Eva-Verena Hanke have shown that while bright lighting promotes reflection, self-awareness, self-regulation, and automatic inhibition of desires and impulses, dim lighting increases creative performance, as subjects experience a diminishment of constraints under reduced illumination.[26] Steidle and Werth (2013) contend that relative darkness "changes a room's visual message," and in doing so shifts concomitant behavior and processing styles to more global, explorative registers.[27] Their results indicate that by subliminally limiting our experience of detail, darkness both leads us to form more abstract representations and increases "psychological distance," defined as a feeling that objects or events are not as concretely present in one's immediate experience of reality.[28] Overall, these results link low-light conditions to more abstract, less detail-oriented thought, implying that we keep our cognitive options open and think more creatively about what we are seeing when lights are low. Steidle and Werth go even further by aligning their results with theories of *cognitive tuning*, which propose that benign, nonthreatening situations elicit positive, attention-expanding emotional states in which we engage in broader, freer patterns of thought and action than we would in high-arousal negative emotional situations.[29] Theatrical performances certainly stand as an example of a nonthreatening context; however, as Edensor reminds us, darkness has its own threatening side.

If we read the visual perception of Forsythe's dark, abstract atmospheres against elements of the "visual dramaturgy" that Lehmann signals as a trait of postdramatic theatre,[30] a space to interrogate his ideas about this style of theatre emerges. Discussing Jan Fabre's work, he notes that

> Actors, lights, dancers, etc. are given over to a purely formal observation; the gaze finds no occasion to detect a depth of symbolic significance beyond the given, but instead—either with pleasure or boredom—remains stuck within the activity of seeing the 'surface' itself...Bereft of its usual crutches of comprehension, the perception of this theatre fails and is forced to engage in a difficult mode of seeing—namely one that is simultaneously formal and sensorially exact. This mode of seeing might produce a more easygoing, more 'negligent' attitude, if it were not for the provocative coldness of the geometry here and the dissatisfied craving for meaning there.[31]

The difficulty indicated by Lehmann—a thwarting of the desire to interpret symbols through the presentation of the formally concrete—is limited by his focus on the semiotics of scenographies that afford clear, easy perception of the concrete "surface" of performance. What happens, though, to the eye and mind when choreo-scenography blurs this surface and renders visual perception unclear and effortful? In such instances, obscuration augments choreography's already abstract nature, further problematizing the performance of interpretive viewing by actually making seeing more difficult. Under such conditions, "seeing harder" can result in only limited improvement. In this, Forsythe's dark works ratify a perceptual paradox: though everyday experience convinces us that our vision is fulsome, accurate, and smooth, our visual perception, which is ecologically optimized for adequacy and energetic economy, is in fact highly selective and imperfect. What we see is in fact a constant blur, out of which we make sufficient but never perfect visual sense. Dancing that is staged in gloaming affords not only a distinct performance of vision but also a distinct and potentially reflexive performance of thinking about vision, one that itself can influence the action of perception.

There is an unforgiving quality to dancing in the dark and the choreo-scenographic choice to deny visual clarity. However, as the "provocative coldness of the geometry" melts away into darkness, what might be considered a counter-warming occurs as the minds' instinctive proclivity to "fill in the gaps" is brought to high activation. Faced with an active stage shrouded in darkness, our instinctive drive to apprehend, recognize, and interpret what we see keeps us from drifting into a dreamy mental reverie. Rather, the flux of appearances and disappearances, the potentials of dark voids, and the continuously changing light conditions keep the eye and mind active beyond the norm, disallowing the relaxed but rapid "contemplation" Lehmann attributes to postdramatic theatre viewing.[32] Whether in conditions of blackout, gloaming, or other vision-dimming scenographic means, choreographies of obscuration take our visual systems to the extremes of their performance. As our eyes actively seek and follow the sometimes more and sometimes less distinct forms of dancers and architectures of light and darkness, we enact a demanding, performative choreography of vision. Lehmann's aesthetic of "meaning in retreat"[33] is underpinned here by an aesthetics of *things* in retreat that scales our awareness of vision's limitations up into consciousness, evoking an altered, poetic engagement with the seen and the not-seen. This is, however, not so much a poetics of failure as a reminder of the perceptual reality that well-lit stages tacitly deny.

NOTES

1. Paul Ben-Itzak, "Art in Fact: William Forsythe's Sounds of Science."
2. Yaron Abulafia, *The Art of Light Onstage*, 110.
3. Anna Kisselgoff, "Brainy With a Contemporary Sense of Fun."
4. Lehmann, *Postdramatic Theatre*, 34–35.
5. Gernot Böhme, "Atmosphere as the fundamental concept of a new aesthetics."
6. See Tonino Griffero, *Atmospheres; Aesthetics of Emotional spaces*.
7. Mikkel Bille et al., "Staging atmospheres: Materiality, culture, and the texture of the in-between," 36.
8. Tim Edensor, *From Light to Dark: Daylight, Illumination, and Gloom*, 189.
9. For Lehmann, "Although it remains debatable to what degree and in what way the audiences of former centuries were taken in by the 'illusions' offered by stage tricks, artful lighting, musical background, costumes and set, it can be stated that dramatic theatre was the formation of illusion. It wanted to construct a fictive cosmos and let all the stage represent—be—a world." *Postdramatic Theatre*, 22.
10. Michael Kirby, *A Formalist Theatre*, 99, cited in Lehmann, *Postdramatic Theatre*, 57.

11. For ideal footage of *Bolero*'s lighting, see Sylvie Guillem's 2008 performance of *Bolero* with the Tokyo Ballet, https://www.youtube.com/watch?v=rybdgpCWk5I (accessed 1 August 2020).

12. Peter Mumford, "Lighting Dance," 49; reprinted in Scott Palmer, *Light*, 248–54.

13. Driver, "William Forsythe and Jennifer Tipton: A Conversation about Lighting, 44–5.

14. Driver, 70–71.

15. Driver, 70.

16. The Forsythe Company, program note for *The Defenders*.

17. For a visual sense of *Limb's Theorem*, see the 2014 Festival d'Automne trailer for the Ballet de l'Opéra de Lyon's performances at https://www.youtube.com/watch?v=6vlCnNUS-Gs (accessed 15 January 2021). It should be noted, however, that the scenes shown are among the more brightly lit sections of the work.

18. For an outstanding analysis, see Steven Spier, "Dancing and drawing, choreography and architecture."

19. Erika Fischer-Lichte, "Limb's Theorem," translation by the author. Original text:

> "Limb's Theorem" ist ein schwarzes Stück…Das Licht sucht verzweifelt nach Öffnungen und Schlitzen, unter der beweglichen Wand hindurch, aus Schächten, aus einem einzigen herumgefahrenen Lichtfluter (bei "Enemy"), oder es verströmt sich eiskalt als nüchternes Arbeitslicht aus dem Schnürboden. Manchmal ist die Bühne so finster, daß sich Bewegung nur mehr schemenhaft erahnen läßt. Bewegung aber verlöscht nicht mit dem Licht, sondern spinnt sich zwanghaft sinnvoll im Kopf des Betrachters weiter…"Limb's Theorem" stellt den Tanz in Fragmenten aus, welche die Vorstellung des Zuschauers zum heilen Ganzen zusammenkittet. Die Lücken füllt die imaginierte Ballettgeschichte.
>
> Der Tanz kurz vor dem Verlöschen schärft die Sinne, weitet die Grenzen der Wahrnehmung. Und dabei wird einem beängstigend kalt. Denn die Abstraktion hat den letzten Rest von Gefühl ausgetrieben. Der intellektuelle Kick sendet Impulse wie Stromstöße. Tanz als Metapher ist Nervenreiz, geschmiert allerdings mit theatralischem Speck.

20. Arnaudde, G., "Black Brown & White Fascinating Limb's Theorem."

21. In one section, the 5 kW light is replaced by fluorescent overhead lighting.

22. W.A. Fletcher and J.A. Sharpe, "Saccadic eye movement dysfunction in Alzheimer's disease."

23. B. Fischer et al., "On the development of voluntary and reflexive components in human saccade genera-tion."
24. D. Guitton et al., "Frontal lobe lesions in man cause difficulties in suppressing reflexive glances and in generating goal-directed saccades," and R. Rafal et al., "Looking forward to looking: Saccade preparation and control of the visual grasp reflex."
25. See, for example, Isen, A.M. et al., "Affect as a factor of organizational behavior," N.H Eklund et al., "Lighting and sustained performance" (2000 and 2001) and R.A. Baron et al., "Effects of indoor lighting (illuminance and spectral distribution) on the performance of cognitive tasks and interpersonal behaviors."
26. A. Steidle et al., "You Can't See Much in the Dark," A. Steidle, et al., "In the dark we cooperate." See also A. Steidle and L. Werth, "Freedom from constraints" and A. Steidle and L. Werth, "In the spotlight."
27. A. Steidle, and L. Werth, "Freedom from constraints," 75.
28. See N. Liberman and J. Förster, "Distancing from experienced self" and Y. Trope and N. Liberman, "Construal-level theory of psychological distance."
29. For a review of this literature, see J. Förster, "Implicit Affective Cues and Attentional Tuning."
30. Lehmann, *Postdramatic Theatre*, 93–94.
31. Lehmann, *Postdramatic Theatre*, 98–9.
32. Lehmann, *Postdramatic Theatre*, 87.
33. Lehmann, *Postdramatic Theatre*, 88.

BIBLIOGRAPHY

Abulafia, Yaron. 2016. *The Art of Light Onstage: Lighting in Contemporary Theatre*. London/New York: Routledge.

Arnaudde, G. 2014. Black Brown & White Fascinating Limb's Theorem—William Forsythe, Theatre du Chatelet, Paris. Accessed 31 December 2014. https://www.scoop.it/topic/culture-and-lifestyle/p/4027608979/2014/09/07/black-brown-white-fascinating-limb-s-theorem-william-forsythe-theatre-du-chatelet-paris

Baron, R.A., M.S. Rea, and S.G. Daniels. 1992. Effects of Indoor Lighting (Illuminance and Spectral Distribution) on the Performance of Cognitive Tasks and Interpersonal Behaviors: The Potential Mediating Role of Positive Affect. *Motivation and Emotion 16* (1): 1–33.

Ben-Itzak, P. 2002, March 29. Art in Fact: William Forsythe's Sounds of Science. *The Dance Insider*. Accessed 8 April 2003. http://www.danceinsider.com/f2002/f0329_2.html

Bille, M., P. Bjerregaard, and T.F. Sørensen. 2015. Staging Atmospheres: Materiality, Culture, and the Texture of the In-between. *Emotion, space and society* 15: 31–38.

Böhme, Gernot. 1993. Atmosphere as the Fundamental Concept of a New Aesthetics. *Thesis Eleven 36* (1): 113–126.

Driver, Senta. 2000. William Forsythe and Jennifer Tipton: A Conversation About Lighting. In *William Forsythe (Choreography and Dance: An International Journal 5 (3))*, ed. Senta Driver, 41–78. Chur: Harwood Academic Publishers.

Edensor, Tim. 2017. *From Light to Dark: Daylight, Illumination, and Gloom.* Minneapolis/London: University of Minnesota Press.

Eklund, N.H., P.R. Boyce, and S.N. Simpson. 2000. Lighting and Sustained Performance. *Journal of the Illuminating Engineering Society 29* (1): 116–130.

———. 2001. Lighting and Sustained Performance: Modeling Data-entry Task Performance. *Journal of the Illuminating Engineering Society* 30 (2): 126–141.

Fischer, B., M. Biscaldi, and S. Gezeck. 1997. On the Development of Voluntary and Reflexive Components in Human Saccade Generation. *Brain Research* 754: 285–297.

Fischer-Lichte, E. 1990. Limb's Theorem: Eine choreographische Reflexion vom William Forsythe in Frankfurt. *Süddeutsche Zeitung*, March 24–25.

Fletcher, W.A., and J.A. Sharpe. 1986. Saccadic Eye Movement Dysfunction in Alzheimer's Disease. *Annals of Neurology: Official Journal of the American Neurological Association and the Child Neurology Society* 20 (4): 464–471.

Förster, J., and R. Friedman. 2010. Implicit Affective Cues and Attentional Tuning: An Integrative Review. *Psychological Bulletin* 136 (5): 875–893.

Griffero, T. 2014. *Atmospheres; Aesthetics of Emotional Spaces.* Translated by S. de Sanctis. Ashgate Publishing.

Guitton, D., H.A. Buchtel, and R.M. Douglas. 1985. Frontal Lobe Lesions in Man Cause Difficulties in Suppressing Reflexive Glances and in Generating Goal-directed Saccades. *Experimental Brain Research* 58: 455–472.

Isen, A.M., and R.A. Barron. 1991. Affect as a Factor of Organizational Behavior. In *Research in Organizational Behavior*, ed. B.M. Staw and L.L. Cummings. Greenwich, CT: JAI Press.

Kirby, Michael. 1987. *A Formalist Theatre*. Philadelphia: University of Pennsylvania Press.

Kisselgoff, A. 2001. Brainy With a Contemporary Sense of Fun. *The New York Times*, December 17. Accessed 21 December 2001. https://www.nytimes.com/2001/12/17/arts/next-wave-festival-review-brainy-with-a-contemporary-sense-of-fun.html

Lehmann, H.-T. 2006. *Postdramatic Theatre*. Translated by K.-J.-Munby. Routledge. Original version: Lehmann, Hans-Thies. 1999. *Postdramatisches Theater*. Frankfurt am Main: Verlag der Autoren.

Liberman, N., and J. Förster. 2009. Distancing from Experienced Self: How Global Versus Local Perception Affects Estimation of Psychological Distance. *Journal of Personality and Social Psychology* 97: 203–216.

Mumford, Peter. 1985. Lighting Dance. *Dance Research: The Journal of the Society for Dance Research* 3 (2): 46–55.

Palmer, Scott. 2013. *Light. Readings in Theatre and Practice.* Basingstoke: Palgrave Macmillan.

Rafal, R., L. Machado, T. Ro, and H. Ingle. 2000. Looking Forward to Looking: Saccade Preparation and Control of the Visual Grasp Reflex. In *Control of cognitive processes: Attention and performance XVIII*, ed. Stephen Monsell and Jon Driver, 155–174. Cambridge MA: MIT Press.

Spier, Steven. 2005. Dancing and Drawing, Choreography and Architecture. *The Journal of Architecture* 10 (4): 349–364.

Steidle, A., and L. Werth. 2013. Freedom from Constraints: Darkness and dim Illumination Promote Creativity. *Journal of Environmental Psychology* 35: 67–80.

———. 2014. In the Spotlight: Brightness Increases Self-awareness and Reflective Self-regulation. *Journal of Environmental Psychology* 39: 40–50.

Steidle, A., L. Werth, and E.V. Hanke. 2011. You Can't See Much in the Dark: Darkness Affects Construal Level and Psychological Distance. *Social Psychology* 42 (3): 174–184.

Steidle, A., E.V. Hanke, and L. Werth. 2013. In the Dark We Cooperate: The Situated Nature of Procedural Embodiment. *Social Cognition* 31 (2): 275–300.

The Forsythe Company. 2008. Program for *The Defenders*.

Trope, Y., and N. Liberman. 2010. Construal-level Theory of Psychological Distance. *Psychological Review* 117: 440–463.

CHAPTER 4

Occlusion: Comings and Goings

As early as 1867, Hermann von Helmholtz theorized that perception arises from a process of active inference through which organisms seek to ratify mental models of the world by comparing real-time occurrences against them.[1] Cognition, in other words, is the posing of hypotheses about event outcomes based on assumptions about the world as the individual has previously experienced it.[2] Events that fail to corroborate predictions prompt us to adjust our hypotheses and assess our own reliability in the specific circumstances. This optimizing process of encoding prediction errors is the foundation of learning. Babies are delighted by games of peek-a-boo because they provide the opportunity for the infant to confirm that things do not cease to exist when they disappear from view. Events of occlusion are among the most effective perceptual cues for object permanence; we don't assume that objects vanishing behind obstructions simply "wink out" of existence.[3] Pioneering developmental psychologist Jean Piaget surmised that the concept of object permanence develops between the ages of 8 and 24 months unless hindered by a cognitive disability,[4] while more recent research indicates that infants possess a rudimentary concept of object permanence as early as three months.[5] Adults continue to enjoy the surprise of objects disappearing in magic shows because appearances and disappearances remain behaviorally relevant events, especially when unanticipated. The hypotheses we make about the world and

© The Author(s), under exclusive license to Springer Nature Switzerland AG 2023
F. Vass, *William Forsythe's Postdramatic Dance Theater*, Cognitive Studies in Literature and Performance,
https://doi.org/10.1007/978-3-031-26658-4_4

behavior of things in it may be sensitive to context but remain primarily driven by evolution.

We thus engage in a constant process of evaluating what is happening, forecasting what will happen next, and evaluating and adjusting our forecasts based on what does in fact happen. In theatrical worlds though, the extradaily qualities of actions, movement, environment, and context can make performances less predictable than our everyday worlds. Appearances and disappearances, however, are fundamental and expected stage events. They attract attention by activating bottom-up process of sensory stimulation like movement and surface contrast, while also simultaneously triggering top-down cognitive processes such as identification and discernment of intention. Classical ballet audiences are accustomed to seeing dancers enter and exit via the wings; their comings and goings follow traditional structures and correspond robustly to musical segments, for example in the *coda* of a *grand pas de deux*, or they occur for dramaturgical reasons. Further, the quality of action during an entrance or exit is critical: from a cognitive standpoint, the locomotion, trajectory, and gaze direction of a performer walking or running out of audience view indicates an intended spatial goal. Unexpected entrances and exits destabilize audience expectations, and unanticipated disappearances are especially surprising. Tacit theatrical conventions are broken when performers exit in mid-action, make sudden, unexpected returns from culturally coded stage exits, or travel behind scenery in mid-phrase. Physical obstructions, however, evoke specific visual-attentional behaviors, upon which, as I discuss below, Forsythe's obstructive choreographies offer performative commentary.

Now You See It, Now You Don't

Obstruction of vision figured prominently in Forsythe's earlier *oeuvre*, perhaps catalyzed by the large stages of the Frankfurt opera house. From 1993 until 2004, Forsythe created works on the stages of the 1200-seat Oper Frankfurt, which has a 15-meter-wide proscenium and a total stage area of 40 × 40 meters, and the 680-seat Schauspiel Frankfurt,[6] with a proscenium width adjustable between 15 and 24 meters and a 24 × 23-meter stage area with a total breadth and depth of 60 × 40 meters. Always highly selective regarding touring venue choices for works created on these stages, Forsythe insists on adequate proscenium width and stage dimensions wherever they are performed. A handful of later Ballett

Frankfurt works were staged at Frankfurt's cavernous Bockenheimer Depot, while almost all of The Forsythe Company's works were created in the ensemble's non-proscenium "home" venues in Frankfurt, Dresden, and Zürich.[7]

Forsythe often further opened these spaces by eliminating wings, backdrops, or both, staging dancing all the way to exposed back walls or beyond the proscenium arch. In works in which choreography continues into the wing space, the theater's architecture becomes a selective obstruction for portions of the audience. During the opening of *Enemy in the Figure*, for example, a woman moves downstage with sharp, sometimes audible smacking gestures along one of the pulled-back side walls, becoming visible to less of the audience seated on the left auditorium side as she progresses. Shortly afterward, the wheeled 5 kW lamp is turned across the upstage to reveal another darkly clad dancer on the opposite wall, frantically wrestling on a wire mesh grid but not visible to those seated at the extreme front right of the auditorium. Forsythe's motivation for such staging was a democratizing one: "I realized that there are people with bad seats, who couldn't afford better ones. So I used the other corners of the space, the back and the sides that were visible to them."[8]

In some works, Forsythe obstructs audience vision with wing flats, set pieces, or large props. One of the costumed "family" figures in *New Sleep* gestures briefly in one of the wing gaps, invisible to the far-left side of the auditorium, while in the crashing interlude of Part III of *Artifact* (1984), a row of diagonally placed square stage flats is knocked down one after the other, revealing a dancer who retreats behind each one before it falls. The huge turning "sail" in *Limb's Theorem* Part 1 (see Chap. 3) blocks and exposes moving dancers, while its own upper contour disappears for audiences seated at the sides of the auditorium. In *Sider*, a 2011 work with dramaturgical foundations in Shakespeare's *Hamlet*, dancers conceal and reveal themselves and others with dinner-table-sized sheets of reinforced cardboard. Strategic obstruction is an overt dramaturgy in this work; as Forsythe explained, Hamlet is compelled to "side" with his father's ghost but obscures his intentions while seeking to discover the truth about his demise (Fig. 4.1).[9]

Forsythe's best-known obstructive device is the 10-meter wide, 3-meter-high undulating wooden wall that sits diagonally on the stage in *Enemy in the Figure* (1989). With its warm and variegated grain, as well as its ability to produce shifting pockets of darkness when lit at angles, the wall is itself a beautiful, visually lively performer. Numerous playful choreographic twists involving the wall interweave *Enemy*'s dynamic scenography of light, set, costume, and space. Shortly after the start, a woman in

Fig. 4.1 The obstructing wooden wall in *Enemy in the Figure*. (Source: photo courtesy of Foteini Christofilopoulou, reproduced with permission of Semperoper Ballet Dresden)

white who has been slowly moving on the floor in an upstage corner stands and walks behind one edge of the wooden wall, coiling up a long rope as she steps in a slow rhythm to the music. Just after she disappears, a man dressed in black appears from the other edge of the wall, also stepping rhythmically and uncoiling rope into the opposite downstage wing. A few moments later, three women in white leotards dancing in unison at one side of the stage move backward behind the wall; as soon as they have disappeared a man, also clad in a white leotard, begins thrusting an arm, leg, or his upper body out briefly from behind the other side. Later in the work, larger groups of performers retreat behind the wall with rhythmic steps as the diagonally positioned 5 kW light makes their blurred, over-sized silhouettes stream out the other side and disappear into the upstage right wing. When a woman in long black pants leaves a duet and runs behind the wall on one side, another woman in black shorts immediately lopes out from behind the other side. These tongue-in-cheek choreographies are interspersed between straightforward instances of dancers passing behind the wall to reappear on the other side, running from behind it and back again, or simply using the wall or the upstage and downstage wing gaps as exits. Taken together, the trajectories and illusory changes of performers deliver a wry and playful commentary on object constancy and action continuity—if in fact they are attended to rather than the solos, duets, and group dancing that is occurring simultaneously, as I discuss in the following chapter.

Numerous programs of vision research have aimed to understand how or whether we maintain stable representations of motion that is momentarily blocked from sight.[10] Most of these laboratory trials use video representations of objects onscreen to ensure parity of viewing experience across research participants. In the studies, moving visual targets such as geometric forms or point-light displays of humans or other animals are momentarily occluded behind visual barriers or objects. In some cases, subjects are tested or questioned about the accuracy of the continued movement, which is manipulated as an experimental variable. In others, eye tracking is used to assess visual attention in a predictive manner.[11] It bears emphasizing that visual attention is a complex phenomenon that involves both bottom-up input from the retina (e.g., neurons firing in response to velocity, acceleration, and angle of motion) and top-down factors such as expectation and memory. When an object becomes occluded, our visual activity is also influenced by whether or not we anticipate it appearing again beyond the occluding surface. If we do, we typically scan to the location where we expect it to reappear. However, though our performance of visual anticipation is generally quite accurate, it is not completely precise: studies have shown that the temporal accuracy of tracked occluded movement is influenced by a variety of factors including the feasibility of biological movement kinematics, gravitational acceleration, and auditory rhythms.[12]

Visual attention also spontaneously increases when objects disappear from view, in response to the perceptual complications that occlusion poses. One study on the simultaneous tracking of multiple objects found evidence of a "high-beams effect" in which a burst of attention was directed at moving objects (in this case, small graphical discs) passing behind narrow occluding rectangles. This was evidenced by increased detection by subjects of small visual probes (square dots) that appeared on the objects as they moved.[13] Another study further investigated this phenomenon through an eye-tracking paradigm in which nine-animated sharks in a 3D tank either occasionally occluded one another or did not. After subjects tracked either two, three, or four specific sharks over 20-second trials, they were asked to indicate whether a highlighted shark was among those originally indicated to track. These trials revealed an increased number of "rescue saccades," or eye movements toward targets that were about to undergo occlusion. The presence of these distinctive eye movement patterns varied with the number of sharks being tracked, with fewer rescue saccades occurring per occlusion if four sharks were being tracked than for two or three. Though the researchers grant that this effect might be a result of potential target confusion rather than occlusion, they hold that their findings indicate an object-tracking system in the brain that occasionally "requests help" from the oculomotor system in order to optimize perception during occluding conditions.[14]

When an object is expected to reappear, it is noteworthy that our eyes do not perform a smooth tracking of the assumed path of the moving object behind the occluding surface. Instead, they linger briefly in the region of the disappearance before making a predictive, relatively time-accurate jump to the presumed site of reappearance. The site of the disappearance also becomes associated with the disappeared object, as shown by research on the phenomenon of "looking at nothing"—the formation of an enduring spatial representation of objects that appeared at a given location.[15] One explanation that has been offered is that the representational strengths of the disappeared object and the occluding object or surface temporarily "compete" with one another at the location of occlusion, with the internal representation of the invisible object failing to overcome that of the present and visually salient occluder.[16]

How does perception perform, though, when discs, virtual sharks, or dancers move behind an occlusion and do not immediately re-emerge? Neurophysiological research on macaque monkeys has shown that further movement is inferred through processes of mental simulation for as long as 11 seconds of occlusion.[17] Such a continuing projection of activity is unlikely when we watch dancers exit into the wings, as we assume them to have stopped dancing and, once we have tracked their exits, relinquish them as targets of attention, especially when there is more action to see onstage. Forsythe performatively acknowledges this tendency in *Enemy in the Figure* by using the rolling 5 kW light at times to throw looming shadows of dancers dancing *behind* the wooden wall onto the back wall of the stage. In effect, Forsythe stages our visual simulation, or at least a potential version of it, in this instance. At another point, he throws the predictive mind an insurmountable challenge when the 5kW lamp is spun behind the wall, out of audience view. Brief fragments of light and the shadows of seen and unseen dancers fly across the stage's walls, and all ability to make associative sense of the unseen action is lost.

The occluding surfaces used in onscreen empirical studies like those mentioned above are of course very narrow and the occlusion timeframes very brief (on the order of 400–700 milliseconds). As such, this research admittedly offers rather limited ground on which to speculate about longer, larger-scale disappearances like those found in the *Enemy in the Figure*. Forsythe's staged disappearances nonetheless arouse our attention and activate predictive faculties by virtue of the bottom-up impact of disappearances and appearances and the top-down relevance of their unexpected occurrences within the performance context. An ironic wink to this occurs in *I don't believe in outer space* (2008), when a performer makes a ping pong ball on a stick "magically" disappear and reappear behind his hand by rotating it to a black-painted side and back again. Though the corny magic trick is easily figured out, the ball's unanticipated change and the performer's attention to it nonetheless draw and heighten our own. Spoken lines delivered during this work tie the little trick to *I don't believe in outer space*'s thematic of our relation to death and the unknowable possibility of continued existence: the line early in the work "I imagine this has a lot to do with disappearances" resonates with lyrics of the song "I Will Survive," which are quoted several times, as well as with a comic sendup of a dancercise class in which "instructor" Yoko Ando shouts "You're gone? You're gone? You're back! You're back!"

In disappearances, as in scenes of darkness or gloaming, Lehmann's "aesthetic of 'meaning in retreat'" is inflected by things themselves retreating from perception. Though Forsythe may have been discussing his staging of darkness when he said, "I like to hide, to make uncertain what takes place onstage (…) and to extend what I call the poetry of disappearance,"[18] a similar poetry is also at work when obscuration occurs by other scenographic means. In a sense, all of Forsythe's choreo-scenographies of disappearances comment on the responses that occur when our received ideas about vision and presence in the theater, and along with them our desire to see, are unsettled by obscuration. In the final chapter of this section, I turn to a different means of making things disappear which, rather than removing them from sight, instead obscures them right out in the open.

NOTES

1. Hermann von Helmholtz, *Handbuch der Physiologischen Optik*.
2. Richard Gregory, "Perceptions as hypotheses."
3. A. Michotte, "On phenomenal permanence: facts and theories"; and J.J. Gibson et al., "The change from visible to invisible: a study of optical transitions."

4. Jean Piaget, *The construction of reality in the child.*

5. See, for example, T.G.R. Bower, *Development in infancy,* Renée Baillargeon and Julia DeVos, "Object permanence in 3.5- and 4.5-month-old infants: further evidence"; *Renée* Baillargeon, "Innate ideas revisited: For a principle of persistence in infants' physical reasoning"; and *Renée* Baillargeon et al., "An account of infants' physical reasoning."

6. Following a fire, the company's Frankfurt performances were exclusively on the Schauspiel stage from 1988 to 1991 during the rebuilding of the Oper.

7. Under the Forsythe Company's multi-party contractual models, partnering cities hosted bespoke world premieres on a yearly basis. The ensemble's home venues were the Bockenheimer Depot (2005–2015), Festspielhaus Hellerau Dresden (2005–2015), and the Schiffbauhalle Zürich (2005–2009). *I don't believe in outer space* was originally staged lengthwise over a 30-meter stage in the Bockenheimer Depot but later adapted for proscenium stage touring.

8. Forsythe quoted in Astrid Kaminski, "Talking Dance."

9. See Freya Vass-Rhee, "Haunted by Hamlet: William Forsythe's Sider."

10. S.J. Bennett and G.R. Barnes, "Human ocular pursuit during the transient disappearance of a visual target"; S.J. Bennett and G.R. Barnes, "Predictive smooth ocular pursuit during the transient disappearance of a visual target"; L. Madelain and R.J. Krauzlis, "Effects of learning on smooth pursuit during transient disappearance of a visual target"; J.J. Orban de Xivry et al., "Evidence for synergy between saccades and smooth pursuit during transient target disappearance."

11. W. Becker and A. Fuchs, "Prediction in the oculomotor system: Smooth pursuit during transient disappearance of a visual target"; J. Findlay, "Spatial and temporal factors in the predictive generation of saccadic eye movements"; E. Kowler et al., "The effect of expectations on slow oculomotor control–IV. Anticipatory smooth eye movements depend on prior target motions"; M. Shelhamer and W. Joiner, "Saccades exhibit abrupt transition between reactive and predictive; predictive saccade sequences have long-term correlations."

12. W. Stadler et al., "Movement kinematics affect action prediction: Comparing human to non-human point-light actions"; G. Orgs et al., "Time perception during apparent biological motion reflects subjective speed of movement, not objective rate of visual stimulation"; F. Lacquaniti et al., "Gravity in the brain as a reference for space and time perception'; I. Indovina et al., "Anticipating the effects of visual gravity during simulated self-motion."

13. J.I. Flombaum et al., "Attentional resources in visual tracking through occlusion: The high-beams effect."

14. G.J. Zelinsky and A Todor, "The role of 'rescue saccades' in tracking objects through occlusions.

15. G.T. Altmann, "Language-mediated eye movements in the absence of a visual world: the 'blank screen paradigm'"; S.A. Brandt and L.W. Stark, "Spontaneous eye movements during visual imagery reflect the content of the visual scene"; R. Johansson et al., "Using eye movements and spoken discourse as windows to inner space"; R. Johansson and M. Johansson, "Look here, eye movements play a functional role in memory retrieval"; B. Laeng and D.S. Teodorescu, "Eye scanpaths during visual imagery reenact those of perception of the same visual scene"; D.C. Richardson and M.J. Spivey, "Representation, space and Hollywood Squares: looking at things that aren't there anymore"; M. Spivey and J. Geng, "Oculomotor mechanisms activated by imagery and memory: Eye movements to absent objects."

16. Y. Munakata et al., "Rethinking infant knowledge: Toward an adaptive process account of successes and failures in object permanence tasks."

17. M.A. Umiltà et al., "I know what you are doing: A neurophysiological study."

18. Roslyn Sulcas, "William Forsythe: The poetry of disappearance and the great tradition," 32.

BIBLIOGRAPHY

Altmann, G.T. 2004. Language-Mediated Eye Movements in the Absence of a Visual World: The 'Blank Screen Paradigm'. *Cognition* 93: B79–B87.

Baillargeon, R. 2008. Innate Ideas Revisited: For a Principle of Persistence in Infants' Physical Reasoning. *Perspectives on Psychological Science* 3: 2–13.

Baillargeon, R., and J. DeVos. 1991. Object Permanence in 3.5- and 4.5-month-old Infants: Further Evidence. *Child Development* 62 (6): 1227–1246.

Baillargeon, R., J. Li, W. Ng, and S. Yuan. 2009. An Account of Infants' Physical Reasoning. In *Learning and the Infant Mind*, ed. A. Woodward and A. Needham, 66–116. New York, NY: Oxford University Press.

Becker, W., and A. Fuchs. 1985. Prediction in the Oculomotor System: Smooth Pursuit during Transient Disappearance of a Visual Target. *Experimental Brain Research* 57: 562–575.

Bennett, S.J., and G.R. Barnes. 2003. Human Ocular Pursuit during the Transient Disappearance of a Visual Target. *Journal of Neurophysiology* 90 (4): 2504–2520.

———. 2004. Predictive Smooth Ocular Pursuit during the Transient Disappearance of a Visual Target. *Journal of Neurophysiology* 92 (1): 578–590.

Bower, T.G.R. 1974. *Development in Infancy*. San Francisco: Freeman.

Brandt, S.A., and L.W. Stark. 1997. Spontaneous Eye Movements during Visual Imagery Reflect the Content of the Visual Scene. *Journal of Cognitive Neuroscience* 9: 27–38.

Findlay, J. 1981. Spatial and Temporal Factors in the Predictive Generation of Saccadic Eye Movements. *Vision Research* 21: 347–351.

Flombaum, J.I., B.J. Scholl, and Z.W. Pylyshyn. 2008. Attentional Resources in Visual Tracking through Occlusion: The High-beams Effect. *Cognition* 107 (3): 904–931.

Gibson, J.J., G.A. Kaplan, H.N. Reynolds Jr., and K. Wheeler. 1969. The Change from Visible to Invisible: A Study of Optical Transitions. *Perception and Psychophysics* 5: 113–116.

Gregory, Richard. 1980. Perceptions as Hypotheses. *Philosophical Transactions of the Royal Society of London, Biological Sciences* 290: 181–197.

Indovina, I., V. Maffei, and F. Lacquaniti. 2013. Anticipating the Effects of Visual Gravity during Simulated Self-motion: Estimates of Time-to-passage along Vertical and Horizontal Paths. *Experimental Brain Research* 229: 579–586.

Johansson, R., J. Holsanova, and K. Holmqvist. 2013. Using Eye Movements and Spoken Discourse as Windows to Inner Space. In *The Construal of Spatial Meaning: Windows into Conceptual Space*, ed. Carita Paradis, Jean Hudson, and Ulf Magnusson, 9–28. Oxford: Oxford University Press.

Johansson, R., and M. Johansson. 2014. Look Here, Eye Movements Play a Functional Role in Memory Retrieval. *Psychological Science* 25 (1): 236–242.

Kaminski, Astrid. 2013. Talking Dance. *Frieze*, August 13. https://frieze.com/article/talking-dance. Accessed 15 April 2019.

Kowler, E., A. Martins, and M. Pavel. 1984. The Effect of Expectations on Slow Oculomotor Control—IV. Anticipatory Smooth Eye Movements Depend on Prior Target Motions. *Vision Research* 24 (3): 197–210.

Lacquaniti, F., G. Bosco, S. Gravano, I. Indovina, B. La Scaleia, V. Maffei, and M. Zago. 2015. Gravity in the Brain as a Reference for Space and Time Perception. *Multisensory Research* 28 (5–6): 397–426.

Laeng, B., and D.S. Teodorescu. 2002. Eye Scanpaths during Visual Imagery Reenact Those of Perception of the Same Visual Scene. *Cognitive Science* 26: 207–231.

Lehmann, Hans-Thies. 2006. *Postdramatic Theatre*. Translated by Karen-Jürs-Munby. Abingdon and New York: Routledge. Original Version: Lehmann, Hans-Thies. 1999. *Postdramatisches Theater*. Frankfurt am Main: Verlag der Autoren.

Madelain, L., and R.J. Krauzlis. 2003. Effects of Learning on Smooth Pursuit during Transient Disappearance of a Visual Target. *Journal of Neurophysiology* 90 (2): 972–982.

Michotte, A. 1950. On Phenomenal Permanence: Facts and Theories. In *Michotte's Experimental Phenomenology of Perception*, ed. Georges Thinés, Alan Costall, and George Butterworth, 122–139. Hillsdale, NJ: Lawrence Erlbaum.

Munakata, Y., J.L. McClelland, M.H. Johnson, and R.S. Siegler. 1997. Rethinking Infant Knowledge: Toward an Adaptive Process Account of Successes and Failures in Object Permanence Tasks. *Psychological Review* 104 (4): 686–713.

Orban de Xivry, J.J., S.J. Bennett, P. Lefèvre, and G.R. Barnes. 2006. Evidence for Synergy between Saccades and Smooth Pursuit during Transient Target Disappearance. *Journal of Neurophysiology* 95 (1): 418–427.

Orgs, G., L. Kirsch, and P. Haggard. 2013. Time Perception during Apparent Biological Motion Reflects Subjective Speed of Movement, Not Objective Rate of Visual Stimulation. *Experimental Brain Research* 227 (2): 223–229.

Piaget, Jean. 1954. *The Construction of Reality in the Child*. New York: Basic.

Richardson, D.C., and M.J. Spivey. 2000. Representation, Space and Hollywood Squares: Looking at Things that Aren't There Anymore. *Cognition* 76 (3): 269–295.

Shelhamer, M., and W.M. Joiner. 2003. Saccades Exhibit Abrupt Transition between Reactive and Predictive; Predictive Saccade Sequences have Long-term Correlations. *Journal of Neurophysiology* 90 (4): 2763–2769.

Spivey, M., and J. Geng. 2001. Oculomotor Mechanisms Activated by Imagery and Memory: Eye Movements to Absent Objects. *Psychological Research* 65 (4): 235–241.

Stadler, W., A. Springer, J. Parkinson, and W. Prinz. 2012. Movement Kinematics Affect Action Prediction: Comparing Human to Non-human Point-Light Actions. *Psychological Research (Psychologische Forschung)* 76 (4): 395–406.

Sulcas, Roslyn. 1991. William Forsythe: The Poetry of Disappearance and the Great Tradition. *Dance Theatre Journal* 9 (1): 4–7 and 32–33.

Umiltà, M.A., E. Kohler, V. Gallese, L. Fogassi, L. Fadiga, C. Keysers, and G. Rizzolatti. 2001. I Know What You are Doing: A Neurophysiological Study. *Neuron* 31 (1): 155–165.

Vass-Rhee, Freya. 2019. Haunted by Hamlet: William Forsythe's Sider. In *The Oxford Handbook of Shakespeare and Dance*, ed. Lynsey McCulloch and Brandon Shaw, 455–476. Oxford and New York: Oxford University Press.

von Helmholtz, Hermann. 1867. *Handbuch der Physiologischen Optik*. Leipzig: Leopold Voss.

Zelinsky, G.J., and A. Todor. 2010. The Role of "Rescue Saccades" in Tracking Objects through Occlusions. *Journal of Vision* 10 (14): 29.

CHAPTER 5

Hiding in Plain Sight: Simultaneity

The strategies of lighting and staging analyzed in previous chapters reflect ways in which our vision is ecologically adapted to the everyday conditions in which we live. The visual system of each unique species has evolved responsively as part of its full perceptual apparatus to optimally fit the organism's needs and the provisions and threats of the environmental niche it is suited to inhabit.[1] Owl's eyes, for example, have five times more contrast-sensitive rod cells per square millimeter than those of humans, while the eagle's dual visual acuity across two foveae in each eye enables it to first spot prey at up to a two-mile distance and then catch it with close-range precision. Our eyes are instead functionally optimized primarily for daylight and far shorter distances. Faced with conditions outside of our common environmental registers, like very low light or very great distance, we run up against the evolutionary limits of our perceptual anatomy.

Our eyes are also optimized for stereoscopic vision of individual targets, though we can of course turn our eyes, heads, and bodies to see what's around us. The protruding, laterally placed eyes of the much slower chameleon function autonomously, though, enabling it not only to see panoramically but also to look in two different directions simultaneously. Thanks to monocular depth mechanisms, chameleons also have depth perception as we do, but unlike us they can visually attend to two things at once. Apparently not everyone is aware of this limitation, as indicated by the behavior of an audience member at a showing of Forsythe's *Heterotopia*

F. Vass, *William Forsythe's Postdramatic Dance Theater*, Cognitive Studies in Literature and Performance,
https://doi.org/10.1007/978-3-031-26658-4_5

(2006), a work performed simultaneously in two spaces separated by a large, opaque floor-to-ceiling screen. A gap at one side, which permitted audience members to pass back and forth, was always packed with spectators as it was the sole point from which both spaces could be viewed. The spectator in question was among the first to enter and, having apparently either attended the show before or received a hot tip, strode resolutely to the gap and stood with their nose against the screen's edge, directing one eye into each space. Obviously disgruntled when they realized that they would not be able to view both rooms at the same time, they chose one of them to start with.

Unless affected by a condition that problematizes smooth visual pursuit, we are also able to effortlessly focus on and track objects as they move. Our world is a busy place, though, cluttered with things and events of casual or vital interest. As a result, we shift our gaze to new attentional targets an average of three to five times each waking second. Our performance of everyday seeing is convincing in its seeming fullness and accuracy but far from perfect under all circumstances. This is brought to our awareness not only by visual illusions and the sleight-of-hand tricks of magicians and scammers, but also by performances that intentionally stage competing regions of visual interest. Pragmatically, the composition of multiple simultaneously salient events is another form of perceptual obstruction, as such instances incite us to divide our visual attention. Focusing on one event leaves others either in peripheral view or literally out of sight, though not necessarily out of mind.

The closer we are to the range of visual targets, the more this obscuring effect is exacerbated. Though the normal human visual field encompasses about 120 lateral degrees at any given moment, our retinal anatomy limits focused foveal vision to a maximum of 2 degrees laterally—approximately the width of 10 letters on this page, or of one's thumb when held at arm's length.[2] Beyond this, parafoveal vision of reduced acuity occurs over a range of eight additional degrees, with mid-range peripheral vision extending to a further 30 degrees. Visual acuity, however, falls precipitously away in mid- and far-range peripheral vision, halving each additional 2.5 degrees from the fovea. Obviously, if our distance from a performance space is increased, as when we sit farther back in an auditorium, more stage area will "fit" into the area of relatively good visual acuity. Increased focal coverage, however, comes at the cost of reduced detail.

As evolutionary compensation for our narrow focal scope, our eyes move very rapidly between visual targets. The quick ballistic eye movements called *saccades* take only about 200 milliseconds to initiate—about the time it takes to blink—and as little as 20 or as much as 200 milliseconds to carry out, depending on the angular distance and activity (the lower figure for reading, the higher for broader gaze shifts). Longer saccades are typically accompanied by a degree of head movement, which the vestibulo-ocular reflex coordinates into quick, calibrated, and largely unperceived re-targetings of attention.

Shifts of gaze between targets involve a constant, largely unconscious dual-attentional process of detailed analysis of foveally fixated objects and the extraction of information from the remaining retinal field to determine targets of future fixation. The possibility of allocating simultaneous attention to multiple targets, along with the level of attention that can be achieved (e.g., detailed viewing of multiple components vs. extracting "the gist" from complex visual scenes), have remained matters of dispute.[3] Attention is thought to be affected by the complexity of stimuli; according to the foveal load hypothesis,[4] increased foveal processing difficulty (e.g., reading uncommon or complex words) results in reduced parafoveal uptake. In other words, less information can be accessed from the peripheral region when more attention is allocated to processing a targeted stimulus. This hypothesis aligns with "bottleneck" theories of attentional resources, which hold attention to be necessarily selective due to processing limitations and constraints.[5] A 2014 study, however, instead showed that foveal processing and peripheral selection occur independently and in parallel, even demonstrating that variations in foveal load caused by increased stimulus complexity do not influence selection and uptake of peripheral information.[6] This study's research team does note that their findings may be contingent on their choice of stimuli and experimental task (identifying pivoting movements among small images of luminant lines). What remains evident, though, is the close connection and interaction between foveal and peripheral processing.

It is also clear that simultaneous *detailed* focus on multiple regions of interest is only possible by relinquishing focus on one attentional target for another—we are not chameleons. Competing attentional targets, then, temporarily obscure each other, as the selection of one elides others from direct focus. Due to the speed and ease with which eyes move from target to target, as well as to the density of salient visual targets in everyday life, we are commonly unaware of not only the limited spatial range of visual attention but also the physical and cognitive effort of attending to multiple targets. However, in busy environments with multiple attentional targets, all of these factors are scaled up into overt experience by virtue of the perceptually taxing conditions, along with the durations over which they may occur. Compositional strategies like those I describe in following tap jointly into the perceptual proclivity to optimize informational uptake and the functional limitations on perceptual performance.

Though theater spaces are more spatially constrained than our real 360-degree world, the onstage worlds of postdramatic theatre are often less visually "linear" than those of previous periods. Lehmann recognizes the heightened perceptual demand of the postdramatic "trait" of simultaneity, citing Forsythe's work as an example. As he comments,

> While dramatic theatre proceeds in such a way that of all of the signals communicated at any one moment of the performance only a particular one is usually emphasized and placed at the centre, the paratactical valency [ambiguous linkage of elements] and ordering of postdramatic theatre lead to the experience of simultaneity. This often—and we have to add: frequently with systematic intent—overstrains the perceptive apparatus (...) Interrogating the intention and effect of simultaneity, one has to state: the *parcelling of perception* here becomes an unavoidable experience. To begin with, the comprehension finds hardly any support in overarching sequential connections of action/plot. But even the events perceived in one moment elude synthetization when they occur simultaneously and when the concentration on one particular aspect makes the clear registration of another impossible.[7]

In visual terms, Lehmann's idea of simultaneity translates to *polycentricity*: the concurrent staging of different regions of interest. Though we live in an inherently polycentric world, the encultured imperative of the *theatron*—which is driven both by economies of perceptual-cognitive effort and by cultural economies of theatre as an extradaily event—encourages close, careful attention to unfolding events lest key details be missed. Despite the speed with which our eyes can shift targets, though, and despite the evolutionary imperative to optimize our intake of sensory information, concurrent spatially distributed events still force attentional choices. The net result, as Lehmann notes, is perceptual overstrain. By dividing attention, polycentric staging elicits greater visual effort, while the duration and context of performance events can tax and fatigue the visual system. Under these circumstances, as with conditions of low light or occlusion, the sensory-cognitive work of attending can bring the usually effortless performance of perception into reflective awareness. The demand of polycentricity sets up a tension between the desire to see as much as possible and the urge to watch individual events play out. Studies of divided attention that rely on simple repetitive actions or static geometric forms fail to capture these extradaily factors.

POLYCENTRISM IN BALANCHINE AND FORSYTHE

European-based concert dance tends not to challenge vision. Unison dancing by groups is parsable with relative ease, while soloists or groupings of dancers yield attentional focus to each other by pausing, relinquishing space, or exiting. When differing dance phrases co-occur, they typically do so in ways that diminish attentional competition through "harmonic" movement structures or choreomusical reflection of accompanying music's layers. This is the case with many of choreographer George Balanchine's abstract, neoclassical ballets dating from the 1920s to 1970s that feature instances of choreographic simultaneity. In, some of these, choreographic complexity produces brief "kaleidoscopic patterns"[8] of differing phrases that subsequently resolve into unison dancing. In *Serenade* (1934), for example, the first refrain of the bright opening movement concludes with a building fugue of differing phrases that clusters the dancers in fours and fives before resolving them into a single diagonal line that "peels off" into the wing. The audience is left with exhilaratingly empty space and silence for a moment before the second refrain begins. Shifting canon patterns feature throughout *Serenade*'s first three movements, with a dizzying phrasal fugue during the brisk third movement (*tema russo*), while the more tranquil and linear staging of the final *élégie* section provides a lyrical closing contrast.[9] In other Balanchine ballets, polycentric counterpoint provides a musically reflective visual contrast between soloists and *corps de ballet*. The two soloists in *Concerto Barocco* (1941) follow Bach's solo violins as the *corps* of eight women provides the visual "voice" of the contrapuntal strings and *basso continuo*. In each of *Symphony in C*'s four movements (1947) a principal couple, two soloist couples, and a *corps* of either six or eight women similarly highlight the melodic fugues of Bizet's orchestral score (Fig. 5.1).

Forsythe's simultaneity is prevalent in his "ballet ballets" and has also taken a wide variety of striking forms in his more theatrical works and performance installations. Sections of several earlier works, including *Impressing the Czar* (1988) and *ALIE/N A(C)TION* (1992), feature stages that are visually or architecturally split, with different choreography and dramatic action occurring in each region and sometimes crossing over. The fourth section of *Impressing the Czar*, titled "Bongo Bongo Nageela," is an

Fig. 5.1 The opening fugue of "Bongo Bongo Nageela" from *Impressing the Czar*. (Source: photo courtesy of Dominik Mentzos)

extreme case of simultaneity, opening with a corps of 32 male and female dancers, identically clad in bobbed pageboy wigs and schoolgirl costumes, performing a wildly diverse 7-group fugue of popular and camp dance moves to a percussive synthesizer variation of the *presto* from Beethoven's *String Quartet No. 14, Op. 131.* New phrases and configurations emerge constantly over "Bongo's" six-minute duration, which is exhilarating and exhausting for performers and spectator-auditors alike (Fig. 5.1). In other pieces, dancers share the stage with printed texts or timekeeping devices, while in others, screen images compete for attention with live performers.[10] *Kammer/Kammer* (2000), most notably, includes several screens hanging above both the stage and audience space, displaying live video feed of performance passages that are either concurrently visible or blocked from view within the "chambers" formed by walls onstage.

Forsythe's reverence to Balanchine is evident not only in the movement aesthetics of his "ballet ballets" but also in the counterpoint formations and canon structures of these and other works. In a 2006 interview, he notes that *Artifact* (1984) is "like a thank-you note to [Balanchine] for everything I've learned by watching his work. And it reflects both my love and my doubts: On one hand, it's reverent; on the other hand it acknowledges the epoch he worked in as something bygone."[11] Compared to Balanchine, though, the distinction between the visual "voices" of soloists and corps de ballet is largely effaced in Forsythe's works. Tamara Tomić-Vajagić highlights not only the complex choreographic organization of the "ballet ballets" but also their uniform costuming as signs of the Ballett Frankfurt's "dissolved hierarchy," noting that soloists in these works are typically indistinguishable from the ensemble.[12]

While Balanchine's classically informed soloist-*corps* counterpoints add satisfying visuosonic depth to his works, Forsythe's counterpoint is more overtly demanding in its perceptual challenge. *Artifact*'s second part opens with an illustrative surprise: a solo couple stands downstage, isolated from the *corps* of dancers framing the sides and back of the stage, but before they begin to move a second couple unexpectedly steps out of the framing *corps* and begins dancing first. Two distinct duets then unfold simultaneously as the *corps* sharply move their arms in unison, following the improvised gestures of a shadowy gray figure standing downstage with her back to the audience. More often, however, Forsythe's counterpoints are shifting and emergent, spatially juxtaposing groups of dancers performing different phrases or interspersing groups of scattered dancers each moving in unison. Dancers often phase in and out of completely different material in solos, duets, or intermeshed groups, and canons tend to be spatially and temporally nonlinear, for example, in the finale of *Playlist (1, 2)*, set to Lion Babe's "Impossible" (Jax Jones remix).[13]

Overt choreomusical synchrony, a powerful attractor of attention,[14] is quite rare in Forsythe's work, as well as far less reflective of melodic lines. Instead, he favors a choreomusical relationship that is "funky"—contrapuntal to rhythms and sound structures. As he explained in a 2013 interview:

I was always interested in bringing another musical sensitivity to ballet. That's what I'm calling my 'funk influence.' It means a certain relationship to the idea of a beat and a multi-layered concept of time. That has now developed into a practice that focuses very little on form and primarily on the time qualities of events (...) Our main focus...has been investigating ways of deriving counterpoint from a two-frame perspective. In one-frame perspective, one has an ergodic, statistical relation to the immediate performative-compositional environment which one 'rides', adapting one's own timings to sustain the compositional whole.[15]

Forsythe's use of the statistical term *ergodic* is telling, as it refers to pro-cesses in which each relevant factor equally represents the whole. In his works, choreography seldom serves as frame or embellishment for other more "important" dancing. Instead, valences of different phrases are typi-cally set into a far more egalitarian dialogue with each other as they mesh and as groups morph into other groupings. In a number of works, inter-estingly, Forsythe also mirrors the attention of the audience by placing watching dancers upstage. Rather than forming a static frame, however, those watching offer their own competition for attention, sometimes mov-ing their arms or making reduced steps.

The qualities above all occur in the standalone ballet *the second detail* (1991), which was also performed as the "prelude" piece to the second version of *The Loss of Small Detail* (1991). Following some initial peram-bulatory place-changing by the 13-member ensemble, a brief opening solo is followed by two independent solos on opposite sides of the stage, then immediately by two more at center and stage left. During these, other members of the ensemble shift positions and strike sharp *tendu* poses on occasional thudding accents in Thom Willems' percussive, build-ing score. A dispersed trio of women performing a brief unison passage is overtaken by a jump that gathers five of the men into a dispersed flock. In the next moment, however, individuals and small groups of dancers simul-taneously perform such a wide range of distinct phrases that any sem-blance of ordered structure blurs. A duet and two closely grouped quartets momentarily come into relative focus, followed by another aggregation of different phrases. Lines of three dancers hint at canon structures, jettison-ing and absorbing solos and duets as they continue. All of this occurs within the first 90 seconds of the 22-minute work, during which some of the ensemble later sit on a row of small square stools upstage, watching as others perform, crossing a leg, or presaging the work's finale by gesturing in canon with their arms.

While Forsythe's staging typically involves shifting groupings or scat-terings of dancers, Balanchine ballets often feature soloists dancing simultaneously with a dancing *corps de ballet* ensemble, rather than being framed by a *corps* that poses or dances simplified steps as is typical in classical ballets. Though Balanchine's soloists stop occasionally in poses or exit while the *corps'* movement takes up reflection of primarily melody, at many points his *corps* perform either distinct full-scale chore-ography or occasional sparse counterpoint movements simultaneously to solos or duets. *Concerto Barocco* provides numerous examples of both of these tactics. The work's busy eight-member *corps* remains onstage throughout the 20-minute piece, while the two soloists occasionally exit. The *corps* has its own choreography throughout the ballet, with the exception of a unison section known as the "mad step"[16] in the first movement and two more unison passages in the work's final moments. In the third and final movement, the *corps* moves in a shifting "star" formation that is literally upstaged by the two soloists, who "cover" or "mask" the star as they trade off phrases of the solo violins' motifs directly downstage of it. The soloists repeat the trade-off passage three times during the third movement, dancing closer to one another each time. Visually, Balanchine's placement of the *corps* behind the soloists seems to tuck the *continuo* and strings in under the solo violins.[17] Created 30 years later, *Stravinsky Violin Concerto*'s first movement features quartets of *corps* dancers framing or offsetting principal dancers or couples, counterpointing and rejoining their steps. In the final *allegro* section with the full ensemble, however, principal couples dance differing choreography directly in front of the 16-member *corps*. At one point, the male soloists mirror each other in front of the split male *corps*—who also mirror each other—while the women's *corps* poses far upstage in lines, creating a subtle but insistent visual diversion by flicking their hands in rhythm.[18]

Balanchine's choreography clearly exploits the harmonic nature of visual and sonic classical aesthetics. In doing so, it too offers moments for attendees to become aware of vision's limitations. His polycentrism, "masking," and swift crossings are not consistently "easy on the eyes" due to ordered clusters moving in unexpected ways both choreographically and spatially. However, the visual-spatial distances between regions of interest in Balanchine's works are relatively short: typically, looking from soloists to *corps* or between *corps* groups in his works involves shifting the gaze more along the z-axis of depth than along the lateral x-axis that a "picture frame" *corps* staging would entail (*Concerto Barocco*'s more laterally counterpointed first movement, however, is a notable exception). In effect, Balanchine's staging keeps the eye *in the dance* and by extension *in the music*, by clustering choreographic elements in near-range peripheral vision rather than spreading them farther out in the periphery. Crucially, the attentional conflict of Balanchine's counterpoint is also regularly resolved in solos, duets, or unison sections, while held poses provide regular respite to the eye.

By contrast, Forsythe's polycentricity involves multiple, distinct visual "voices" that seldom coalesce into easy coherence. *Artifact* Part 2's opening, with its two duets and the *corps* following the gestures of the gray figure downstage, creates four and later six distinct regions of interest as the framing *corps* becomes three independently moving lines. Here and elsewhere, including *In the Middle, Somewhat Elevated* (*Impressing the Czar*'s Part 2), Forsythe's staging occasionally reflects Balanchine's front-to-back blocking and crossing, as it does in other "ballet ballets" like *Herman Schmerman* (1992) and the recent *Blake Works 1* (2016) and *Playlist* pieces.[19] In many other works, however, different choreographic patterns are scattered almost randomly among each other, as mentioned above. "Bongo Bongo Nageela's" seven groups and concentric circles swap phrases and occasionally move in unison, but do so unpredictably and irregularly. In *the second detail,* five or more distinct choreographic phrases often unfold simultaneously, with brief synchronies unexpectedly ceasing or re-forming into others. *One flat thing, reproduced* (2000), set to a thrumming Willems soundtrack, is a non-stop, all-star/no-star "baroque machinery" of gestural cues, temporal alignments, and independent phrases.[20] The multilinear and polycentric choreography and shifting patterns of activity in these works make it impossible for the eye to take in more than a fraction of the overall choreography. In parallel, Willems' scores are filled with constant phrasal shifts and unexpected injections of sonic detail.

You See?

Polycentric choreographies are events of overtly lossy perception that call awareness to the deep and even confrontational elusiveness of complex dance works. Forsythe seems to have dilated, or perhaps deconstructed, Balanchine's more fleeting polycentricity by making it more of a constant in his "ballet ballets" and other works. Whether this obscuration of dancing by hiding it in plain sight delights or unsettles audiences—or both—is largely a factor of expectation and of awareness of one's own scopic desire. Audience members might feel compelled to see the ballets a second time, only to find that even more has been missed than first surmised. This points squarely to the discrepancy between the "what you think you see" blithely mentioned by *Artifact*'s "Woman in Historical Costume," and what you actually do.

Forsythe's performative investigations of vision are all underpinned by the profuseness of his movement aesthetics and choreographic structuring. Occasionally, though, he has stood his "hyperkineticism" on its metaphorical head. In the original version of *7 to 10 Passages* (2000),[21] a wide line of dancers far upstage moves glacially forward for more than 10 minutes, each independently executing articulations of limbs and torso that are nearly invisible as the dancers first emerge from the dim distance, and evoking close, focused attention as they slowly loom into clearer view. For critic Pieter T'Jonck the effect of their "almost unnoticeable," trajectory and movement that "hangs against a complete standstill" is that

After a while you also start to notice the enormous differences in the way in which the dancers complete this extremely difficult task. The performance also plays with the viewer's attention in a subtle way. Partly due to the lingering music of Thom Willems, there is a moment when your own brain just doesn't seem to stop while staring. An unnoticed change then breaks through that paralysis of perception time and again.[22]

The works discussed in Part 1 have largely been set to rhythmic music. Part 2 considers Forsythe's soundscapes that diverge from rhythmical musical accompaniment, in order to investigate his experimentation with sound and movement. Like different registers of illumination, the range of soundscores developed over the twentieth century also provides ground for perceptual inquiry through choreo-scenographic processes.

NOTES

1. Roswell Johnson first used the term *niche* in 1910 to describe this environmental contingency, with Joseph Grinnell further elaborating it a few years later in an extended program of research.
2. R.P. O'Shea, "Thumb's rule tested: visual angle of thumb's width is about 2 degrees"; and Groot et al., "Thumb rule of visual angle: a new confirmation."
3. Bert Jans et al., "Visual spatial attention to multiple locations at once: The jury is still out"; and Kyle Cave et al., "Split Attention as Part of a Flexible Attentional System for Complex Scenes: Comment on Jans, Peters, and De Weerd." See also additional commentary articles from both research groups in the same volume.

4. J.M. Henderson and F. Ferreira, "Effects of foveal processing difficulty on the perceptual span in reading: implications for attention and eye movement control."

5. There are three principal models of selective conscious attention: Broadbent's filter model (1958), Deutsch and Deutsch's late selection model (1963), and Treisman's theory of attenuation (1964).

6. Ludwig et al., "Foveal analysis and peripheral selection during active visual sampling."

7. Lehmann, *Postdramatic Theatre*, 87. Emphasis original.

8. Nancy Reynolds *Repertory in Review: 40 Years of the New York City Ballet*, 6.

9. Balanchine's *Serenade* reverses the order of the final two movements of Tchaikovsky's composition.

10. For comprehensive views of Forsythe's use of new media technologies, see Kerstin Evert, *DanceLab. Zeitgenössischer Tanz und Neue Technologie* and Nik Haffner, "Zeit erkennen."

11. Forsythe quoted in Gabriela Ferrari's interview.

12. Tamara Tomić-Vajagić, "The dancer at work: The aesthetic and politics of practice clothes and leotard costumes in ballet performance," 100.

13. See English National Ballet's trailer of *Playlist (1, 2)*'s Track 2 at https://www.youtube.com/watch?v=hLBpVsBpah0 (accessed 4 April 2020).

14. M. Woolhouse and R. Lai, "Traces across the body: influence of music-dance synchrony on the observation of dance."

15. Forsythe quoted in Astrid Kaminski, "Talking Dance."

16. So named because of the energetic attack required to execute the step's quick *ronds de jambe* into *tendu*. Stagers of *Concerto Barocco* tell the dancers that "You have to get mad at [the phrase] to stay on time." See the online discussion Jack Reed, "Ashley and Goldner Remember Balanchine."

17. It is worth noting, however, that audiences seated in the balconies will see both formations more clearly than those seated at orchestra level.

18. Stephanie Jordan has analyzed the choreomusical structure of numerous Balanchine ballets in close detail (1993a, 1993b, 2000, 2007, and others).

19. Forsythe created *Playlist (1, 2)* for the English National Ballet in 2018 and extended this work into *Playlist (EP)* for the Boston Ballet in 2019.

20. The complex score of *One flat thing, reproduced* has been visually notated and diagrammed in the project *Synchronous Objects for One flat thing, reproduced*, an interactive online project produced by William Forsythe, Maria Palazzi, and Norah Zuniga Shaw for The Ohio State University.

21. A revised version of *7 to 10 Passages* was performed in Dresden in September 2010.

22. Pieter T'Jonck, "Forsythe extreem trag en extreem snel."

BIBLIOGRAPHY

Broadbent, Daniel. 1958. *Perception and Communication*. New York: Pergamon.

Cave, K., W. Bush, and T. Taylor. 2010. Split Attention as Part of a Flexible Attentional System for Complex Scenes: Comment on Jans, Peters, and De Weerd. *Psychological Review* 117 (2): 685–695.

Deutsch, J.A., and D. Deutsch. 1963. Attention: Some Theoretical Considerations. *Psychological Review* 70 (1): 80–90.

Eriksen, C., and J. St James. 1986. Visual Attention Within and Around the Field of Focal Attention: A Zoom Lens Model. *Perception & Psychophysics* 40 (4): 225–240.

Evert, Kerstin. 2003. *DanceLab. Zeitgenössischer Tanz und Neue Technologie*. Würzburg: Königshausen & Neumann.

Ferrari, G. 2006. Interview with William Forsythe. *BOMB Magazine*, July 1. Accessed 16 August 2006. https://bombmagazine.org/articles/william-forsythe/.

Forsythe, W., M. Palazzi, and N. Zuniga-Shaw. 2009. *Synchronous Objects for One flat Thing, Reproduced*. The Ohio State University. Accessed 27 April 2010. https://synchronousobjects.osu.edu/.

Grinnell, J., and H.S. Swarth. 1913. *An Account of the Birds and Mammals of the San Jacinto Area of Southern California with Remarks upon the Behavior of Geographic Races on the Margins of Their Habitats*. Vol. 10. Berkeley: University of California Press.

Groot, C., F. Ortega, and F.S. Beltran. 1994. Thumb Rule of Visual Angle: A New Confirmation. *Perceptual and motor skills* 78 (1): 232–234.

Haffner, Nik. 2004. Zeit erkennen. In *William Forsythe: Denken in Bewegung*, ed. Gerald Siegmund, 133–144. Berlin: Henschel Verlag.

Henderson, J.M., and F. Ferreira. 1990. Effects of Foveal Processing Difficulty on the Perceptual Span in Reading: Implications for Attention and Eye Movement Control. *Journal of Experimental Psychology: Learning, Memory, and Cognition* 16 (3): 417–429.

Jans, B., J. Peters, and P. De Weerd. 2010. Visual Spatial Attention to Multiple Locations at Once: The Jury is Still Out. *Psychological Review* 117 (2): 637–682.

Johnson, R.H. 1910. *Determinate Evolution in the Color-Pattern of the Lady-beetles*. Washington DC: Carnegie Institution of Washington.

Jordan, Stephanie. 1993a. Agon: A Musical Choreographic Analysis. *Dance Research Journal* 25 (2): 1–12.

———. 1993b. Music Puts a Time Corset on the Dance. *Dance Chronicle* 16 (3): 295–321.

———. 2000. *Moving Music: Dialogues with Music in Twentieth Century Ballet*. London: Dance Books.

————. 2007. *Stravinsky Dances: Re-Visions Across a Century*. London: Dance Books.

Kaminski, A. 2013. Talking Dance. *Frieze*, August 13. Accessed 15 April 2019. https://frieze.com/article/talking-dance.

Lehmann, H.-T. 2006. *Postdramatic Theatre*. Translated by Karen-Jürs-Munby. Abingdon/New York: Routledge. Original version: Lehmann, Hans-Thies. 1999. *Postdramatisches Theater*. Frankfurt am Main: Verlag der Autoren.

Ludwig, C.J., J.R. Davies, and M.P. Eckstein. 2014. Foveal Analysis and Peripheral Selection During Active Visual Sampling. *Proceedings of the National Academy of Sciences* 111 (2): E291–E299.

O'Shea, R.P. 1991. Thumb's Rule Tested: Visual Angle of Thumb's Width is about 2 Degrees. *Perception* 20 (3): 415–418.

Reed, J. 2004. Ashley and Goldner Remember Balanchine. *Ballet Alert!* Accessed 28 March 2019. https://balletalert.invisionzone.com/topic/17976-ashley-and-goldner-remember-balanchine/.

Reynolds, Nancy. 1977. *Repertory in Review: 40 Years of the New York City Ballet*. New York: Dial Press.

T'Jonck, P. 2000. Forsythe extreem trag en extreem snel. *De Standaard*. Archived at SARMA, February 2. Accessed 10 February 2022. http://dighum.ua.ac.be/ptj/html/2000-02-25_Forsythe_extreem_traag_en_extreem_snel.html.

Tomić-Vajagić, Tamara. 2014. The Dancer at Work: The Aesthetic and Politics of Practice Clothes and Leotard Costumes in Ballet Performance. *Scene* 2 (1–2): 89–105.

Treisman, Anne M. 1964. Selective Attention in Man. *British Medical Bulletin* 20 (1): 12–16.

Woolhouse, M., and R. Lai. 2014. Traces Across the Body: Influence of Music-dance Synchrony on the Observation of Dance. *Frontiers in human neuroscience* 8: 965.

PART II

Unsettling Hearing: Thresholds of Attention and Perception

Without a doubt, we are a profoundly visual species. When it comes to affective experiences, however, the auditory system has certain perceptual advantages. "The space of hearing is not ungoverned in comparison to the space of the eye; but it is differently governed," Steven Connor notes.[1] Though we can selectively allocate attention to both sounds and visual objects, we can only see limited segments of its totality at any time. Sound instead surrounds and immerses us in a perceptual field whose physical contours are less clearly discernible, while situating us, as Walter Ong puts it, "in the middle of actuality and in simultaneity" rather than "in front of things and in sequentiality."[2] Marshall McLuhan concurs, rather cheekily reminding us that

> [t]he ear favors no particular "point of view." We are enveloped by sound. It forms a seamless web around us. We say, "Music shall fill the air." We never say, "Music shall fill a particular segment of the air."[3]

The auditory perceptual channel is also constantly receptive, even in sleep; we may close or avert our eyes, but we cannot close our ears. Within this watery and more volatile sonic field, co-present sound-objects impinge ceaselessly upon our ears, blending with and altering each other in ways that are for the most part beyond our control.

The subtle and often subliminal effects of sound have profound effects on the atmospheres of spaces. Theater environments and technologies are remarkable in that they are optimized not only to enhance sound quality and audition but also to facilitate swift and global atmospheric changes.

Current audio technologies also offer a seemingly limitless range of possibilities to alter live or recorded sounds and to produce layered scores of music, text, ambient noise, or other elements. Additionally, sonic components can be localized in space or moved in ways that make space *perform* as it never has before. These versatile and agile sonic environments also offer unprecedented challenges to attention and perception, as well as access to experiences of the uncanny, the transcendent, and the sublime. The influence on Forsythe's soundscores of his most frequent compositional partner, Thom Willems, cannot be overstated, and the reader is encouraged to refer to the outstanding writings on the Forsythe-Willems collaboration by Chris Salter, who collaborated with the Ballett Frankfurt in the 1990s when Forsythe's exploration of the technological affordances of theatrical sound was at its peak.[4]

Lehmann has highlighted how postdramatic theatre is a "decomposed" theatre in which different layers of performance, formerly agglomerated and localized within bodies and contingent on places, are freed to be treated as autonomous "languages" of presentation.[5] David Roesner responds to this idea by positing a "composed theatre" that is not a genre but rather an expansion on Lehmann's language-focused discussion of postdramatic theatre's "musicalization."[6] I obliquely take up this direction in Chap. 11 of this volume; aligning with Roesner, however, I am interested in the "theatricalization of music" but more broadly still of soundscapes, which in postdramatic theatre are often composed of elements that we do not commonly categorize as music.[7]

Forsythe has used sound in both straightforward ways as accompaniment and in performative ones. Like the visual compositional strategies described in the previous section, performative soundscores not only call attention to the limits and tendencies of the auditory perceptual system, but in Forsythe's works critically also interface with the performative potentials generated by their choreo-scenographies. This is the focus of the chapters in this section, which examine a range of sonic conditions that recur across Forsythe's oeuvre. As such, the three chapters do not offer a choreomusical focus on Forsythe along the lines of Stephanie Jordan's excellent analyses. Rather, by considering silence (argued here to be *silences*), minimalist music, and scenes of sonic overwhelm, my focus is on the perceptual demands that arise beyond conditions in which dancing "goes together" with accompanying music. This is distinct from the choreomusical independence or incongruence that Allen Fogelsanger and Kathleya Afanador investigate in their valuable study.[8] Instead, I turn to the ways that registers of sound and music are deployed by Forsythe—whose choreographic career has been driven by the question "How can this be otherwise?"[9]—to performatively investigate how dance, sound, and theatrical environment and context can be otherwise composed.

NOTES

1. Steven Connor, *Dumbstruck: A Cultural History of Ventriloquism*, 15.
2. Walter Ong, *The Presence of the Word*, 128.
3. Marshall McLuhan and Quentin Fiore, *The Medium is the Massage: An Inventory of Effects*, 111.
4. See Chris Salter, *Entangled: Technology and the Transformation of Performance*, and "Timbral Architectures, Aurality's Force."
5. Hans-Thies Lehmann, *Postdramatic Theatre*, 51.
6. Hans-Thies Lehmann, *Postdramatic Theatre*, 91–93.
7. See Matthias Rebstock and David Roesner, eds., *Composed Theatre: Aesthetics, Practices, Processes*. See also Lynne Kendrick and David Roesner, *Theatre Noise: The Sound of Performance*.
8. Allen Fogelsanger and Kathleya Afandour, "Parameters of Perception: Vision, Audition, and Twentieth-Century Music and Dance."
9. Rehearsal notes 2006–2013; see also Linda Caruso Haviland, "Dancing Forsythe's Dances: From Outside In and Inside Out."

BIBLIOGRAPHY

Connor, Steven. 2000. *Dumbstruck: A Cultural History of Ventriloquism*. New York: Oxford University Press.

Fogelsanger, Allen, and Kathleya Afanador. 2017. Parameters of Perception: Vision, Audition, and Twentieth-Century Music and Dance. *AVANT. Pismo Awangardy Filozoficzno-Naukowej* 1: 59–73.

Haviland, Linda Caruso. 2013. Dancing Forsythe's Dances: From Outside in and Inside Out. Pennsylvania Ballet website, July 10. Accessed 25 July 2013.

Kendrick, Lynne, and David Roesner, eds. 2012. *Theatre Noise: The Sound of Performance*. Newcastle upon Tyne: Cambridge Scholars Publishing.

Lehmann, Hans-Thies. 2006. *Postdramatic Theatre*. Translated by Karen-Jürs-Munby. Abingdon and New York: Routledge. Original Version: Lehmann, Hans-Thies. 1999. *Postdramatisches Theater*. Frankfurt am Main: Verlag der Autoren.

McLuhan, Marshall, and Quentin Fiore. 1967. *The Medium is the Massage: An Inventory of Effects*. New York: Bantam Books.

Ong, Walter J. 2000. *The Presence of the Word: Some Prolegomena for Cultural and Religious History.* 2nd ed. Binghamton: Global Publications.

Rebstock, Matthias, and David Roesner, eds. *Composed Theatre: Aesthetics, Practices, Processes.* Bristol and Chicago: Intellect Books.

Salter, Chris. 2010. *Entangled: Technology and the Transformation of Performance.* Cambridge, MA and London: MIT Press.

———. 2011. Timbral Architectures, Aurality's Force. In *William Forsythe and the Practice of Choreography: It Starts from Any Point,* ed. Steven Spier, 54–72. Abingdon and New York: Routledge.

CHAPTER 6

Quiet: Hush, Caesurae, and Deep Silence

Live dance performances are rarely entirely silent. Even without accompanying music or other soundscore, dancers make sounds when they move: shoes squeak or clatter and costumes rustle, feet or other body parts strike or slide over the stage and occasionally smack or thud against each other. Breathing is sometimes heavy or made deliberately louder. If you are seated far enough back in the auditorium, you may miss much of the sound that dancing makes; the closer you are, though, the harder its sounds are to ignore. Audiences make sounds of their own as well, rustling, coughing, whispering, sighing, gasping, blowing noses, or even audaciously unwrapping sweets. A cell phone rings and suddenly a dancer performing "in silence" is dancing to music.

It is anyone's guess how John Cage might have felt about ringing cell phones. Cage chose a benefit concert at the barnlike open-air Maverick Concert Hall in rural upstate New York for the 1952 premiere of his controversial *4′33″*, which soloist David Tudor performed on a bill of experimental works by Morton Feldman, Earl Brown, Pierre Boulez, and others. During the first half-minute-long movement of the work, wind could be heard in the trees outside; rain began to patter on the wooden roof during the almost three-minute-long second one, and during the shorter third movement, as Cage noted, "the people themselves made all kinds of interesting sounds as they talked or walked out."[1] Views and criticisms of the work's meaning and worth proliferated following the premiere, so the cat

© The Author(s), under exclusive license to Springer Nature Switzerland AG 2023
F. Vass, *William Forsythe's Postdramatic Dance Theater*, Cognitive Studies in Literature and Performance,
https://doi.org/10.1007/978-3-031-26658-4_6

was almost immediately out of the bag. Douglas Kahn noted in 1997 that "in every performance [of *4'33"*] I've attended the silence has been broken by the audience and become ironically noisy."[2]

Though *4'33"* is a "silent" performance, it is far from a motionless one. The original score dictates a page turn at the end of the first movement, three during the second, and one during the third. Given the work's time signature, this amounts roughly to a page turn every 30 seconds.[3] A filmed performance late in Tudor's life shows him also operating a stopwatch as he closes and opens the keyboard lid three times while reading and turning the score's pages. Each time, he places the stopwatch on the closed lid and then moves his hands to his thighs, occasionally shifting their position before taking up the stopwatch again. Tudor's posture and gaze also shift constantly as he attends to the score and stopwatch.[4]

4'33" famously extended the conceptual realm of soundscores. As Kahn points out, though, the work also performatively exploited the concert-manners propriety on which the silence was contingent by "transpos(ing) the performance onto the audience members both in their utterances and in the acts of shifting perception toward other sounds."[5] The silencing of the performer in *4'33"*, in other words, draws audiences' attention to both the overt and covert potentials of their own individual and collective performance *as* an audience—an assembly of listeners.[6] As George Home-Cook highlights, when theatre worlds are quiet, we crane both to hear and to see. Perceived silences provoke an awkward, even painful "purgatory of listening" that we seek to fill by "stretching ourselves,"—in other words, our attention.[7]

Silent typically stands for *without speech* in theatre, and for *without music* when dance performance is being discussed. But as Cage noticed and perhaps instigated, aural perception shifts in a fluid manner that conceptual framing of soundscapes does not. This is evident in Sheila Orysiek's observations in a review of Forsythe's *The Room as It Was* (2002):

> The "music" is silence…Never once did I hear pointe shoe connect with the stage. However, bare legs in pointe shoes lays [sic] bare the physical scaffolding that make the shoes work (…) My attention was drawn to these details because my attention had to be drawn to something. The only other alternative was constantly flailing arms, unflagging percussive movement, countless hip swivels, contractions and twists. Another layer of "interest" were [sic] the pantings, gruntings and martial arts gusts of vocalizations from the performers.[8]

Her comment in turn ratifies composer and music scholar Barbara White's view that "We are so accustomed to the absence of, or our own lack of attention to, the sounds dancers make that it is possible to describe a music-less dance piece as being 'silent.'"[9] These paradoxical views invite recognition of an array of *silences* with distinct perceptual effects and capabilities to evoke differing performative responses, as well as the ways in which choreographers have experimented and continue to experiment with them.

Dancing in Silence(s)

In London's proto-modern Elizabethan theaters, audience quiet served as a barometer for quality. Ross Brown notes that the ears of noisy, unpoliced attendees demanded more than just stories, and so the dramas of the period were accordingly couched within a counterpointed "sonic dramaturgy" that drew audiences into the theatrical event and the presented narrative. Interpolated music regenerated and retained interest: overtures and finales, trumpet heralds and alarums, musical interludes, and sonic flourishes. In conventional modern theatre performances, by contrast, the "body bristles in omnidirectional attentiveness to the strangeness of the environment."[10] Audiences fall into anticipatory quiet at the start of performances and remain so until the time comes to applaud, except in the case of overwhelming disapproval. With auditory attention thus focused, sound becomes a delicate theatrical medium through which silences can speak volumes virtually without risk of interruption. At the same time, the anxiety provoked by the silent stage has opened ground for the performative staging of silences.

Nowhere is this anxiety more acute than in dance performance, where musical accompaniment or at least by some form of sound is anticipated while dancers are in motion. Western concert dance performances are in fact permeated by short-term silences, with breaks occurring between passages and movements of compositions and pregnant pauses accentuating drama onstage. While classical ballets bracket their constituent parts with silences, for example, between *divertissements* or the traditional sections of *grand pas de deux*, silences also lend dramatic or even interventive effects in modern dance works and abstract ballets. However, choreographic structures and *leitmotifs* directly reflect the brevity of caesurae within the compositions to which they are choreographed. Those familiar with the compositions or with conventional classical or modern music forms will expect musical pauses when they commonly occur. Dance movement during these interstitial silences is an unexpected break with this conventionality. In Glen Tetley's elegiac 1973 work *Voluntaries*, for example, soloists make preparatory steps, turns, or exits during the silences within Poulenc's *Organ, String and Percussion Concerto in G minor*, moving in empty sonic space. Given that *Voluntaries* was created as a homage immediately following John Cranko's sudden death, its silences bear a deep and visceral poignance. I contend, though, that the brevity of such instances, together with the returns to movement-music correspondence immediately afterward, limits their power in terms of perceptual performativity and renders them dramatic but not reflexive. By contrast, when choreography includes silences that are unanticipated or of unexpected duration, there is a clear rupture of presentational conventions. Our expectations are thwarted and an anticipatory response occurs that is both anxious and sensorially arousing.

Conventional patterns of sound and silence were challenged in German *Ausdruckstanz* (expressionist dance) of the early twentieth century through the production of choreographies without music. As Dada pioneer Hugo Ball wrote in his diary, "The nervous systems have become extremely sensitive. Absolute dance, absolute poetry, absolute art – what is meant is that a minimum of impressions is enough to evoke unusual images. Everyone has become mediumistic."[11] Influenced by the ideas coming out of Zürich, Rudolf von Laban asserted the idea of dance's independence from music, while Sophie Taeuber-Arp reduced performance sound to ringing gong strikes. It was Mary Wigman, though, who began including at least one unaccompanied "absolute dance" in her programs from 1917 onward.[12] Half a century later, postmodern choreographers—many influenced by Cage—also explored the performative potentials of dance without music. Yvonne Rainer's multiple scores for *Trio A* (1966), which included silence, Wilson Pickett's "In the Midnight Hour," and a recording of a lecture about the piece itself,[13] stand as a comparative experiment on visuosonic effects. Commenting on Merce Cunningham's *Walkaround Time* (1968), Sally Banes and Noël Carroll note how silence and stillness render the work "fixed, static, highly legible, and transparent."[14] Steve Paxton, who danced with Cunningham before becoming a choreographer and the creator of Contact Improvisation, produced a number of slow or seemingly still choreographies performed without music, highlighting how the body's visual "silence," like auditory silence, is never absolute. Writing in the *Contact Quarterly* in 1976, he reflects poetically on "silent" dance's effect on his own perception of movement:

normal tends to be unnoticed (avisible)
quiet may be contrasted with normal
movement or self-conscious movement

self conscious movement influences
subsequent quiet. Normal movement
influences subsequent quiet.

When quiet, I am contrasting
experiences or modes of experience and
may be able to see the avisible and the visible.

What comes before influences what comes after.
The quality of vision will influence
the avisible and the visible to come.[15]

Silence plays a key role in the work of contemporary choreographic duo of Jonathan Burrows and composer/performer Matteo Fargion. The title of their 2005 work *The Quiet Dance* seems to promise a low-volume performance; however, the entire 35-minute piece sustains a dynamic of unexpected alternations of silence with sound, rhythm, and movement. After they take their places on stage, Fargion emits loud descending vocal *glissandi*, crying "Aaaaaaaaaaahhhh!" to accompany Burrows' jerky, striding passages across the stage. Caught off guard, audiences respond with laughter. Burrows and Fargion vary the length of pauses and silences between each of Burrows' many crossings, sustaining the anticipation and humor of the repetitive movement phrase. Both then suddenly exchange tasks and volume level, with Fargion crossing several times while Burrows accompanies with a quiet "Shhhhhhhh." After several repetitions, a somewhat longer pause and silence occurs; then Fargion's loud "Aaaaaaaaaaahhhh!" returns as Burrows resumes crossing, to gales of audience laughter. The interplay of silence, stillness, and their rupture continues throughout the work.

Thom Willems recalls the process of subtraction by which Forsythe's *The Room as It Was* (2002) came to be performed almost entirely without music:

We had tried way too hard. Were cramped. It was one big construction, just construction. Then three hours before the start he threw out all the music and dancing and had the dancers dance in stillness for twenty minutes. Only in the last two minutes can you hear my music. Yes, that was hard to swallow, but I saw what it served: something happened, then music – that's the beauty of a privileged moment.[16]

Willems' observation and the choreographies above reflect theorizations of silence from within the laboratory of artistic practice, as does Ball's comment on the "highly sensitive" nervous systems of Post-World War 1 Europeans. Modern dance pioneer Doris Humphrey also advanced a theory of silence's effect in her 1958 volume *The Art of Making Dances*, written shortly before her death. She explicitly cites unaccompanied dance as improving focus on the dancing, noting that

> the dance without music – the absence of sound on a program which is otherwise ear-filling in musical opulence – has a contrary effect to that which might be expected. It does not seem empty, or as though the bottom had dropped out, but increases concentration and attention to movement to an astonishing degree (…) the original point, that dance can stand alone, has been proved over and over, but the main virtue of the silent dance is its power to simplify concentration and rest the ear. After a section or a whole dance with no music, sound is new again and fresher than if it had been continuous.[17]

The twofold perceptual shift Humphrey indicates—heightened attention to the visual, followed by a "refreshed" experience of hearing when music returns—expresses a hypothesis that the experience of dance performance is optimized through dynamics of variance from multimodal (visual and sonic) to monomodal (visual only) and back again. Her use of volumetric terms ("ear-filling," "empty," "bottom dropped out") reflects a conceptual metaphor of perceptual experience as a container or reservoir whose partial emptying affords easier and enhanced focus on the dancing.[18] Dance performed in silence, in other words, facilitates perception of the dynamic and rhythmic qualities of movement when the augmentative perception of interplay between sound and movement is jettisoned. At the music's return, Humphrey holds, perceptual focus is renewed and improved, and auditory perception "refreshed."

A few of Forsythe's works or longer sections of works seem to ratify Humphrey's theory. One of his earliest works, *In Endloser Zeit* (From the Most Distant Time) (1978), begins with 27 minutes of extremely slow movement in a silence periodically broken by an unseen speaker reciting brief Tang dynasty poems. The silences between the poems last approximately two and a half minutes each, after which the work concludes to György Ligeti's 16-minute *Double Concerto for Flute and Oboe*. This sonic structure finds a parallel four decades later in Forsythe's *A Quiet Evening of Dance* (2018), which opens with a soundscore of quiet birdsong (in *Catalogue (Second Edition)*) and a section of "silence" except for the dancers' breath and squeaks of their sock-covered shoes (in *Dialogue (DUO2015)*). Then the sparse tones of Morton Feldman's 1951 *Nature Pieces for Piano, No.1*—itself a study in silences and cessations—are followed by Jean-Philippe Rameau's *ritournelle* from *Hippolyte et Aricie, Act 3* (1733). *The Room as It Was*, as mentioned above, also concludes with a section of music as a curtain slowly rises to reveal the unused upstage and two performers moving in a slow embrace.

Half a decade after Humphrey's publication, however, musicologist Barbara White instead claims that it is accompanying music, rather than silence, that allows us "to see the movement more clearly," while dance, "drawing our eyes away from the orchestral pit toward the stage, highlights the sounds for us…they support, challenge, and reshape each other, mutually."[19] In the opposition between Humphrey and White's views, dance's visuo-sonority stands as a matter of contention, notwithstanding their potential practice-based biases. In following, I interrogate Humphrey and White's contentions on the basis of three types of Forsythe's performative engagements with silence.

HUSH

Sound is perceived as the result of a vibratory medium—air, in the case of land-dwelling mammals like ourselves—first striking our selectively amplifying and sound-canceling pinnae (external ears) and ear canals before eventually being refracted against our eardrums. The vibrations of air within the middle ear are then translated into motion of the three ossicles (malleus, incus, and stapes), which similarly optimize aspects of the continually arriving vibrations. Air pressure is translated into motion of fluid within the cochlea, which is then translated again into electrical firing of neurons as sensory hair cells lining the cochlea's organ of Corti are moved. Though relative stillness along this roughly three-centimeter motion channel gives us a perception of silence, the auditory system also conveys the body's own organic noises—our own breath, heartbeat, and other bodily sounds, which are constantly present but rarely noticed. During Cage's 1951 visit to an anechoic chamber, where background noises are actually measured in negative decibels, he reported hearing a high tone and a lower one: the hum of his nervous system and the movement of his blood.[20] Though the near-silence of the chamber allowed these sounds to emerge, Cage's auditory system will also have involuntarily attuned to them. The ear, like the eye, abhors a vacuum and will "crane" for stimulus, even producing aural hallucinations to fill the perceptual void.[21]

Auditory attention is influenced both bottom-up by stimuli and top-down by experience, expectations, and goals, with perceptual load (the amount of information involved in cognitive task processing) also having an impact. This explains why we may sometimes be slow to notice impinging sounds when concentrating on a specific task. We are able to voluntarily attune to specific sounds; however, for most individuals this faculty is poorly developed and taxing to sustain. Our perceptual systems have evolved to habituate to both ongoing quiet sounds and relatively static auditory information, screening these out as background or ambient noise in order to preserve attentional resources for potentially more meaningful auditory events.

Sounds with very low volume exist near our average threshold of attention and can easily escape notice. Attention to these over time requires effortful focusing of attention; however, this remains a less-than-perfect performance of perception, particularly when other salient stimuli are present. This is reflected in some sections of Forsythe's works that are commonly considered "silent" but that actually include extremely reduced soundscores. The quiet, sparse, and often subliminal soundscapes of these conditions of *hush* are not so much danced *to* as danced *in*, as they do not afford the choreomusical congruity offered by rhythmic or melodic scores. Instead, these quiet and often sporadic sonic undercurrents inflect the atmosphere of scenographic worlds in same the manner as subliminal underscores and sound "beds" in film and other media.

Though Thom Willems is known for his intense, rhythmic synthesizer compositions for Forsythe's "ballet ballets," he has added hushed underscoring to many other Ballett Frankfurt and Forsythe Company works, performing live and responsively from the back of the auditorium where Forsythe and technical team were also stationed. *Duo* (1996), which features a "breath score" (discussed in detail in Chap. 10) of performers' breathing, footfall, and limb-on-limb contact, contains quiet melodic interpolations, while *N.N.N.N.* (2002), another work with seemingly only a breath score, has a full, almost-inaudible soundtrack of brief, sporadic synthesizer gestures. At one point in the longer work of *Stellentstellen* (2012), low contrabass "fill-ins" (Forsythe's term) flower into a section of overt, lively music before fading back to periodic, almost-inaudible inclusions. Sections of *The Returns* (2009) had a faint burbling sub-aquatic subscore befitting the piece's references to piracy, while an ominous, visceral subwoofer rumble sneaks in at the close of the 2010 work *Whole in the Head*.[22]

Hushed soundscores facilitate spatial and temporal performative effects in other Forsythe works. Sound technicians Dietrich Krüger and Niels Lanz created a faint, extremely high-pitched score element they referred to as the "crystals" or "needles," which is played through speakers around perimeter of the auditorium space during the second, primarily text-focused part of *Three Atmospheric Studies* (2006).[23] The delicate wisps of tone, which are actually a section of Monteverdi's *Tancredi e Clorinda* processed through a DSP (Digital Signal Processing) system,[24] are meant not only to gently impinge on the ear but also to delineate and draw awareness to the audience's environment. As Krüger explained, "We draw a space; we make a box with the needles." For *Human Writes* (2005, co-created with law professor Kendall Thomas), Krüger, Lanz, and Willems collaborated on a soundscape for the large halls in which the three to four-hour long performance installation was staged. As attendee-participants perambulated among an array of 40 or more tables upon which performers laboriously attempted to write phrases from the Universal Declaration of Human Rights, Willems' score of thin, extended tones and intermittent subwoofer rumbles joined the sounds of the task at hand,[25] while recordings of key human rights speeches emanated quietly and selectively from individual small speakers around the perimeter of the installation space. The volumes of the soundscore components oscillated at a glacial pace, a subtle sonic presence that influenced attendant-participant's trajectories and pauses within the space.[26] Together with slow changes of global light levels, the soundscore accentuated the passage of time, and with it the ongoing and largely futile writing actions of the performers.

Forsythe's hushed but not silent stage environments seem to point to the fact that even when perceived as silent, our actual soundscape harbors sounds that define spaces, giving them character or atmosphere that is not only heard but felt. Philosopher Michel Serres highlights the deeply mingled nature of our senses, describing the explicit anatomical connection between aurality and tactility and the linkage of sound and movement within our phylogenic history:

> We hear through our skin and feet. We hear through our skull, abdomen and thorax. Our body-box, strung tight, is covered head to toe with a tympanum. We live in noises and shouts, in sound waves just as much as in

spaces…Plunged, drowned, submerged, tossed about, lost in infinite rever-
berations and making sense of them through the body (…) The body
remembers its previous aquatic life, guiding itself through the sound waves
by instinct and force of will. Humanity in shoals swims through these waters.[27]

Sound, then, quite literally *moves* us. We are immersed in it, surrounded
by and responsive to the waves traveling through the air. Given this, it is
unsurprising that ecological psychologist James J. Gibson excludes silence
from his analysis of the auditory environment, instead considering only
the structure and sensory pickup of "vibratory events."[28] Silence essentially does not exist; when artificially approximated, we "stretch" our sensory systems or they "stretch" themselves, filling in the perceptual gap
with heightened attention or with hallucinated sound. In the hushed
instances described here, Forsythe's dancers matter-of-factly move and
pause, seemingly oblivious to the quiet, nonrhythmic wash but in fact
highly attuned to the theatrical valences created by such subliminality.
These choreographies of quiet, in which Lehmann's "independent auditory semiotics"[29] is perhaps less independent when considered along atmospheric lines, open moments in which attendees may notice their own
imperfect performances of aural attention, which parallel the performances
of vision in low light and deeper darkness.

CAESURAE

The non-existence of absolute silence aside, how do we perceive the condition that we classify as silence? Despite its lack of the discernible qualities
of sounds—loudness, pitch, timbre, directionality—we do in fact apprehend, listen to, and hear in silence. Philosopher Roy Sorensen emphasizes
that the sensory experience of silence is not a cessation or failure of perception but is instead "successful perception of an absence of sound."[30] Given
that silences at least potentially possess salience, he further notes, we treat
them in a similar manner as we do sounds. When either occurs unexpectedly, our meaning-seeking parsing of the sonic environment becomes
more sharply attuned through a heightening and focusing of attention.[31]
With obvious contingency on context, lengthy intervals of near-silence are
highly uncomfortable for many individuals, but shorter ones evoke
responses ranging from awkwardness to pleasure. This range offers a fruitful domain for performative experimentation in contemporary theatre
and dance.

Home-Cook flags the perceptual performativity that theatrical silence engenders by noting how silence in performance manifests a profound reflexivity in which both the silence and the intersubjective act of noticing it are noticed. As he comments, theatrical silence is "manipulated (or held in grasp) by all concerned, in such a way as to endow it with a particular hue, effect, or significance."[32] In other words, in moments of silence, audience members are implicated in the performance in a directly apprehensible and agentive manner, both experiencing and curating the present thing that is also an absence. Awkwardness, for Home-Cook, emerges as we become aware "of our own uncomfortable existence as silently present subjects within a larger collectivity of silent selves."[33] Brown similarly notes how the conventional theatrical requirement of silent stillness engenders a corporeal engagement that has commonalities with the maintenance of public memorial silences. He clarifies that "the corporeal attentiveness to circumstance experienced subjectively by the performer [of the silence] belongs to a genre-related state of *audience*"—in other words, of apprehending the silence as it is being communally maintained. Brown also explicitly signals the perceptual performativity of experiencing theatrical silence when he notes that this heightened awareness is "a perceptual experience of the whole body and one which creeps more into the perceptual foreground during moments of pause."[34]

It is only recently that silence has become an object of greater empirical interest, particularly within the contexts of music and meditative practices.[35] As potent as theatrical silence can be, though, it has not been empirically studied for its own affect or effect, and monomodally focused studies of silences in music offer limited relevance to visuosonic forms like dance, theatre, and film. Given its frequent inclusion as a compositional element in music, theatre works, and modern and contemporary dance, silence also warrants deeper consideration from a phenomenological perspective. Though silences may not be a "vibratory events," they are nonetheless experienced as *moving* events. Corinna da Fonseca-Wollheim, a music critic with a research background in psychology, explains that

> What unites music's negative spaces – whether they are designed for comedy, drama or mysticism – is their power to propel the listener from the role of passive consumer to active participant. As in a limerick recited with the last word missing, the brain jumps in to complete the rhyme.[36]

Composed silences not only arouse the brain, though, but also arouse the sensing body, causing it to strain for the vibratile touch of sound, seeking motion in the seemingly still air. In doing so, silences open a new angle on Lehmann's observation that postdramatic theatres of "muteness and silence" are not indebted to minimalism but rather to "a basic motif of *activating* theatre" [emphasis mine].[37]

One manner that Forsythe composes silence taps the drive for auditory sensation by stopping and restarting musical accompaniment or sound-scores at unexpected junctures. During these caesurae, dancers typically continue to move as though the soundscape had continued. Forsythe's witty 1996 *Trio* begins without music, with the three performers matter-of-factly displaying different parts of their bodies to the audience: an elbow, a ribcage, a flank, a shin. As this develops into an accelerating improvised theme, the silence becomes punctuated by the sounds of their grips and steps. Once the lilting *minuet* of Beethoven's *String Quartet No. 15, Op. 132* begins a few moments later, they swing airily together through complex, twining choreography. The music then suddenly stops at the end of a phrase but the dancers continue, the sounds of their movement suddenly audible. The music begins again from the start, but then stops again at the same place and restarts again. Over the 13-minute work, the Beethoven and Berg string quartets continue breaking off at increasingly unpredictable junctures but the dancers continue, at one point running from the stage to leave both silence and stillness before returning again (Fig. 6.1).[38]

Contrasting to the light mood of *Trio*, the original version of *Yes We Can't* (2008)[39] opened with a series of hand-cued cutoffs[40] of a loud, threatening motif reminiscent of a strongly amplified double bass as danc-ers entered and exited, performing high-energy dance passages while roar-ing, yelling, or vocalizing at two microphones. The ears were left ringing in the silences, as if a sonic blanket had been suddenly whipped aside to reveal bareness. In one instance, a female performer (Elizabeth Waterhouse) entered on the cutoff, lobbing herself into the air and landing silently while two male performers made "squishy" sounds and gesticulations at the microphones. Other cutoffs were marked by faint, sporadic bell tones or the sounds of the dancers performing hand-clapping games, while at one juncture there was a more complete silence until a performer began speaking. In this instance, though, the staging of a sight gag drew audible laughter from audience members.

Fig. 6.1 Elizabeth Waterhouse soars in silence as Ander Zabala and Christopher Roman "squish" in *Yes We Can't* (2008 version). (Source: photo courtesy of Dominik Mentzos)

Other choreographers have also made a *leitmotif* of unexpected musical caesurae. In Pina Bausch's *Blaubart* (1977, subtitled *while listening to a taped recording of Béla Bartók's opera* Duke Bluebeard's Castle), the central male character obsessively repeats specific sections of Bartók's opera by switching an onstage tape player on and off, a detail Anna Kisselgoff includes in her inventory of the work's "assault on the senses."[41] But where *Blaubart* shows the music ostensibly being controlled by a performer onstage, *Yes We Can't* and *Trio*'s music is an "invisible" capricious presence. The first musical interruption in these works, together with the continuation of dancing in the silence, triggers a "terror of error" in spectators, arousing anxiety that something has gone wrong. Once musical rupture is established as a *leitmotif*, though, the perceptual mechanism shifts to an anticipatory questioning of whether, when, and how the soundscape might stop and return. These works thus offer audiences a literal change of mind, from initial fright to pattern recognition to inquisitive prediction. The fire curtain that notoriously and repeatedly closes during Forsythe's *Artifact* Part 2 has the same effect (though as with Cage's composition, the cat was also almost immediately out of the bag and remains so).

When music is anticipated by audiences but not provided, or when music suddenly stops at unexpected junctures, attention to the sound-scape increases along with arousal and suspense. Commenting on audio-visual attention and the interplay between sound and silence in film, Jeff Smith observes that "Music may paradoxically be most noticeable in its absence, during those moments...when it is most commonly expected."[42] He refers to the phenomenon of "inattentional blindness" (failure to notice fully visible objects due to attention being captured by other ones),[43] arguing that film audiences suffer from "inattentional deafness" in which they do not actively perceive film music but assume its presence due to the auditory norms of cinematic presentation. Psychomusicologist Annabel Cohen provides further evidence of this, citing a survey in which audience members questioned after viewing a film provided positive evalu-ations of its musical score when in fact none was present.[44] However, as Smith notes, though film music often remains below the threshold of awareness, it nonetheless strongly influences the experience of cinema, as do moments of cinematic silence.[45] Given that musical accompaniment is also an expected component of theatrical dance performance—perhaps even more so than in film—Smith's observations certainly apply to dance as well.

In the instances described above, the introduction of brief sounds into silence or the abrupt cessation of ongoing sound highlights two contrast-ing ways in which auditory attention intensifies and focuses in response to novel signal quality. Though auditory attention can be voluntarily shifted across different streams or aspects of sonic information, it also shifts invol-untarily in response to sudden changes in the soundscape. The presence of new and potentially important information triggers a reflex first described by Ivan Pavlov in 1927 as an "investigative" or "what-is-it" reflex and later referred to as the orienting reflex. Typically, this reaction elicits increased attention, stilling of behavior, and autonomic arousal.[46] Later studies by Evgenii Sokolov and others further refine understanding of the orientation response by linking it with memory and with processes of habituation to stimuli,[47] while further research investigates the role of stimulus significance to the perceiver.[48] These studies' conclusions on the roles played by expectation, habituation, and meaning in attentional arousal support Humphrey's view that sound is perceived as "new again and fresher" following a period of silence. However, they complicate her observation that silence "rests the ear." Humphrey's view is perhaps understandable given the overwhelming tendency in both commonsense assessments and perceptual research to consider silence to be a cessation of hearing. But as ratified by empirical research and corroborated by the analyses of Sorensen and Home-Cook, our auditory systems actively seek to *make sense* of silence and will even construct fallacious perceptions of sound.

There is a further conflict within Humphrey's claim that silence both simplifies and increases "concentration and attention to movement" by permitting a solely visual focus. Humphrey clearly considers the co-presence of movement and music to be more perceptually taxing than movement on its own. Whether the presence of sound actually complicates attention to movement is a matter of contention among cognitive researchers, with studies of the effect on visual perception of attentional capture by unexpected sounds offering conflicting results. Some experiments measuring subjects' performance of visual tasks while exposed to changes in soundscape show that attention-capturing sounds with no relevant relation to the visual task impair task performance, while others instead show that such stimuli instead enhance performance.[49] The latter results would align with White's claim that music enhances movement perception by "allowing us to see the dance more clearly." The sounds, visual tasks, and laboratory settings used in such experiments of course differ greatly from the social, often alcohol-fuelled experience of attending live dance performances. Nonetheless, it can be surmised that sonic offsets and inserts in dance performances do have an effect on the visual experience of the works, be it enhancement of focus on movement or detraction through the intrusion of sound. Weighing these against the high value that Forsythe places on the quality of attention that audiences bring to performance, along with the perceptually performative means by which he seeks to enhance it, it would appear that Forsythe aligns more with Humphrey when it comes to silences, but favors White's view when it comes to his more choreomusically congruent "ballet ballets."[50]

It is noteworthy that almost without exception in Forsythe's works with unexpected, abrupt sound changes, dance movement and overall levels of action onstage continue unabated and in the same high-dynamic range through the sonic transitions. In other words, the visual environment retains a relatively steady level and quality of stimulus in contrast to the extreme dynamic shifts of caesurae. Forsythe clearly avoids creating congruent or oppositional multimodal shifts by limiting change to the auditory channel. One reason for this is likely that stopping both the music and the dancing could trigger applause. By stopping only the music, however, he also specifically and performatively isolates and taps the reflex responses of the auditory system, enhancing the experience of the spectacular hush of such moments. Notably, Forsythe also does not stage single instances of sonic shift with continuing visual action within works, and strategically varies the timing of caesurae each time. This keeps audiences guessing when (or whether) the soundscape will drop out again, as well as when and how it will be reintroduced if it does. As I have discussed elsewhere with regard to a filmic installation piece by Forsythe,[51] these irregular iterations "refresh" performative effects over and over again, extending the perceptual experiment and creating a sustained opportunity for viewer-auditors to become aware of the phenomenological experience of attending. Forsythe's playful, perhaps even frustrating repetition of auditory shifts reveals the robustness and "hardwired" quality of the orienting response and produces a visuosonic "independence"[52] that amounts to a meta-discourse on perceptual performativity.

Deep Silence

When audiences enter the auditorium for *Artifact*, Forsythe's first creation as director of the Ballett Frankfurt in 1984, they find the curtain already open to reveal a bare, dimly cross-lit stage. While they are taking their seats, a ghostly, barefooted, gray-painted figure begins crossing the stage, stepping very slowly forward through *tendus en arrière* and moving her arms through even slower *ports de bras*. Identified in the program as the "Other Person," she passes straight across and into the wings before appearing again after a brief interval from another wing. Uncertain whether the performance has already started, audience members self-consciously negotiate the transition from settling and chattering into quiet stillness as she continues her slow passages. Finally, the house lights slowly dim as a woman in a powdered wig and long, ornate dress walks slowly but deliberately to the center of the stage. Lightly whirling to face the audience, she claps her hands ceremonially, and a bright passage from a Bach *chaconne* rings out from an unseen piano. Sweeping floridly forward with exaggerated, courtly dance movements, the "Woman in Historical Costume" arrives downstage at the end of a musical phrase. "Step inside," she says.

Music scholar Julie Sutton notes how initial silences mark the temporal boundary of performances, signal performer readiness, and establish audience expectancy.[53] Theatrical conventions elicit a culturally defined parallel choreography from audiences in which they respond to the signaling of imminent performance beginnings by hushing themselves and quietly waiting. At *Artifact*'s opening, however, Forsythe stages an audio-visual paradox: the entering audience finds the "Other Person" already in motion with the house lights up but without accompanying music, moving formally but not yet dancing in a conventional sense. In rendering the point of the work's actual beginning indistinct, *Artifact*'s initial silence performatively addresses expectations of music in dance performance. Forsythe staged this "Vorschau" device ("before-show" or pre-view) again in later works such as *Kammer/Kammer* (2000) and *I don't believe in outer space* (2008). In these two works, though, onstage dialogue, action, or accompanying music soften the demanding effect achieved at *Artifact*'s "silent" start.

Like Cage's *4'33"*, *Artifact*'s initial silence has a sensitizing effect on audiences, who carefully reduce but seldom fully eliminate the noises they make. It is worth noting that Forsythe takes pains to eliminate any ambient sounds within the auditorium or stage space, including asking for air conditioning to be turned off at crucial points, wherever the work is performed. He is also willing to wait until the desired depth of silence occurs; the number of the "Other Person's" crossings and the intervals between them varies not only according to auditorium size and front-of-house signaling conventions (e.g., closing auditorium doors to indicate that the foyer is empty), but also audience haste and noisiness.[54] The desired result is a deep hush of anticipation, generated and sustained not only by the "Other Person's" unsettlingly repeating reappearances but also by the trajectories of her crossings, which pass again and again through points on the stage where dancing typically commences.

Full silence heightens anticipation and expectation in a different manner in a striking scene in *Die Befragung des Robert Scott†*, a work created in 1986 and revisited as source material several times over the following 15 years.[55] Near the work's end, the stage empties and Thom Willems' sustained airy pitches fall away as one female performer begins swiftly circling her arms into an open-handed V-position, emitting a short, high-pitched scream each of the 100 times she performs the gesture. Her 101st repetition occurs in silence, and as she holds the V-position briefly and then allows her arms to slowly fall, the abrupt shift from visual and sonic rhythm into silent stillness catches the audience off guard. Her gesture's

drawn-out decay, repeated several more times, further sustains and augments the tension. Willems' long, static tones then quietly recommence
and a solo slowly begins elsewhere onstage.

"Moving" silences in Forsythe's work are often enhanced through similar visual dynamics that alternate movement with stillness. Occasionally,
though, Forsythe has choreographed onstage silence involving cessation of
both sound and movement. In a section of *Decreation*, a 2003 work with
a narrative derived from Anne Carson's book *The Beauty of the Husband: A
Fictional Essay in 29 Tangos* and a further essay,[56] a dancer who plays the
role of the husband's male lover performs a harrowing kinetic-vocal improvisational modality, rapidly enacting incomplete physical expressions of
multiple and conflicting emotions. The result is a string of truncated,
incomplete gestures and sputtering, gasping utterances.[57] During this solo,
a section of an argumentative dialogue between a husband and wife is
shared among six performers and repeated several times, each time ending
with the phrase "So he gestured to his attorney: five minutes" and a freeze
by all speakers with an arm raised and five fingers open. The first freeze is
typically close to a full minute in length, the second 30 seconds, and the
third, during which composer David Morrow begins playing quiet single
piano tones, typically lasts well over a minute and a half. The chaotic, stum-
bling solo of the "lover" spills noisily over into each of freezes before peter-
ing out to a tensed stillness, while his gasping voice falters away to leave
complete silence onstage. Breathing visibly but inaudibly and with sweat
dripping from his face, he holds the stillness with the other performers,
resuming the solo with full force when Forsythe cues the text's continuation from the auditorium.[58] Subsequent repetitions then accelerate sub-
stantially, catapulting the dialogue into the next raucous section of the work.

The cessations of sound and action in the "5 minutes" scene extended
from the stage to the spectators, who seemed to hold their breath and
refrain from moving as they watched and waited for one of the speakers to
break the silent stillness. Forsythe timed the follow-on cues responsively,
gauging audience attention each performance by watching and listening
for signs that they were becoming restless. However, the performers who
re-initiated the scene's action by speaking (Richard Siegal and Dana
Caspersen in the roles of husband and wife) were also attuned to audiences' attentional levels and, according to Forsythe, would often spontaneously continue just as he prepared to cue them.[59]

Whether absolute or not, silences can be spectacular, as Vivian Sobchack
points out in reference to films by Douglas Trumbull and Stanley Kubrick.[60]

While prolonged silence provokes arousal on its own, the sonic rupture of dance performance is one of an arsenal of choreo-scenographic techniques through which moments of perceptual performativity can be engendered. Forsythe curates audience silence in *Artifact* by relying on audience awareness of conventional and expected theater behavior, surprises with unexpected silence in *Robert Scott* and in works involving abrupt caesurae, and brings *Decreation*'s audiences to the unsettling edge of collective patience during the long intervals described above. In all of these anxious and often literally breathtaking moments, attention is strongly focused not only on the uncertain vista of potential action but also on the collective performance of *attendance*. Quieted and transfixed, audience and performers are united in the creation and performance of moving moments of silences.

NOTES

1. Cage quoted in Richard Kostelanetz, *Conversing with Cage*, 65.
2. Douglas Kahn, "John Cage: Silence and Silencing," 560.
3. Cage produced several different score formats. See Larry *Solomon, "The Sounds of Silence: John Cage and 4'33."" m
4. Sangmi Sim, John Cage—4'33" by David Tudor, https://www.youtube.com/watch?v=-rP1DIU0m7M.
5. Douglas Kahn, "John Cage: Silence and Silencing," 560.
6. *4'33"* was motivated by the way Robert Rauschenberg's "white paintings" amplify attention to detail and ambient conditions. See John Cage, "On Robert Rauschenberg, artist, and his work."
7. George Home-Cook, *Theatre and Aural Attention: Stretching ourselves*, 127–130.
8. Sheila Orysiek, review of Ballett Frankfurt mixed bill.
9. Barbara White, "'As if they didn't hear the music,'" 79.
10. Ross Brown, "Towards Theatre Noise," 9–10.
11. Hugo Ball, *Flight out of Time*, 108.
12. Isa Partsch-Bergsohn, *Modern Dance in Germany and the United States*, 30–31.
13. Sally Banes, "Yvonne Rainer: The Aesthetics of Denial," 52–53.
14. Sally Banes and Noël Carroll, "Cunningham and Duchamp," 117–118.
15. Steve Paxton, "A model for formulae."
16. Anette Embrechts, "Elke millimeter telt."
17. Doris Humphrey, *The Art of Making Dances*, 142.
18. See George Lakoff, *Metaphors We Live By*, 29.
19. White, "'As if,'" 80.
20. John Cage, *A Year from Monday*, 134. See also Cage, "Indeterminacy."

21. Oliver Mason and Francesca Brady, "The Psychotomimetic Effects of Short-Term Sensory Deprivation."

22. This rumble was also often ready in Willems' programmed synthesizer sound bank for interpolation in other works at Forsythe's request.

23. Originally the second part of *Clouds After Cranach* (2006). *Three Atmospheric Studies*, which premiered as a two-part work in 2005, was first performed as a three-part evening in Berlin in early 2006, with its original second part following *Cranach*'s first and second parts.

24. DSP (Digital Signal Processing) programming and voice treatments for *Three Atmospheric Studies* were executed by Andreas Breitscheid, Olivier Pasquet, and Manuel Poletti in collaboration with Staatsoper Stuttgart's Forum Neues Musiktheater.

25. The task for performers of *Human Writes* was to attempt to write passages of the Declaration onto paper covering the tabletops, but to devise physical or cognitive strategies that would hinder the writing. Audience members would be asked "help" with the task, only to discover that they were to participate in further hindrance of the process rather than to actually facilitate the accomplishment of the writing. The frustrating and often-messy interactions between performers and public were intended to generate dialogue about the difficulty of enacting human rights, in line with the work's physical metaphor: "continuing to do the best one can under the worst possible circumstances" (Forsythe). The installation and images of the writing can be seen at https://www.williamforsythe.com/installations.html?&no_cache=1&detail=1&uid=16 (accessed 10 July 2021).

26. A similar effect was achieved in a 2000 installation work by Hans Peter Kuhn titled *Aquarium*. Here, an array of speakers hung above the installation space emitted abstract unidentifiable sounds that could only be heard when standing very nearby. The attention of the installation's mobile audience members was subliminally drawn by the localized sounds, causing them to move through the space like the fish in an aquarium. As they did, they were viewed by other spectators from a gallery overlooking the installation space. See Christa Brüstle, "Auf Klänge aufmerksam (gemacht) werden: Strategien der Klangkunst" and image at https://hanspeterkuhn.com/installations/aquarium/.

27. Michel Serres, *The Five Senses: A Philosophy of Mingled Bodies*, 141.

28. James J. Gibson, *The Senses Considered as Perceptual Systems*, 53.

29. Hans-Thies Lehmann, *Postdramatic Theatre*, 91.

30. Roy Sorensen, *Seeing Dark Things: The Philosophy of Shadows*, 267.

31. Sorensen, *Seeing Dark Things*, 277.

32. Home-Cook, *Theatre and Aural Attention*, 129.

33. Home-Cook, *Theatre and Aural Attention*, 129.

34. Ross Brown, "Noise, Memory, Gesture: The Theatre in a Minute's Silence," 208.

35. See, for example, the special Research Topic "Neurophysiology of Silence: Neuroscientific, Psychological, Educational and Contemplative Perspectives," *Frontiers in Psychology* vol. 12 (2021), https://www.frontiersin.org/research-topics/10734/neurophysiology-of-silence-neuroscientific-psychological-educational-and-contemplative-perspectives.

36. Corinna Da Fonseca-Wollheim, "How the Silence Makes the Music."

37. Hans-Thies Lehmann, *Postdramatic Theatre*, 90.

38. For a focused analysis of *Trio*, see Elizabeth Waterhouse, "Choreographic Re-mix."

39. This version was performed in Dresden and Frankfurt in 2008 and 2009, with Forsythe making substantial changes to scenes and texts there and on tours to Paris and Munich. In 2010, Forsythe produced a fully new version of *Yes We Can't* in Barcelona, to which he made further changes in eight other venues through its final performances in 2014.

40. Cutoffs in this work coincided with specific events onstage (e.g., movements or dancers' arrivals at specific locations onstage) but were cued by Forsythe himself.

41. Anna Kisselgoff, "Dance: A *Bluebeard* by Pina Bausch Troupe."

42. Jeff Smith, "Music," 194.

43. See, for example, Ulric Neisser, "The control of information pickup in selective looking," and A. Mack and I. Rock, *Inattentional Blindness*.

44. Annabel Cohen, "Film Music: Perspectives from Cognitive Psychology," 366.

45. Jeff Smith, "Unheard Melodies? A Critique of Psychoanalytic Theories of Film Music," 239. Smith borrows from Peter Kivy to argue that the apprehension of film music taps a range of modes of musical cognition between subliminality, which primarily evokes physiological response, and close attentive appreciation, through which listeners engage interpretively and emotionally.

46. Ivan Pavlov, *Conditioned Reflexes: An Investigation of the Physiological Activity of the Cerebral Cortex*. See also R. Näätänen, *Attention and Brain Function*, and J. Gavin Bremner and Alan Fogel, eds., *Blackwell handbook of infant development*, 243.

47. See E. Sokolov, "Higher Nervous Functions: The Orienting Reflex"; A. Öhman, *The Orienting Response, Attention and Learning: An information-processing perspective*; and Peter Lang et al., eds. *Attention and Orienting: Sensory and Motivational Processes*.

48. A. Bernstein, "To what does the orienting response respond?" Alvin Bernstein, "The orienting response as novelty *and* significance detector"; Irving Maltzman, "Orienting reflexes and significance: a reply to O'Gorman"; and David LaBerge, "Attentional Processing in Musical Listening: A Cognitive Neuroscience Approach."

49. See the review article by I. San Miguel et al., "Attention capture by novel sounds: Distraction versus facilitation." See also N. Wetzel et al., "Distraction and facilitation—two faces of the same coin?"
50. William Forsythe, *Decreation* post-performance talk, Haus der Berliner Festspiele, Berlin, January 21, 2009.
51. Freya Vass-Rhee, "Turning the Tables: William Forsythe's *Antipodes I/ II*," 297.
52. Hans-Thies Lehmann, *Postdramatic Theatre*, 91.
53. See Julie Sutton, "The Pause that Follows," 30.
54. Forsythe in personal discussion with the author, August 23, 2010.
55. Revised versions of *Die Befragung des Robert Scott†* have been produced periodically since its initial premiere. For a comprehensive study of related works, see Gerald Siegmund, "Of Monsters and Puppets: After the 'Robert Scott Complex.'"
56. Anne Carson, "Decreation: How Women Like Sappho, Marguerite Porete, and Simone Weil Tell God."
57. I am grateful to Georg Reischl, who originated the role, for providing this description. Personal discussion with the author, August 29, 2010.
58. Forsythe cues the resumption of the texts from the back of the house either with a small hand-held light or, if he can be seen from stage, by gesturing or nodding his head.
59. Personal discussion with the author, Berlin, January 22, 2009.
60. See Vivian Sobchack, *Screening Space: The America Science Fiction Film*, 159 and 175.

Bibliography

Ball, Hugo. 1917. *Flight Out of Time*. New York: Viking Press.

Banes, Sally. 1997. Yvonne Rainer: The Aesthetics of Denial. In *Terpsichore in Sneakers: Post-Modern Dance*, 41–53. Middletown: Wesleyan University Press.

Bernstein, A. 1969. To What Does the Orienting Response Respond? *Psychophysiology* 6 (3): 338–350.

———. 1979. The Orienting Response as Novelty *and* Significance Detector. *Psychophysiology* 16 (3): 263–273.

Bremner, J. Gavin, and Alan Fogel, eds. 2002. *Blackwell Handbook of Infant Development*. Hoboken: Wiley-Blackwell.

Brown, Ross. 2009. Noise, Memory, Gesture: The Theatre in a Minute's Silence. In *Performance, Embodiment and Cultural Memory*, ed. Colin Counsell and Roberta Mock, 203–221. Newcastle upon Tyne: Cambridge Scholars Publishing.

————. 2012. Towards Theatre Noise. In *Theatre Noise: The Sound of Performance*, ed. Lynne Kendrick and David Roesner, 1–13. Newcastle upon Tyne: Cambridge Scholars Publishing.

Brüstle, Christa. 2006. Auf Klänge aufmerksam (gemacht) werden: Strategien der Klangkunst. In *Wege der Wahrnehmung: Authentizität, Reflexivität und Aufmerksamkeit im zeitgenössischen Theater*, ed. Erika Fishcher-Lichte, Barbara Gronau, Sabine Schouten, and Christel Weiler, 140–152. Berlin: Theater der Zeit.

Cage, John. 1961a. On Robert Rauschenberg, Artist, and His Work. In *Silence: Lectures and Writings*, 98–108. Middletown: Wesleyan University Press.

————. 1961b. Indeterminacy (Lecture Transcription). In *Die Reihe* 5, English ed., eds. Herbert Eimert and Karlheinz Stockhausen, 115. Malvern, PA: Theodore Presser Co.

————. 1967. *A Year from Monday: New Lectures and Writings*. Middletown: Wesleyan University Press.

Carson, Anne. 2002a. Decreation: How Women Like Sappho, Marguerite Porete, and Simone Weil Tell God. *Common Knowledge* 8 (1): 188–201.

————. 2002b. *The Beauty of the Husband: A Fictional Essay in 29 Tangos*. New York: Knopf.

Cohen, Annabel. 2000. Film Music: Perspectives from Cognitive Psychology. In *Music & Cinema: Flappers, Chorus Girls, and Other Brazen Performers of the American 1920s*, ed. D. Neumeyer, C. Flinn, and J. Buhler, 360–377. Middletown: Wesleyan University Press.

Da Fonseca-Wollheim, Corinna. 2019. How the Silence Makes the Music. *The New York Times*, 2 October. https://www.nytimes.com/2019/10/02/arts/music/silence-classical-music.html. Accessed 12 February 2020.

Embrechts, Anette. 2002. Elke millimeter telt. *de Volkskrant*, 11 April 2002. https://www.volkskrant.nl/nieuws-achtergrond/elke-millimeter-telt~b3c76cbd/. Accessed 20 June 2022.

Gibson, James J. 1966. *The Senses Considered as Perceptual Systems*. Boston: Houghton Mifflin.

Home-Cook, George. 2015. *Theatre and Aural Attention: Stretching Ourselves*. London and New York: Palgrave Macmillan.

Humphrey, Doris. 1959. *The Art of Making Dances*. Princeton, NJ: Princeton Book Company.

Kahn, Douglas. 1997. John Cage: Silence and Silencing. *The Musical Quarterly* 81 (4): 556–598.

Kisselgoff, Anna. 1984. Dance: A *Bluebeard* by Pina Bausch Troupe. *The New York Times*, 16 June.

Kostelanetz, Richard. 1988. *Conversing with Cage*. 2nd ed. London and New York: Routledge.

LaBerge, David. 1995. Attentional Processing in Musical Listening: A Cognitive Neuroscience Approach. *Psychomusicology* 14: 20–34.

Lakoff, George, and Mark Johnson. 2008. *Metaphors We Live By*. Chicago: University of Chicago Press.

Lang, Peter, Robert Simons, and Marie Balaban, eds. 1997. *Attention and Orienting: Sensory and Motivational Processes*. Mahwah: Psychology Press.

Lehmann, Hans-Thies. 2006. *Postdramatic Theatre*. Translated by Karen Jürs-Munby. Abingdon and New York: Routledge. Original version: Lehmann, Hans-Thies. 1999. *Postdramatisches Theater*. Frankfurt am Main: Verlag der Autoren.

Mack, A., and I. Rock. 1998. *Inattentional Blindness*. Cambridge, MA: MIT Press.

Maltzman, Irving. 1979. Orienting Reflexes and Significance: A Reply to O'Gorman. *Psychophysiology* 16 (3): 274–282.

Mason, Oliver J., and Francesca Brady. 2009. The Psychotomimetic Effects of Short-Term Sensory Deprivation. *The Journal of Nervous and Mental Disease* 197 (10): 783–785.

Näätänen, R. 1992. *Attention and Brain Function*. Mahwah: Lawrence Erlbaum.

Neisser, Ulric. 1979. The Control of Information Pickup in Selective Looking. In *Perception and Its Development: A Tribute to Eleanor J. Gibson*, ed. A.D. Pick, 201–219. Hillsdale, NJ: Lawrence Erlbaum.

Öhman, A. 1979. *The Orienting Response, Attention and Learning: An Information-Processing Perspective*. Mahwah: Lawrence Erlbaum Associates.

Orysiek, Sheila (Anjuli Bai). 2004. Review of Ballett Frankfurt Mixed Bill. http://www.ballet.co.uk/magazines/yr_04/jul04/ab_rev_ballett_frankfurt_0604.htm. Accessed 12 September 2010.

Partsch-Bergsohn, Isa. 2011. *Modern Dance in Germany and the United States: Crosscurrents and Influences*. Vol. 1. Oxon and New York: Routledge.

Pavlov, I. 1927. *Conditioned Reflexes: An Investigation of the Physiological Activity of the Cerebral Cortex*. Translated by G.V. Anrep. London: Oxford University Press.

Paxton, Steve. 1976. A Model for Formulae. *Contact Quarterly* 2 (1): 22.

Sally, Banes, and Noël Carroll. 1994. Cunningham and Duchamp. In *Writing Dancing in the Age of Postmodernism*, ed. Sally Banes, 109–118. Middletown: Wesleyan University Press.

San Miguel, I., D. Linden, and C. Escera. 2010. Attention Capture by Novel Sounds: Distraction Versus Facilitation. *European Journal of Cognitive Psychology* 22 (4): 482–483.

Serres, Michel. 2008. *The Five Senses: A Philosophy of Mingled Bodies*. Translated by Margaret Sankey and Peter Crowley. London and New York: Continuum. Original version: 1985. *Les Cinq Sens*. Paris: Editions Grasset et Fasquelle.

Siegmund, Gerald. 2011. Of Monsters and Puppets: After the 'Robert Scott Complex'. In *William Forsythe and the Practice of Choreography: It Starts from Any Point*, ed. Steven Spier, 20–37. London and New York: Routledge.

Smith, Jeff. 1996. Unheard Melodies? A Critique of Psychoanalytic Theories of Film Music. In *Post-Theory: Reconstructing Film Studies*, ed. David Bordwell and Noël Carroll, 230–247. Madison, WI: University of Wisconsin Press.

———. 2009. Music. In *The Routledge Companion to Philosophy and Film*, ed. Paisley Livingston and Carl Plantinga, 184–195. London and New York: Routledge.

Sobchack, Vivian. 1993. *Screening Space: The America Science Fiction Film*. 2nd ed. New York: Unger.

Sokolov, E. 1963. Higher Nervous Functions: The Orienting Reflex. *Annual Review of Psychology* 25: 545–580.

Solomon, Larry J. 1998. The Sounds of Silence: John Cage and 4'33". https://web.archive.org/web/20180109031457/http://solomonsmusic.net/4min33se.htm. Accessed 12 February 2022.

Sorensen, Roy. 2008. *Seeing Dark Things: The Philosophy of Shadows*. Oxford and New York: Oxford University Press.

Sutton, Julie. 2002. The Pause That Follows. *Nordic Journal of Music Therapy* 11 (1): 27–38.

Vass-Rhee, Freya. 2010. Turning the Tables: William Forsythe's *Antipodes I/II*. In *Theater ohne Fluchtpunkt/Theatre Without Vanishing Points: Das Erbe Adolphe Appias: Szenographie und Choreographie im zeitgenössischen Theater/The Legacy of Adolphe Appia: Scenography and Chorography in Contemporary Theatre*, ed. Gabriele Brandstetter and Birgit Wiens, 293–301. Berlin and Köln: Alexander Verlag.

Waterhouse, Elizabeth. 2019. Choreographic Re-mix. William Forsythe's *Trio* (1996) and Beethoven's *String Quartet No. 15 in a Minor* Op. 132. In *Rund um Beethoven: Interpretationsforschung Heute*, ed. Thomas Gartmann and Daniel Allenbach, 487–504. Schliengen: Edition Argus.

Wetzel, N., A. Widmann, and E. Schröger. 2012. Distraction and Facilitation—Two Faces of the Same Coin? *Journal of Experimental Psychology: Human Perception and Performance* 38 (3): 664–674.

White, Barbara. 2006. 'As If They Didn't Hear the Music,' Or: How I Learned to Stop Worrying and Love Mickey Mouse. *The Opera Quarterly* 22 (1): 65–89.

CHAPTER 7

Lull: *Ostinati* and Drones

In the 1960s, postmodern dance choreographers rejected both classical ballet's formal-ornamental artificiality and modern dance's harmonic expressionism. Sally Banes explains how they instead opted to create works in which movement "became like an object, something to be examined coolly without psychological, social, or even formal motives."[1] This was accomplished by making dances that were stripped of their spectacular trappings, producing what Banes refers to as an "aesthetics of denial." Yvonne Rainer's famous "no" to spectacle succinctly captures the rejectionist attitude of the era.[2] Forsythe's performative stance toward spectacularity's immersive tendencies has operated along different lines: instead of excising visual and sonic spectacle, he has instead deployed it as a substrate upon which to stage perceptual interventions.

In essence, Forsythe says both yes and no to spectacle, alternating between its inclusion and rupture to produce a distinctly perceptual ideology of performativity. In some works, this takes the form of a scene that punctuates a through-going aesthetic of relative formality with its opposite. One of the most raucous scenes in any Forsythe work occurred in early versions of the evening-long *ALIE N/A(C)TION* (1992).[3] A kaleidoscope of dozens of hot pink geishas (three of them blasting trumpets) on risers and white-clad figures on benches danced to a blaring, drum-heavy sample loop while Stephen Galloway pontificated like a high priest of funk in an electric green kimono, black wig, and thick-framed glasses. A

© The Author(s), under exclusive license to Springer Nature Switzerland AG 2023
F. Vass, *William Forsythe's Postdramatic Dance Theater*, Cognitive Studies in Literature and Performance,
https://doi.org/10.1007/978-3-031-26658-4_7

sing-song chant emerged from the aural and visual chaos, echoing a huge banner reading I DON'T WANT TO BE HYPNOTIZED that hung across the stage. Often, though, such interruptions in Forsythe's works occur on a far more reduced scale, as an unsettling substrate that impinges on hypnotic atmospheres. This chapter explores instances in Forsythe's works of *lulling* dynamics of sound and movement and their perturbations, while the following chapter looks at his more overt and larger-scale scenic interventions.

Immersion, Absorption, and Intrusion

In his critique of the ideological work of music in society, Jacques Attali posits a contrast between music and unorganized sound, which he terms noise, primarily in terms of ideological valence but along the lines of their perceptual effects. Attali holds that noise has "always been viewed as disorder, dirt, pollution," while music, as noise that has been channeled into orderly and acceptable patterns through composition, affirms the possibility of societal order by functioning as "pure order" itself.[4] Using death as a metaphor, he compares the two by arguing

> that listening to noise is a little like being killed; that listening to music is to attend a ritual murder, with all the danger, guilt, but also the reassurance that goes along with that; that applauding is a confirmation, after the channelization of the violence, that the spectators of the sacrifice could potentially resume practicing the essential violence.[5]

In effect, Attali claims that music and noise both produce states of altered ideology in which music, by generating collective belief in order and protective agency, causes the possibility of a carnivalesque liberty to be forgotten.[6] His analysis tacitly marks music as a soothing sonic spectacle that literally *enchants* societies (literally, to spellbind through song) into a turn away from the potential release offered by the real, noisy world. Film theorist Jean-Louis Baudry comments similarly about the cinematic image, noting how spectators are "chained, captured, or captivated" by its spectacular and illusory representation of reality, which is harnessed and controlled by the filmic apparatus and projected into the dark, safe space of the movie theater.[7]

Though Attali and Baudry's views are ideological, they also obtain at the level of perception. The veridicality of film imagery and sound convinces us that what we see are real worlds rather than two-dimensional staged, edited, underscored simulations. Musical structure, meanwhile, harbors many simultaneous orders, including but not limited to melody, harmony, motifs, instrumentation, timbres, and historical or cultural styles. Like film, music is also highly immersive; rather than listening *to* it, we listen *into* it, allowing ourselves to become absorbed and moved by its manifold perceptual currents. We no more apprehend music as collections of notes or noises than do we view films as series of shots, sounds, and effects of the filmic apparatus—unless, that is, the composer or filmmaker effectively inserts grit into the perceptual oyster. And many twentieth-century composers and filmmakers have performatively countered the immersive qualities of music and filmic images by crafting works that establish and then undermine immersion.

The middle of the 1960s saw an increase in research interest on consciousness, out of a confluence between the cognitive turn in psychological research, a popular turn to Eastern transcendental traditions, and increased use of recreational drugs. Non-ordinary states of consciousness (NOSCs), often referred to as "altered states of consciousness,"[8] can arise spontaneously as a result of certain illnesses, injuries, trauma, or states of physical deprivation, but can also be induced by a variety of means, including meditative mental or physical practices, the use of psychoactive drugs, or specific patterns of sensory information. NOSCs encompass a very broad array of experiences including not only meditative states and experiences of expanded consciousness, trance, ecstasy, and hysteria, but also everyday phenomena like daydreaming, absorption, and productive states of concentrated focus. Peter Hess and Sabine Rittner draw a distinction between high-arousal, physiologically stirring trance (ergotropic), and calming and focusing, low-arousal trance (trophotropic).[9] Among considerations of less extreme NOSCs are Mihalyi Czikszentmihalyi's extensive investigation of "flow" (pleasurable immersive states of concentrated activity)[10] and examinations of everyday music listening that evokes either transcendent (eudaimonic) experience,[11] or what Ruth Herbert, interrogating and augmenting the ergotropic-trophotropic continuum, refers to as "secular trancing in everyday life."[12] However, by focusing primarily on pleasurable music and positively arousing responses, only limited consideration has been given to musical experiences that may be discomforting for the perceiver.[13]

The work of Charles Tart, Gilbert Rouget, Judith Becker, and others indicates that specific sound types are one of several means of sensory "driving" by which autonomic or brainwave entertainment can be induced, leading to shifts of conscious state and perception. These include repetitive aural patterns such as drumming, chanting, and instrumental drones.[14] While there is no fixed sound structure that universally produces trance as a causal effect, general characteristics include continuous intensification of tempo or volume, extremely consistent tonality (monotony) or minimal tonal variation, narrow tonal range, and longer durations of sound presentation.[15] According to David Aldridge and Jörg Fachner, certain sounds can also function as transitional "acoustic triggers" of trance, including complex multivocal structures that do not permit resolution, low pulses of sound, and sudden high-pitched tonal modulations.[16] Together, these studies broaden the range of sounds studied; however, they provide little ground upon which to address the spectatorial experiences of movement performance in tandem with sound. Further, though numerous ethnographic studies have in fact examined the structure and psychology of dance practices in which trance or possession play a key role,[17] these primarily focus on the experience of the performer rather than of those watching. The NOSC experience of the spectator-auditor, not only of concert dance but of other forms as well, is neglected.

Additionally, the nature of the stimuli presented in experimental trials on sound and states of consciousness leaves out an element that is pervasive in many of Forsythe's soundscapes: sounds that unsettle by impinging on and competing with music. In order to induce and study NOSCs, experimental subjects are presented with uninterrupted music or sound believed to be capable of causing a shift in state. However, sonic intrusion is an inherently taxing occurrence, requiring added cognitive effort first to segregate and identify signals within the "cocktail" of sound entering the ear, and then directing of attention to or away from specific sound sources.[18] Beyond the increased demands on processing and memory, disruptions are also shown to be experienced as annoying, frustrating, mentally demanding, and lacking in respect, with greatest effects being registered when interruptions occur in mid-task.[19]

Zoologist Vincent Dethier notes that while interruption implies disruption of prioritized informational streams by incongruous elements, they are in fact essential from a physiological perspective. Though interruptions may be experienced as aggravating, they produce counteracting effects on habituation, the adaptive tendency to disattend to continuous, unchanging perceptual signals. As Dethier shows, organisms have evolved a wide variety of physical mechanisms to self-impose intermittent interruption of stimuli uptake, ranging from small involuntary eye movements (saccades, drift, and tremor) to subconscious behaviors such as sniffing and twitching. He further points out how environments or situations with little interruption, such as calm waters, monotonous sounds, or conditions of sensory deprivation, often elicit psychological discomfort, heightened sensitivity, or even hallucinations.[20] Essentially, interruptions may be perceptually stressing, but they in fact alleviate stress that would be generated in their absence. This complicating view illustrates the complexity that underlies our response to disturbances.

Dethier also extends his analysis to consider the importance of the perceptual effects of interruption within artistic contexts. Looking at experimental forms in music and visual art of the mid-twentieth century, he highlights the divergence between minimalist trends, in which interruption tends to be reduced, and paradigms such as 12-tone composition and Op Art, of which increased complexity of stimulation are hallmarks.[21] Just prior to this period, inclusion of discordant figures broke with "orderly" structural traditions of classicism, in which musical figures relate harmoniously to supporting orchestration. Stravinsky's punctuations of melodic or *ostinato* ground structures with jarring figures, for example, in the early 20th century ballets *Petrushka*, *Les Noces*, and *Le Sacre du Printemps*, are examples of this dramatic employment of intrusion.[22] The presence of such musical figures complicates Attali's distinction between noise as disorderly "dirt" and music as orderly and "pure." Closer to our time, the experimentations of postmodern and contemporary choreographers both ratified and tested the effects of sonic stress by experimenting at both ends of the spectrum: the minimalism of Steve Paxton, Lucinda Childs, and David Gordon contrasts with the sensory assault of Karole Armitage and Michael Clark's raucous punk-driven works and the loud, hyperkinetic "Eurocrash" aesthetics of Wim Vandekeybus and Édouard Lock. As I detail below, the experimental approach that Forsythe has taken aligns with Stravinsky's aesthetics of intrusion, albeit more subtly and to postdramatic rather than dramatic ends. Through push-pull dynamics of lull and intrusion, instances in his works instantiate Lehmann's trait of "play with the density of signs," while also showing an approach to choreographing attention that is both experimental and contingent on wider scenographic factors.

MINIMALISM AND DISTURBANCE

A number of scenes in Forsythe's works or entire shorter works are under-pinned by what is commonly termed "minimalist music," a term coined in the 1970s by composer and music critic Michael Nyman that eventually supplanted terms like "hypnotic," "pulse," "trance," "process," "modu-lar," and "systemic" music.[23] Its predominant characteristic is rhythmic, tonal, or timbral patterning that remains relatively constant, transforming only very gradually over longer periods. Among the forms this relative stasis takes are reiterative musical figures such as *ostinati* (short melodic phrases or rhythmic patterns which repeat at the same pitch and with the same instrumentation), pulses, sustained drones, and phase shifting (multiple performers slightly varying the tempo of their playing before once again "locking in" to a common tempo). As the terms above show, minimalist music is noted for its hypnagogic qualities. These are also found in both traditional and "new age" music, in which long passages of chanting, vocal or instrumental drones, and repetitive figures are intended to produce relaxation or support meditative states. "Trance" music associated with rave culture also features these and similar characteristics, albeit with more complex structure, higher volume levels, and accelerated tempi. However, though trance music tends to energize listeners, it too is noted for its ability to induce shifts of conscious experience. Notably, trance music is often accompanied by light shows whose complexity and crossmodal coordina-tion further support the occurrence of non-ordinary subjective experiences.

Under receptive conditions, repetitive sound patterns and sustained static sound structures can lead to an attentional shift called reduced lis-tening (*écoute réduite*) first theorized by musicologist and *musique concrète* pioneer Pierre Schaeffer.[24] Typically, we process emergent features of sound streams as perceptual cues, aiming to establish associations between sounds and sound patterns heard and those stored in memory. Because repeating sound patterns and static tones offer little new auditory infor-mation or cues, the focus of listening shifts away from comparative, memory-based activity and toward the intrinsic, molar qualities of the iter-ating sound. When engaged in reduced listening, we essentially *re-attune* ourselves to it by focusing on fundamental aspects like pitch, rhythms, timbres, and textures. This shift of attentional focus is likely to contribute to its hypnotic effects. However, though reliant on reduction of novelty for its effect, minimalist and trance music is rarely completely monotonous or repetitive. Instead, hypnotic sound typically features minor structural alterations in the form of shifts of pattern, volume, or density.

Forsythe engenders and sustains a perceptual performativity by delicately but decisively disrupting conditions of visuosonic *lull* through the iterative inclusion of what he has termed "disturbers"[25] that unexpectedly intrude on underlying patterns. This practice, which aligns with what theater sound designer and scholar Ross Brown calls "design through annoyance,"[26] stages a performance of perception in which the enchanting effect of lulling music is mitigated by sonic elements, usually but not always of a delicate scale and sometimes including the highly salient human voice, that activate both bottom-up and top-down attentional processes. This sonic strategy of interruption finds a parallel in Forsythe's peripheral staging of figures that intrude upon established regions of focal interest, instances of which are discussed in Chap. 5.[27]

OSTINATI

Several of Forsythe's works are either scored entirely to music with *ostinato* patterning or contain *ostinato* sections. Some earlier evening-length works feature brief rhythmic *ostinato* passages during which Forsythe staged complex, often balletic canons performed by large numbers of dancers. *Ostinato* passages figure prominently in the first and final acts of *Artifact* (1984), whose piano scores are Eva Crossman-Hecht's variations on a Bach *chaconne* that accompanies the work's second act.[28] Forsythe explains the dramaturgical importance of *Artifact*'s *ostinato* patterns by pointing out that *Artifact* engages with ballet as a historical construct and *ostinati*, like ballet, have figured in numerous musical epochs from the Baroque period to contemporary popular music.[29] Four of the fifteen mostly brief scenes in *Artifact*'s first act are accompanied by *ostinato* motifs with durations of no more than six seconds, while the ballet's fourth act contains five *ostinato* passages out of a total of nine distinct musical scenes. Referred to by Forsythe and stagers of *Artifact* by names like "Hypno" and "Herd," these scenes are the longest in the acts, ranging from just over one minute to almost seven minutes. All are marked by subtle melodic augmentations and slow *crescendo*, while repetitive interlocking clapping patterns provide an additional repetitive overlay to four of them.[30]

During *Artifact*'s *ostinati*, large groups of dancers move in relatively dim light or are silhouetted in stark backlighting as they perform lush, rhythmic, movement canons, and occasional unison dancing in linear and geometric formations that reflect the spatial patterns of classical *corps de ballet*. The danced canon phrases are of different lengths than the *ostinato* music phrases, which produce constantly shifting relations between the repeating musical and movement motifs. However, the ensemble shares these scenes with three anomalous figures: a silent, pale gray figure named in the program as the "Other Person," who emerges from under the stage to provide a visual counterpoint to the ensemble's visually harmonious gestures, and two speaking characters, the "Woman in Historical Costume" and the "Man with Megaphone"[31] who pass among them at several junctures. The speakers' permutative language, which derives from a small vocabulary of terms (inside/outside, I/you, remember/forget, always/never, see/hear/think/say/do, rocks/dirt/sand/soot/dust), creates a rhythmicity of its own, as in when they verbally enjoin the audience to "forget the dust, forget the sand, forget the dirt, forget the rocks."[32]

Another rhythmic *ostinato* section occurring in the evening-length *Eidos:Telos* (1995) features similar movement structures of irregular lengths relative to the accompanying music. During a nine-minute scene, the "ranks of the dead"—a large *corps de ballet* of male and female dancers in long, bustled skirts—weave in lines through the stage space and around speaking characters, performing complex canons of broad, lush *pas de valse* steps. Through its reference to the classical codex, this scene evokes the "white acts" of romantic and classical ballets; however, Antony Rizzi undermines the broad, sweeping harmony as he staggers about, spouting an angry litany of futile obscenities ("I'm fucking dead, man! I'm gonna shit on your table and make you eat it! I'm gonna scratch your CDs! I'm gonna cut your head off and fuck your neck hole!") More recently in a scene from *I don't believe in outer space* (2008) not incidentally referred to in rehearsals as "Voodoo," the members of the *corps* move to a slow, quietly percussive sample loop by Thom Willems, performing counterpointed phrases of footwork while Dana Caspersen slowly overlays lyrics from Screamin' Jay Hawkins' song "I Put a Spell on You."

A number of Forsythe's later one-act works are staged entirely to *ostinati* with longer and less rhythmic phrases. *Quintett* (1994) is performed to Gavin Bryars' 1971 composition "Jesus' Blood Never Failed Me Yet," in which a 26-second-long hymnlike phrase sung by an unidentified homeless man repeats over 60 times. Music builds slowly under the frail yet confident voice of the singer, which begins alone and is joined first by soft strings and then by quiet brass. *Pivot House* (1994) is performed to part of the gamelan composition *Sirimpi (Provisions for Death)* from the Kraton Surakarta, as is Part I of the two-part *Endless House* (1999),[33]while *Hypothetical Stream* (1997) is a resonant wash of long, low tones and intermittent hush by Stuart Dempster (*Standing Waves* (1976)) and Ingram Marshall (*Fog Tropes* (1979)).

Forsythe's choreo-scenographic choices during *ostinati* fall into two distinct patterns of musical reference, ensemble size, and aesthetic style that align with tempo and phrase length. To shorter, rhythmic *ostinati*, Forsythe sets large groups of dancers moving in balletic canons of irregular lengths, while to the longer, slower *ostinato* phrases found in more recent works, Forsythe stages smaller groups of dancers moving at irregular and usually far more rapid tempi.[34] In both cases, the reduction of novel information through repetition in the music, the steps, or both underpins the scenes' hypnotic qualities. However, against the lull of musical and choreographic repetition, Forsythe stages or includes elements that encroach on the flow of visual or sonic action. *Artifact*'s "Man with Megaphone" wanders at one point among the women's *corps*, periodically tapping the floor as if trying to locate the silent, ghostly "Other Person" beneath the stage, while in other scenes, the two speaking characters cross the stage space while arguing loudly with each other (Fig. 7.1). *I don't believe in outer space*'s milling "Voodoo" *corps* becomes a backdrop for two speakers, a silent "percussionist," and a duet and quartet of rapidly twining dancers, two of whom emit periodic crying noises.[35] Even *Quintett*, perhaps the most tranquil of Forsythe's *ostinato* works, contains a brief instance of rhythmic, audible stamping.

Sonic "disturbers" also include musical accents which, due to their energy or the sonic qualities, stand out as figures against lulling musical

Fig. 7.1 Enemies in the figure: Kate Strong (Woman in Historical Costume) and Nicholas Champion (Man with Megaphone) intrude on one of *Artifact*'s balletic canons. (Source: photo courtesy of Wilfried Hösl, reproduced with permission of Bayerisches Staatsballett)

backgrounds. The *keprak* (wooden block) accents and shouted calls punctuate the *Sirimpi*, and Thom Willems also often overlays sample loops in his compositions with brief, improvised bits of organic or electronic sounds.[36] Referring to the music of Willems, who has composed over 80 works for Forsythe including *The Loss of Small Detail*, *Eidos:Telos*, and *I don't believe in outer space*, Eva-Elisabeth Fischer notes the variety of forms these sonic overlays take and draws an explicit parallel to the encroaching noise of the postmodern world:

> [W]e are dealing here with the 'melody' of today's urban life, as might be heard in Amsterdam, Tokyo, Hong Kong or New York. Harsh synthesizer blasts give the impression that someone living in a busy street has suddenly opened his double windows. And even when the windows, so to speak, are shut again, there remains, in the background of these passages - sometimes rarefied, sometimes rhythmically excited - a disturbing murmur that reminds one that there is a threatening world outside and leaves traces of sound.[37]

In the works of Willems, Eva Crossman-Hecht (*Artifact*), Ekkehard Ehlers (*Woolf Phrase*, with Willems), and others, disruptions fleck the sonic "carpet" of *ostinati*, evoking brief orienting returns of perception to associative processing of the emergent figures before giving way again to the flow of the background. In this regard, minimalist soundscapes featuring such interruptions function similarly to scenes of *hush* (see Chap. 6), in which the depth of attention to sound is repeatedly shifted through dramatic changes in volume level.

Hypnotic Drones

Similar dynamics of informational reduction and visuosonic intrusion occur in scenes choreographed to musical drones, another characteristic form in minimalist music that shares the hypnotic qualities evoked by *ostinato* repetitions. In contrast to the more active choreography set to *ostinati*, Forsythe's choreography in drone scenes tends to be reduced in both scale and complexity, and scenes are far longer in length. The 1991 version of *The Loss of Small Detail* opens with 10 minutes of a slowly building, increasingly discordant drone, during which dancers calmly reposition small stools and perform brief, unannounced solos of soft, disfocused movement. Dana Capsersen, bending over a table onstage while whispering almost inaudibly into a microphone, is lifted smoothly away by a male performer again and again before being released to return and resume whispering. In the original version of *7 to 10 Passages* (2000),[38] a line of dancers moves slowly downstage to Thom Willems' texturally rich drone for the work's first 13 minutes, articulating small internalized motions of the "Tuna" phrase of choreography that underpins several of Forsythe's works created between 1986 and 2010.[39] Punctuating this section are two timed freezes and texts spoken by performers seated at tables.

Forsythe's use of drones often subserves strategies of sonic overwhelm described in the following chapter. As Chris Salter comments on the third part of *Eidos:Telos*:

> Here, Willems and (Joel) Ryan push *Eidos:Telos*'s sonic evolution to its (ironically) ultimate telos, building up thundering waves of sound based on the same multi-tap delay technique of mutating individual notes played by the trombones into drone-like lines and layering these drones into a wall of sound that has the sonic force of a tidal wave.[40]

Similarly, during two scenes in *Decreation*, the ensemble blends their voices into a building drone, producing lush resonances that fill the auditorium. In the climactic instance, David Morrow's keyboard and the combined voices of 11 singing dancers build and sustain a rich major ninth chord for over three and a half minutes. During this extended drone, five singing dancers lope lightly forward and backward in uncharacteristically warm and slowly brightening light. Interruptions come in its sustained peak: the "husband" figure calls loudly off-mic to another male performer "Come here, I want to hold you," while one of the women bends almost double to produce a high, loonlike cry and another writhes toward a held microphone, vocalizing gutturally as she moves downstage. Finally, the miked voices of three male performers boom out slow, echoing lines of Anne Carson's text: "The floor was on fire...The world was on fire."[41] The chord slowly dissipates as the lights begin to fade and cool, and the next scene commences. In this scene, as in others described above, the tempo of visual and sonic structuring undergoes extreme slowing relative to other scenes. Light, smooth, and subtle movement supports the hypnotic quality of the music through reduction of broad gesture and elimination of sharp accents. The "density of signs" thins out as the drones sustain but build relatively static aural structure, and the dance movement undergoes a softening and simplification that permits the sound to become the more dominant sensory focus.

By unsettling viewer-auditors from non-normative state of consciousness through unpredictable inclusions of novel sounds and movements, Forsythe brings the attention-arousing dynamics of habituation and dishabituation into play. Irregularly timed disruptions to smooth flows of music and visual action cause a cyclic process of shift between ground and figure in which viewer-auditors, deeply immersed in the mesmerizing spectacle, are unexpectedly pulled to the surface level of recognition and association, before being released to settle again into the washes of sound and fluid movement. The confrontation with disruption in Forsythe's works is simultaneously a confrontation with the desire to be and remain "hypnotized" by harmony and unmindful of the real—forgetting the dust, the sand, the dirt, and the rocks.

NOTES

1. Sally Banes, "Yvonne Rainer," 43.
2. Yvonne Rainer, "Some retrospective notes on a dance," 178.
3. As with many Forsythe works, *ALIE N/A(C)TION* was changed numerous times over the period in which it was performed.
4. Jacques Attali, *Noise*, 31.
5. Jacques Attali, *Noise*, 28.
6. Ibid., 27.
7. Jean-Louis Baudry, "The Ideological Effects of the Basic Cinematographic Apparatus," 44.
8. The term "altered state of consciousness" (ASC), first used in 1966 by Arnold Ludwig and popularized three years later by Charles Tart, is widely used to denote experiences which differ subjectively from everyday waking experience. In this chapter, I instead use the term "non-ordinary state of consciousness" (NOSC), which was coined by Stanislav Grof and which bears less of the former term's associations with meditative and narcotic means of manipulating conscious function. See Arnold Ludwig, "Altered States of Consciousness," Charles Tart, ed., *Altered states of consciousness: a book of readings*, and Stanislav Grof, *The Adventure of Self Discovery*.
9. Peter Hess and Sabine Rittner, "Verändertes Wachbewusstsein," 401.
10. See Mihalyi Czikszentmihalyi, *Beyond Boredom and Anxiety: Experiencing Flow in Work and Play; Flow: The Psychology of Optimal Experience*; and later writings.
11. See, for example, A. Gabrielsson, "Strong experiences with music," A. Lamont, "University students' strong experiences of music: pleasure, engagement, and meaning," Ruth Herbert, "Musical and non-musical involvement in daily life: the case of absorption," L. Harrison et al.,

"Thrills, chills, frissons, and skin orgasms: toward an integrative model of transcendent psychophysiological experiences in music," T. Schäfer et al., "How music changes our lives: a qualitative study of the long-term effects of intense musical experiences," and Ruth Herbert, *Everyday Music Listening: Absorption, Dissociation and Trancing.*

12. Ruth Herbert, "Reconsidering music and trance: Cross-cultural differences and cross-disciplinary perspectives," 203. See also Judith Becker, *Deep listeners: Music, emotion, and trancing.*

13. A few studies have compared the experience of listening to pleasant and unpleasant music, including A. Blood et al., "Emotional responses to pleasant and unpleasant music correlate with activity in paralimbic brain regions" and D. Sammler et al., "Music and emotion: electrophysiological correlates of the processing of pleasant and unpleasant music."

14. See Charles Tart, *Altered States*, Gilbert Rouget, *Music and trance: A theory of the relations between music and possession*, and Judith Becker, "Music and Trance." Becker also emphasizes that trance is experienced differently across cultures; see 41–42.

15. See Jörg Fachner, "Wanderer between worlds: Anthropological perspectives on healing rituals and music"; cf. R. Brandl, "Musik und veränderte Bewusstseinszustände" (music and altered states of consciousness).

16. David Aldridge and Jörg Fachner, *Music and Altered States: Consciousness, Transcendence, Therapy and Addiction*, 22.

17. See, for example, Gregory Bateson and Margaret Mead, *Trance and Dance in Bali*, Kathy Foley, "The Dancer and the Danced: Trance Dance and Theatrical Performance in West Java," and Wolfgang Jilek, "Therapeutic use of altered states of consciousness in contemporary North American Indian dance ceremonials."

18. For a general overview, see Josh McDermott, "The cocktail party problem."

19. See, for example, Tony Gillie and Donald Broadbent, "What makes disruptions disruptive?" and Piotr Adamczyk et al., "If not now, when? The effects of interruption at different moments within task execution."

20. Vincent Dethier, "Sniff, Flick, and Pulse: An Appreciation of Interruption," 170–171.

21. Vincent Dethier, "Sniff, Flick, and Pulse: An Appreciation of Interruption," 175–176.

22. See Jann Pasler, "Music and Spectacle," and Edward Cone, "Stravinsky: The Progress of a Method."

23. Edward Strickland, *Minimalism: Origins*, 17.

24. Pierre Schaeffer, *Traité des objets musicaux.* See also Michel Chion, *Guide des objets sonores: Pierre Schaeffer et la recherche musicale.*

25. Forsythe, in rehearsal with Thom Willems for *Whole in the Head*, November 16, 2010.

26. Ross Brown, *Sound: A Reader in Theatre Practice*, 137.
27. A valuable comparison can be made to Pieter Verstraete's concept of "auditory distress." See Verstraete, *The Frequency of Imagination*, "The Listener's Response," and "Radical Vocality, Auditory Distress and Disembodied Voice."
28. Johann Sebastian Bach, *Chaconne* from *Partita Nr. 2 in d minor* (BWV 1004), in Nathan Milstein's 1968 recorded rendering. For impressions of *Artifact*, see the Bayerische Staatsoper's documentary at https://www.youtube.com/watch?v=Rtxd_TjbPV4.
29. Forsythe, personal discussion with the author, March 9, 2010.
30. See also Chris Salter, "Timbral architectures," 69–70.
31. These figures are also named as "Person in Historical Costume" and "Person with Megaphone."
32. See Gerald Siegmund, "The space of memory: William Forsythe's ballets," 129–132.
33. See also Chris Salter, *Unstable Events*, 91–93.
34. Though these two categories can be said to correspond to his earlier and later works, they do overlap across his *oeuvre*. It is worth noting that, in many cases, the scores of Forsythe's works are composed or mixed during rehearsals, in response to movement material being created or scenes being staged.
35. This description refers to versions performed from 2009 onward.
36. To clarify, when Willems plays live in Forsythe's performances, he does not play "free" improvisations but augments preplanned sound structures (often underlying tone loops) with musical gestures or phrases in improvised response to the dance performance. See also Vass-Rhee, "Dancing Music," 74–90.
37. Eva-Elisabeth Fischer, "Thom Willems."
38. A revised version of *7 to 10 Passages* was performed in Dresden in September 2010.
39. *7 to 10 Passages* is one of several Forsythe works whose dramaturgy centers on the failed expedition of Robert Scott and its attendant ideas about technological prowess and human fallibility. The "Tuna" phrase is referenced in all of these. See Gerald Siegmund, "Of Monsters and Puppets: After the 'Robert Scott Complex,'" and Freya Vass-Rhee, "Schooling an ensemble: The Forsythe Company's *Whole in the Head*."
40. Chris Salter, "Timbral architectures," 64.
41. From Anne Carson, (2001), *The Beauty of the Husband: A Fictional Essay in 29 Tangos*.

BIBLIOGRAPHY

Adamczyk, P.D., and B.P. Bailey. 2004, April. If Not Now, When? The Effects of Interruption at Different Moments Within Task Execution. In *Proceedings of the SIGCHI Conference on Human Factors in Computing Systems*, 271–278.

Aldridge, David, and Jörg Fachner. 2009. *Music and Altered States: Consciousness, Transcendence, Therapy and Addiction*. London: Jessica Kingsley Publishers.

Attali, Jacques. 1985. *Noise: The Political Economy of Music*. Translated by Brian Massumi. Minneapolis: University of Minnesota Press. Original version: 1977. *Bruits: essai sur l'économie politique de la musique*. Paris: Presses Universitaire de France.

Banes, Sally. 1987. Yvonne Rainer: The Aesthetics of Denial. In *Terpsichore in Sneakers: Post-Modern Dance*, 41–53. Middletown: Wesleyan University Press. First published in 1977 by Houghton Mifflin.

Bateson, Gregory, and Margaret Mead. 1951. *Trance and Dance in Bali*. New York: New York University Film Library.

Baudry, Jean-Louis. 1974–1975. The Ideological Effects of the Basic Cinematographic Apparatus. *Film Quarterly* 28 (2): 39–47.

Becker, Judith. 1994. Music and Trance. *Leonardo Music Journal* 4 (1): 41–51.

———. 2004. *Deep Listeners: Music, Emotion, and Trancing*. Bloomington & Indianapolis: Indiana University Press.

Blood, A., R. Zatorre, P. Bermudez, and A. Evans. 1999. Emotional Responses to Pleasant and Unpleasant Music Correlate with Activity in Paralimbic Brain Regions. *Nature Neuroscience* 2 (4): 382–387.

Brandl, R. 1993. Musik und veränderte Bewusstseinszustände. In *Musikpsychologie: Ein Handbuch*, ed. H. Bruhn, R. Oerter, and H. Rösing, 599–610. Reinbek: Rowohlt Verlag.

Brown, Ross. 2010. *Sound: A Reader in Theatre Practice*. New York: Palgrave Macmillan.

Carson, Anne. 2001. *The Beauty of the Husband: A Fictional Essay in 29 Tangos*. New York: Alfred A. Knopf.

Chion, Michel. 1994. *Guide des objets sonores: Pierre Schaeffer et la recherche musicale*. Paris: Buchet/Chastel.

Cone, Edward. 1962. Stravinsky: The Progress of a Method. *Perspectives of New Music* 1 (1): 18–26.

Czikszentmihalyi, Mihalyi. 1975. *Beyond Boredom and Anxiety: Experiencing Flow in Work and Play*. San Francisco: Jossey-Bass.

———. 1990. *Flow: The Psychology of Optimal Experience*. New York: Harper and Row.

Dethier, Vincent. 1987. Sniff, Flick, and Pulse: An Appreciation of Interruption. *Proceedings of the American Philosophical Society* 131 (2): 159–176.

Fachner, Jörg. 2007. Wanderer Between Worlds: Anthropological Perspectives on Healing Rituals and Music. *Music Therapy Today* 8 (2): 166–195.

Fischer, Eva-Elisabeth. Thom Willems. www.frankfurt-ballett.de/thom_willems. htm. Accessed 31 May 2003.

Foley, Kathy. 1985. The Dancer and the Danced: Trance Dance and Theatrical Performance in West Java. *Asian Theatre Journal* 2 (1): 28–49.

Gabrielsson, A. 2010. Strong Experiences with Music. In *Handbook of Music and Emotion: Theory, Research, Applications*, ed. P.N. Juslin and J.A. Sloboda, 547–574. Oxford: Oxford University Press.

Gillie, T., and D. Broadbent. 1989. What Makes Interruptions Disruptive? A Study of Length, Similarity, and Complexity. *Psychological Research* 50: 243–250.

Grof, Stanislav. 1988. *The Adventure of Self Discovery*. Albany: State University of New York Press.

Harrison, L., and P. Loui. 2014. Thrills, Chills, Frissons, and Skin Orgasms: Toward an Integrative Model of Transcendent Psychophysiological Experiences in Music. *Frontiers in Psychology* 5: 790.

Herbert, Ruth. 2011. Reconsidering Music and Trance: Cross-Cultural Differences and Cross-Disciplinary Perspectives. *Ethnomusicology Forum* 20 (2): 201–227.

———. 2012. Musical and Non-musical Involvement in Daily Life: The Case of Absorption. *Musicae Scientiae* 16: 41–66.

———. 2016. *Everyday Music Listening: Absorption, Dissociation and Trancing*. Routledge.

Hess, P., and S. Rittner. 1996. Verändertes Wachbewusstsein. In *Lexikon Musiktherapie*, ed. H.H. Decker-Voigt, P. Knill, and E. Weymann, 398–403. Göttingen: Hogrefe.

Jilek, Wolfgang. 1989. Therapeutic Use of Altered States of Consciousness in Contemporary North American Indian Dance Ceremonials. In *Altered States of Consciousness and Mental Health: A Cross-cultural Perspective*, ed. C. Ward, 167–185. Newbury Park, CA: Sage.

Lamont, A. 2011. University Students' Strong Experiences of Music: Pleasure, Engagement, and Meaning. *Musicae Scientiae* 15: 229–249.

Ludwig, Arnold. 1996. Altered States of Consciousness. *Archives of General Psychiatry* 15 (3): 225–234.

McDermott, J.H. 2009. The Cocktail Party Problem. *Current Biology* 19 (22): R1024–R1027.

Pasler, Jann. 1988. Music and Spectacle in *Petrushka* and *The Rite of Spring*. In *Confronting Stravinsky: Man, Musician, and Modernist*, ed. Jann Pasler, 71–73. Berkeley: University of California Press.

Rainer, Yvonne. 1965. Some Retrospective Notes on a Dance for 10 People and 12 Mattresses Called 'Parts of Some Sextets,' Performed at the Wadsworth Atheneum, Hartford, Connecticut, and Judson Memorial Church, New York, in March, 1965. *Tulane Drama Review* 10 (2): 168–178.

Rouget, G. 1985. *Music and Trance: A Theory of the Relations Between Music and Possession.* Chicago: University of Chicago Press.

Salter, Chris. 1997. *Unstable Events: Theater at the Verge of Complexity.* PhD dissertation. Stanford University.

———. 2011. Timbral Architectures, Aurality's Force. In *William Forsythe and the Practice of Choreography: It Starts from Any Point*, ed. Steven Spier, 54–72. Abingdon and New York: Routledge.

Sammler, D., M. Grigutsch, T. Fritz, and S. Koelsch. 2007. Music and Emotion: Electrophysiological Correlates of the Processing of Pleasant and Unpleasant Music. *Psychophysiology* 44 (2): 293–304.

Schaeffer, Pierre. 1966. *Traité des objets musicaux.* Paris: Seuil.

Schäfer, T., M. Smukalla, and S.A. Oelker. 2014. How Music Changes Our Lives: A Qualitative Study of the Long-Term Effects of Intense Musical Experiences. *Psychology of Music* 42: 525–544.

Siegmund, Gerald. 2011a. Of Monsters and Puppets: After the 'Robert Scott Complex'. In *William Forsythe and the Practice of Choreography: It Starts from Any Point*, ed. Steven Spier, 20–37. Abingdon and New York: Routledge.

———. 2011b. The Space of Memory: William Forsythe's Ballets. In *William Forsythe and the Practice of Choreography: It Starts from Any Point*, ed. Steven Spier, 128–138. Abingdon and New York: Routledge.

Sloboda, John. 1991. Music Structure and Emotional Response: Some Empirical Findings. *Psychology of Music* 19 (2): 110–120.

Strickland, Edward. 2000. *Minimalism: Origins.* Bloomington: Indiana University Press.

Tart, Charles, ed. 1969. *Altered States of Consciousness: A Book of Readings.* New York: John Wiley.

Vass-Rhee, Freya. 2011. Dancing Music: The Intermodality of The Forsythe Company. In *William Forsythe and the Practice of Choreography: It Starts from Any Point*, ed. Steven Spier, 73–89. Abingdon and New York: Routledge.

———. 2018. Schooling an Ensemble: The Forsythe Company's *Whole in the Head. Journal of Dance and Somatic Practices* 10 (2): 219–233.

Verstraete, Pieter. 2009. *The Frequency of Imagination: Auditory Distress and Aurality in Contemporary Music Theatre.* Enschede: Ipskamp Drukkers BV.

———. 2010. The Listener's Response. *Performance Research*, 15 (3): 88–94.

———. 2011. Radical Vocality, Auditory Distress and Disembodied Voice: The Resolution of the Voice-Body in The Wooster Group's La Didone'. in *Theatre Noise: The Sound of Performance*, ed. Lynne Kendrick and David Roesner, pp. 82–96. Newcastle upon Tyne: Cambridge Scholars Publishing.

CHAPTER 8

Overwhelm: Audio-Visual Stress

Forsythe's first concert program as new director of the Ballett Frankfurt in 1984 was a three-part evening titled *Audio-Visual Stress*. *France/Dance*, created one year earlier for the Paris Opera Ballet, featured a sound collage of music by Johann Sebastian Bach, animal sounds, and text spoken by a dwarf (Sabine Roth) moving between cutouts of animals and historic monumental buildings. The 1984 film *Berg AB*, set to Alban Berg's forceful *Three Pieces for Orchestra, Op. 6*, was filmed and photographed in the cellars of the Vienna State Opera,[1] while the closing work, *Say Bye Bye* (1980, for the Netherlands Dance Theater) juxtaposed aggressive physicality with Latin and pop music, screaming dialogue, and Chinese fireworks. As was the case with Forsythe's *Gänge*, created the preceding year for the Frankfurt company, theatergoers expecting the typical sights and sounds of ballet performance were surprised or even offended to hear dancers breaking the aural "fourth wall" through which only the occasional hand clap or tambourine jingle typically passes.

Just as a substantial number of Forsythe's works are characterized by multicentric action onstage (see Chap. 5), many Forsythe works are also characterized by overlays of competing sound events, which include not only the "disturbing" overlays of minimalistic lulls discussed in the previous chapter but also works or sections of works set to cacophonic music, sound collages, dancers speaking or shouting, and noises made by props. In the first part of *Gänge* (1982),[2] one of Forsythe's earliest large-scale

© The Author(s), under exclusive license to Springer Nature   139
Switzerland AG 2023
F. Vass, *William Forsythe's Postdramatic Dance Theater*, Cognitive
Studies in Literature and Performance,
https://doi.org/10.1007/978-3-031-26658-4_8

works, Michael Simon's stage set featured a floor and two onstage walls studded with microphones that amplified and echoed the sounds of dancers moving and striking them, which joined Thomas Jahn's jarring soundscore and shouted texts.[3] A profusion of short, frenetic scenes was punctuated again and again by sudden blackouts and jarring shifts of lighting. As Forsythe recounts, *Gänge*'s chaotic choreo-scenography was not to everyone's liking:

> When I first began in Frankfurt, at the end of the performance at the [1369-seat] Opera House, there were only 60 people left in the audience: 30 of them were booing and 30 of them were cheering!...It started out full because it was by subscription. And then all hell broke loose. I thought it was great that people felt so strongly about culture. I remember when I stepped out on stage to talk to the audience I was greeted with such an extraordinary wall of acoustic aggression. It was like nothing I've ever experienced in my life! (…) The dramaturgs at Frankfurt Opera, where I worked in the 1980s, were all students of Theodor Adorno, and the message to me was that I was responsible for redefining the practice. Therefore, the dramaturgical team was very happy with the *Gänge* performance. Obviously the public was not of entirely the same mind as them![4]

While *Gänge*'s overwhelming dynamic is sustained throughout the entire work, Forsythe included similar relatively short scenes in many of his later evening-length works. Interestingly, these often occurred roughly two-thirds of the way through and prior to a buildup into finale scenes, a temporal position that corresponds to that of the *scherzo* in classical compositions as well as the "eleven o'clock number" in musicals. Around half of *Artifact*'s nine-minute third act is a chaotic maelstrom of shouted text, rapid solos and duets, and scenery flats being knocked down in hard crosslight or near-darkness, set against a recording of construction site noise.[5] The 1991 version of *The Loss of Small Detail*[6] also contains an approximately four-and-a-half-minute section of frightening intensity in which the blacked-out stage and auditorium are filled with Thom Willems' percussive rhythms and the shouting, technologically warped voice of David Kern. Other dancers, one naked save for full body paint, perform frenetic solos in a small lighted "pool" of snow or silhouetted against multiple screens projecting strobed and jittery video images. Lighting and music briefly lift to the work's bleached-out, drone-accompanied main mode, only to plunge back into darkness and cacophony again. In a scene from *Decreation* (2003), Dana Caspersen urgently quotes an extended passage of text by French mystic Marguerite Porete against David Morrow's *sforzando* keyboard scoring, two other performers belting fragments of ballads, eleven rapid, angular dance solos, and jolting changes of light cued by hugely amplified and echoing slams of folding metal chairs. The uneven timings of these sonic fragments and accents, along with the sharp, shifting movements of the dancers, undercut the ongoing monologue, jutting out from the massed sound and movement. Early in the third act of *Three Atmospheric Studies* (2005), stage lights dim and Thom Willems apocalyptic synthesizer score rises to a roar as dancers dodge erratically on ominous half-light before being hurtled to the floor. Once there, they are dragged away from and scrabble back to microphones that translate their frantic cries into grating, unintelligible static.

Critics zeroed in early on Forsythe's noisy tactics, with Anna Kisselgoff complaining in 1988 that he had settled into a "formula" of permutative choreography fragmented by lighting changes and presented within clashing, multi-component soundscores.[7] In a 1986 review of *Artifact* titled "The Sound and the Flurry of William Forsythe," her highest praise goes to the work's second act, which, despite its repeatedly slamming fire curtain, she singles out as "the passage that has the least interruptions."[8] Many others, however, simply ignored the cacophonous scenes or mentioned them only in passing. In doing so, however, a facet of Forsythe's perceptual exploration is missed. Chris Salter, who collaborated with Forsythe's sound team from 1993 to 1995, vividly captures the power of such scenes in a section of his "casebook" detailing the making of *Eidos:Telos* (1995):

> Bill talks quickly about building a complex acoustic scenery to match the abrupt shifts of "light and darkness," in the mood as well as visually. From this moment on, all chaos breaks loose. In real time, we literally start composing with a combination of samples, CD's Maxim [Franke]'s violin playing and Dana [Caspersen]'s body microphone. A mistakenly played heart beat suddenly becomes integrated into the scene's aural topography, along with streams of animal noises, crashes, fragments of text from Goddard's *Alphaville*, pygmy sounds, a Chinese violin player. At one point, we actually sample the sound of the HMI [light] turning on, a horrible static buzz that lasts the length of an instant but is so distinctive that it sounds like the earth itself opening up (...) The hours we spend building this world seem completely out of control. There is so much happening on stage between Dana, Bill, the lights, Maxim and the music, that we are all dumbfounded even as we are caught in the flow. I am running back and forth between the orchestra

pit, Bill and Dana, listening to things and trying to keep track of the event flow in order that we might have some way to notate and perhaps, reproduce the chaos. The environment that we are creating is in itself the event. It is a fluid, dynamic architecture of the rawest of emotions and states; a breathing body and universe where the only law is possession, madness, intoxication.[9]

Salter's account illuminates the complexity and density not only of informational flow in Forsythe's choreo-scenographic process, but also the kinds of sonic qualities that come into play in his noisiest and most chaotic scenes. Research has sought to draw out the cognitive distinction between noise and music (which is of course a form of noise) and to understand the perception, judgment valences, and ideologies associated with these categories. Our evaluation of sounds as music or noise, however is also encultured and fluid. My aim, though, is not to interrogate this categorization but instead to posit a category of dancing, and by extension of choreo-scenography, that is "noisy" in the sense of its visuosonic composition. As with the soothing effects of lulling music, responses to hyperkinetic performance and visually overwhelming dancing and scenography reflect Jacques Attali's distinction between music and noise, as discussed in Chap. 7. Noise in all forms intrudes and impinges, striking our ears and influencing our perceptions of the environments that generate it.[10] But how does "noisy" dancing and staging impact the performance of perception?

Plethora and Sublime Excess

One way to view Forsythe's scenes of overwhelm is as simple contrast or perceptual counterweight: thunderous and busy *entremets* to cleanse the visuosonic palate before a final and comparatively more palatable course of dancing. In Forsythe's case, however, these instances have a refocusing effect on his already hyperkinetic classicism, one that demands a reassessment of claims levied that his choreography—particularly during his first decade at the Ballett Frankfurt—was in some way a destruction (or as some more generously frame is, a de*con*struction) of classical form.[11] Though the scenes mentioned above are comparatively brief, they occur at points in the works at which audience perception has already been highly aroused and taxed by the contrasting and demanding informational and perceptual dynamics of prior scenes or acts. These hypervisual and hypersonic intermezzi further stress the senses, heightening the relief of return to the less overpowering visuosonic dynamics and relative order that follow.

Like the reduced action in conditions of *lull* described in the previous chapter, visually "noisy" scenes also reflect a facet of "play with the density of signs" that Lehmann signals as a trait of postdramatic theatre. He highlights the presence of a "dialectic of *plethora and deprivation,* plenitude and emptiness [italics Lehmann]" in which, on one hand, slowness, silences, and repetition invoke the imagination of the spectator to fill in the gaps, while on the other, "scenic overabundance" creates confusing and even disturbing densities of information that disorient and overwhelm the attendee.[12] Dance theater works that Lehmann associates with this trait include those of late 1980s "Eurocrash" representatives Johann Kresnik, Wim Vandekeybus/ Ultima Vez and Édouard Lock's company La La La Human Steps. Prior to these, "punk ballet" emerged in the late 1970s as an explosive subversion of both ballet and modern dance's formal order and postmodern dance's minimalist tendencies, while the musical choices in these works reflected a desire to move away from not only highbrow classical music but also silence and *musique concrète.* The dancing, however, retained an overtly nose-thumbing connection to the classical aesthetic by transmuting balletic movement into an explosive response to the music's volume, raw energy, and speed. Karole Armitage's works from this period were marked by broad movement at shocking velocities, fractured lines, violent partnering, and disunity, while Michael Clark's frenetic, punk/rock scored works and psychedelic *mise-en-scènes* were decried by some critics in tones similar to those aimed at Forsythe (often by the same critics) in the 1980s.[13]

Subjective judgments of dance quality are typically positively responsive to what Julia Christensen et al. refer to as "rounded" shapes (curved and visually balanced extension of limbs rather than straight limbs and pointed forms), "impressive" movements that display a high degree of skill,[14] and smoothness and predictability of movement.[15] Symmetry and compositional synchrony of both individuals' movements and those of groups align with general principles governing visual aesthetic appreciation, in line with Rudolf Arnheim's Gestalt psychology.[16] Though the choreographies mentioned above feature a high degree of virtuosity, movement is often spiky or jerky and compositional formations, if they exist, tend toward chaotic, "noisy" disorganization. In the absence of visual harmony and of structures that meet predictive expectations, our evaluative categories fall short, leaving us in the unsettled space of incomprehension and unable to parse what we are seeing.

Occasionally, choreographers have used this categorical failure to subserve humor. In an extremely brief duet between scenes of Twyla Tharp's 1976 *Push Comes to Shove*, the principal couple execute a pas de deux that is a frantic, disorganized series of movements, pausing for a moment of nonchalance, then relaunching into another flurry of steps that propels them into the wings. It is not incidental that this 20-second duet evokes wry laughter: "noisy" dancing irritates precisely through its incoherent busy-ness, and laughter is a spontaneous and socially acceptable response to incongruity.[17] The duet's visual chaos is further underscored by a lack of music—the only unscored section in a ballet that opens with a jaunty ragtime orchestration and then continues with sections of a bright Haydn symphony. Set among far more structurally typical choreography, the duet plays with the doubled effect of hyperkineticism's ability to outstrip of the eye and thwart the search for "sensible" organization.

Yvonne Rainer's *Trio A* stands as an interesting compositional counterpole to the physical and visual din of choreographic plethora. Rainer sought to avoid creating steps that shared qualities of other ones in the piece; as a result, *Trio A* contains virtually no repetitive movement.[18] Instead, as she explains, it involves "one *discrete* thing following another," the sequences progressing smoothly without accents, pauses between steps, or a relation to music. Her perceptual experiment in *Trio A* is clear in the two assumptions she lays out:

> (1) A movement is a complete and self-contained event; elaboration in the sense of varying some aspect of it can only blur its distinctiveness; and (2) Dance is hard to see. It must either be made less fancy, or the fact of that intrinsic difficulty must be emphasized to the point that it becomes almost impossible to see.[19]

At its premiere, critics derided *Trio A* as "a long business," "a sort of boring continuum," and likened it to "woolen underwear."[20] Despite its seemingly lackluster quality, though, *Trio A*'s movement is deceptively complex due to its large vocabulary of different movements, as well as points at which the choreography requires use of the body—borrowing Forsythe's formulation—in a "many timed" manner by executing different simultaneous geometries and temporal dynamics across its parts.[21] Despite their differing aesthetics, *Trio A* moves forward offering virtually no relational structure, like the "noisy" choreographies above—all motif and no synthesis.

Negative reactions to choreo-scenographic overload come as no surprise when considered from a cognitive perspective. In a 1974 paper discussing settings that are extremely saturated with sensory information, behavioral scientist Joachim Wohlwill draws a distinction between the terms *sensory overload* and *sensory overstimulation,* reserving the former term for conditions under which individuals do not experience a more passive exposure to concurrent or competing stimuli but instead *must* process information in order to produce an appropriate response.[22] Wohlwill holds that a full breakdown of response is only likely to occur in situations in which overlapping streams of information require differential responses.[23] Other studies from the 1970s heyday of empirical research on consciousness revealed how exposure to intense auditory and visual stimuli, such as randomly patterned colored lights and cacophonous sounds, readily induces psychedelic effects including hallucinations, distorted perceptions of time and body image, mood shifts, or symptoms of paranoia, as well as reduced performance on cognitive tasks.[24] On a less invasive but also detrimental level, environmental noise has been shown to negatively influence evaluations of life quality due to increased annoyance and tension.[25] While these and other studies sought to measure impairment of subjective state and task performance rather than to pinpoint the breakdown of response capability, they show that both cognitive function and psychophysiological well-being are negatively impacted by extreme surfeits of information.

Despite the orientation of this period's research toward "altered" states of consciousness and the detrimental effects of urban environments, it nonetheless invites comparison to the demands that "noisy" contemporary performance makes on audiences, as well as to subjective experience of this demand. However, more recent studies of both everyday and aesthetic experiences have revealed an opposing process that warrants consideration. This body of research instead focuses on the hedonic value of *fluent processing* of stimuli, regardless of the content of the stimulus. What has been shown is that we experience an early-stage boost of pleasure when perception occurs with ease, speed, and accuracy, and this response is independent of and may even precede our recognition of and reaction to what we are perceiving.[26] The picture becomes more complex as exposure time extends beyond initial apprehension of low-level properties like contrast and symmetry, and higher-order properties like memory, taste, and expertise come into play. Considering both of these processes, it seems possible that the disharmonious, temporally extended "noise" of hyperkinetic dance may indeed *lengthen* the timeframe of this hedonic effect to a point when it is overridden by the perceptually taxing effect of sensory overstimulation. Instances of dance hyperkineticism could be ideal potential stimuli for further investigation of these effects and their interactions.

As torrents of sound agglomerate into cacophony, compete for attention, and override each other, the aggregation of multiple disharmonious overlays effectively creates a sonic obscuration that overwhelms the ear. The torrential sound of "noisy" scenes, which are further complemented by distorting effects, extremes of lighting, and disharmonious choreography, keep any one percept from establishing itself as dominant figure for any length of time. Instead, tumultuous pluralities of sound and movement tax the senses, filling the eye and ear with relentless activity whose impetus and intentions are rendered unclear by the interference of the whole. The contrast between these relatively brief scenes and more subdued "musical" sections of works highlights instances of audio-visual stress as events of otherness, subverting expectations in arresting displays of "excesses of power."[27] During the perceptual onslaughts of what Lehmann terms "concrete theatre," any attempt to extract dramatic depth via higher-order processes is thwarted by the paradoxically opaque sensuous surface, which stuns the senses and hinders critical reflection. Instead, audiences are met with a "radical refusal: the confrontation with a figuratively 'silent' and dense presence of bodies, materials and forms...Perception finds itself thrown back onto the perception of structures."[28]

Though Forsythe's brief scenes of jarring visuosonic overwhelm might be considered spectacular, they have much in common with the organized, harmonic displays of massed bodies and/or sounds commonly associated with the sublime. Film scholar Greg Tuck clarifies the distinction thus:

> At simplest level both the spectacular and the sublime can be understood as visually extraordinary experiences, albeit in distinct ways (...) Both spectacle and sublime are perceptually impressive at a cognitive level, but only the latter produces an often-fearful sense of wonder, while the former is about the pleasure of wondering how it was done. The spectacular and the sublime have an inverse relationship with regard to our faith 'in' and understanding 'of' the conceptual and perceptual aspects of such displays. Spectacles might be impressive and fun, but there is something shallow or depthless about

them, while the sublime is the complete opposite, a moment of extraordinary metaphysical density.[29]

In the grip of the sublime, then, the pleasure of spectacular beauty is subverted by the raw force of disorder and sensory overwhelm. Confronted with these intense worlds, whether natural or made, we fail not only to perceive their totality but also to come to grips with our own experience. Forsythe's overwhelming interludes offer Attali's state of potential release, which demands a daring plunge into the depths of our sensing experience but which can yield a deeper engagement with existential awe.

NOTES

1. See Roslyn Sulcas, "Forsythe and Film," 97–98.
2. The first part of *Gänge* was created in 1982 for the Netherlands Dance Theater. It subsequently opened the three-part *Gänge* (subtitled *Ein Stück Über Ballett*) that Forsythe choreographed a year later as his first evening-length work in Frankfurt, prior to becoming Director.
3. See illustrations in Michael Simon, *Michael Simon – FERTIG gibt's nicht. Bühnenbild. Prozesse.*
4. Forsythe interviewed by Ana Bogdan, "No one has any idea what really works."
5. In 2017, this section of *Artifact* was replaced with a new rhythmic dance-and-vocal version for the Boston Ballet, which performed the work under the title *Artifact 2017*.
6. The 1991 version of evening-length *The Loss of Small Detail* includes the one-act work *the second detail* (1991) as a prelude. An intermission occurs between the works.
7. Anna Kisselgoff, "Dance View: When a Choreographer Settles into a Formula."
8. Anna Kisselgoff, "The Sound and the Flurry of William Forsythe."
9. Chris Salter, *Unstable Events: Theater at the Verge of Complexity*, 148.
10. Jacques Attali, *Noise*.
11. See Adeline Chevrier-Bosseau, "Renewing the Discipline."
12. Hans-Thies Lehmann, *Postdramatic Theatre*, 89–91.
13. In a review titled "An Occasion for Tears," for example, Clement Crisp mourned that Clark had become

    a child of his time, that most corrupting of states, and punk dance, wild extravagance and all the deadly paraphernalia of self-indulgence in the 1980s claimed him, and corroded his talent. I recall evenings of frustration—mine quite as much as what I guessed was his—where crass dance and barbarous din were allied to aggressive costuming, urchin obscenity, and the feeling that here was a beautiful dancer deriding his own gifts so as to give maximum affront to a stuffy public, and provide youthful fans with a nose-thumbing at a fusty establishment.

14. See Julia Christensen et al., "Affective responses to dance."
15. See Guido Orgs et al., "Learning to like it: Aesthetic perception of bodies, movements and choreographic structure."
16. See Rudolf Arnheim, *Art and visual perception: A psychology of the creative eye* and Ian McManus, "Symmetry and asymmetry in aesthetics and the arts." See also Kreitler & Kreitler, *Psychology of the Arts.*
17. J. Vaid and V.S. Ramachandran, "Laughter and humour,"426.
18. More recently, Rainer made a performed a version in 2010 titled *Trio A: Geriatric with Talking.*
19. Yvonne Rainer, *A Woman Who...: Essays, Interviews, Scripts,* 35.
20. Carrie Lambert, "Moving Still: Mediating Yvonne Rainer's 'Trio A,'" 90.
21. Paul Kaiser, "Dance Geometry: William Forsythe in dialogue with Paul Kaiser," 66.
22. Joachim Wohlwill, "Human Adaptation to Levels of Environmental Stimulation," 131, n.3.
23. Joachim Wohlwill, "Human Adaptation to Levels of Environmental Stimulation," 142.
24. See, for example, L. Gottschalk et al., "Effect of sensory overload on psychological state: changes in social alienation-personal disorganization and cognitive-intellectual impairment," J. Haer, "Alterations in consciousness induced by sensory overload," J. Haer, "Field dependency in relation to altered states of consciousness produced by sensory overload," A. Ludwig, "'Psychedelic' effects produced by sensory overload," and Z. Lipowski, "Sensory information and overload: Behavioral effects."
25. See Jack Westerman and James Walters, "Noise and Stress: A Comprehensive Approach."
26. Piotr Winkielman et al., "The hedonic marking of processing fluency: Implications for evaluative judgment," and Rolf, Reber et al., "Processing fluency and aesthetic pleasure: Is beauty in the perceiver's processing experience?"
27. See Baz Kershaw, "Spectacles of performance: Excesses of power."
28. Lehmann, Postdramatic Theatre, 99.
29. Greg Tuck, "When more is less: CGI, spectacle, and the capitalist sublime," 251–252.

BIBLIOGRAPHY

Arnheim, Rudolf. 1954. *Art and Visual Perception: A Psychology of the Creative Eye.* Berkeley, CA: University of California Press.

Attali, Jacques. 1985. *Noise: The Political Economy of Music.* Translated by Brian Massumi. Minneapolis: University of Minnesota Press. Original version: *Bruits: essai sur l'économie politique de la musique.* Paris: Presses Universitaire de France, 1977.

Bogdan, Ana. 2018. No One has Any Idea What Really Works. Interview with William Forsythe. *The Talks*, January 24. https://the-talks.com/interview/william-forsythe/. Accessed 4 August 2021.

Chevrier-Bosseau, A. 2020. Renewing the Discipline: William Forsythe's Blake Works I. *Revue francaise detudes americaines* 165 (4): 82–97.

Christensen, J.F., F.E. Pollick, A. Lambrechts, and A. Gomila. 2016. Affective Responses to Dance. *Acta Psychologica* 168: 91–105.

Crisp, Clement. 2001. An Occasion for Tears. *Financial Times*, October 26.

Gottschalk, L.A., J.L. Haer, and D.E. Bates. 1972. Effect of Sensory Overload on Psychological State: Changes in Social Alienation-Personal Disorganization and Cognitive-Intellectual Impairment. *Archives of General Psychiatry* 27 (4): 451–457.

Haer, J. 1970. Alterations in Consciousness Induced by Sensory Overload. *Journal for the Study of Consciousness* 3: 161–169.

———. 1971. Field Dependency in Relation to Altered States of Consciousness Produced by Sensory Overload. *Perceptual and Motor Skills* 33 (1): 192–194.

Kaiser, Paul. 1999. Dance Geometry: William Forsythe in Dialogue with Paul Kaiser. *Performance Research* 4 (2): 64–71.

Kershaw, Baz. 2007. Spectacles of Performance: Excesses of Power. In *Theatre Ecology: Environments and Performance*, 206–238. New York and Cambridge: Cambridge University Press.

Kisselgoff, Anna. 1987. The Sound and the Flurry of William Forsythe. *The New York Times*, July 19. https://www.nytimes.com/1987/07/19/arts/the-sound-and-the-flurry-of-william-forsythe.html. Accessed 9 November 2007.

———. 1988. Dance View: When a Choreographer Settles into a Formula. *The New York Times*, July 3. https://www.nytimes.com/1988/07/03/arts/dance-view-when-a-choreographer-settles-into-a-formula.html. Accessed 10 November 2007.

Kreitler, Hans, and Shulamith Kreitler. 1972. *Psychology of the Arts.* Durham, NC: Duke University Press.

Lambert, Carrie. 1999. Moving Still: Mediating Yvonne Rainer's "Trio A". *October* 89: 87–112.

Lehmann, Hans-Thies. 2006. *Postdramatic Theatre.* Translated by Karen-Jürs-Munby. Abingdon and New York: Routledge. Original Version: Lehmann, Hans-Thies. 1999. *Postdramatisches Theater.* Frankfurt am Main: Verlag der Autoren.

Lipowski, Z. 1975. Sensory Information and Overload: Behavioral Effects. *Comprehensive Psychiatry* 16 (3): 199–221.

Ludwig, A. 1972. "Psychedelic" Effects Produced by Sensory Overload. *American Journal of Psychiatry* 128 (10): 1294–1297.

McManus, I.C. 2005. Symmetry and Asymmetry in Aesthetics and the Arts. *European Review* 13 (S2): 157–180.

Orgs, G., N. Hagura, and P. Haggard. 2013. Learning to Like It: Aesthetic Perception of Bodies, Movements and Choreographic Structure. *Consciousness and Cognition* 22 (2): 603–612.

Rainer, Yvonne. 1999. *A Woman Who...: Essays, Interviews, Scripts*. Baltimore, MD: The John Hopkins University Press.

Reber, R., N. Schwarz, and P. Winkielman. 2004. Processing Fluency and Aesthetic Pleasure: Is Beauty in the Perceiver's Processing Experience? *Personality and Social Psychology Review* 8 (4): 364–382.

Salter, Chris. 1997. *Unstable Events: Theater at the Verge of Complexity*. PhD diss., Stanford University.

Simon, Michael. 2022. Michael Simon – FERTIG gibt's nicht. Bühnenbild. Prozesse, ed. Tilman Neuffer and Stephan Wetzel. Berlin: Theater der Zeit.

Sulcas, Roslyn. 2003. Forsythe and Film: Habits of Seeing. In *Envisioning Dance on Film and Video*, ed. Judy Mitoma, 96–102. Abingdon/New York: Routledge.

Tuck, Greg. 2008. When More is Less: CGI, Spectacle, and the Capitalist Sublime. *Science Fiction and Television* 2 (2): 249–273.

Vaid, J., and V.S. Ramachandran. 2001. Laughter and Humour. In *The Oxford Companion to the Body*, ed. Colin Blakemore and Sheila Jennett, 426–427. Oxford: Oxford University Press.

Westerman, Jack, and James Walters. 1981. Noise and Stress: A Comprehensive Approach. *Environmental Health Perspectives* 41: 291–309.

Winkielman, P., N. Schwarz, T. Fazendeiro, and R. Reber. 2003. The Hedonic Marking of Processing Fluency: Implications for Evaluative Judgment. In *The Psychology of Evaluation: Affective Processes in Cognition and Emotion*, ed. Jochen Musch and Karl Klauer, 189–217. Hove: Psychology Press.

Wohlwill, Jochen. 1974. Human Adaptation to Levels of Environmental Stimulation. *Human Ecology* 2 (2): 121–147.

PART III

Sounding Dancing: The Senses in Concert

One of my favorite Instagram clips was posted by former Ballett Frankfurt dancer Stephen Galloway, who has also designed costumes for many of Forsythe's ballets. It shows a lighthearted moment in a dressing room at the Royal Ballet of Flanders; Stephen supports Nancy Osbaldeston as she does finger pirouettes, her foot in a low *coupé*, her free arm wound behind her back, and a wide grin on her face. Were this a typical classical supported pirouette, Nancy might finish with a sustained pose like *developpé à la seconde*, her leg floating effortlessly up to the side. Instead, she throws her leg into a swift, high *battement* and sharply stabs it down into an overcrossed fourth position. What I love about the clip, though, is Nancy's gleeful shout of "Bam!" on her *battement* and Stephen's approving "Hah!" as she hits the *croisé* pose.

Dancers think of movement in a synesthetic manner, as evidenced by their tendency to deploy non-textual aspects of utterance like pitch, volume, prosody (speech melody), variance of syllabic duration, and timbre to describe movements. If you walk into any dance studio, you will likely hear dancers and coaches using their voices in illustrative ways to indicate actual or desired qualities of movement. At times, this may sound like singing along to accompanying music, while at others their vocalizations reflect anticipatory exhortation and warning or post hoc congratulation or resignation. The linguistic register is inflected by a translatory scaffolding practice of *sounding movement*. Sonification of visualizations and intentions, however, is far from unique to dancers: onomatopoeia, the creation of sounds that describe qualities of things, may in fact be a universal human mimic ability. When movement is translated into utterance, though, it is not just what is seen or heard that inflects vocalization but also what is felt, both in our kinesthetically empathetic projection of movement and in our vocal re-presentation of it. And movement is notoriously ineffable, a word whose roots mean "not capable of being said."

Translation has been a broad hallmark of Forsythe's choreographic approach. Extrapolating from dance theorist and pedagogue Rudolf von Laban's model of the kinesphere (a three-dimensional geometric form that surrounds the body and delineates its spatial range as it moves), Forsythe re-imagined the dancing body as a constellation of non-hierarchized centers rather than a single, all-encompassing kinesphere, with all points, axes, and dynamics given potentially equal importance. His "algorithmic" or "modality" based approach to improvising with balletic form involves the transposition of dance's geometric traces from one body part to another, or the derivation of spatial relations between multiple moving parts or locations in space, be they real or virtual, or static or moving.[1] Any point, part, or area, including internal body structures, can also potentially serve as a locus—or as one of multiple synchronous or "many-timed"[2] loci—for geometrically inscriptive thinking and movement. In this translatory mode of improvising, the balletic vocabulary of steps—or any other systematic dance structuring—affords an immense proliferation of combinatory possibilities, while also blurring the conceptual boundary between choreography and improvisation. Forsythe has also drawn on other extracorporeal sources of information as translational prompts: In *Limb's Theorem*, two-dimensional architectural drawings of Daniel Libeskind (one of which was projected onto a large curved "sail" in the work's third part) were rendered into improvised three-dimensional dancing, as Nik Haffner describes:

> The same drawing on a sheet of paper is translated in a different and individual way by each dancer. The timing of the movement is determined by the manner and speed with which I, let us say, "read" a drawing. It is a matter of how much time it takes to go through certain parts of the drawing...This information is available as an offer to every dancer when improvising. The dancer decides what to select.[3]

During the final years of the Ballett Frankfurt and the ensemble's transition into The Forsythe Company, Forsythe extended his consideration of the translatory possibilities of choreography and the relation between dance and sound by investigating the performative potentials of dance's own sounds. In describing dance as "a kind of music—maybe a visual music," Forsythe reveals an intuitive understanding of the common physiological and cognitive ground shared by visual and aural perception. He also reminded his dancers that sound is fundamentally a product of movement: sound begins when vibrating objects set air molecules into motion, while sound perception begins when this moving air initiates a chain of motion in the organs of the ear.[4] The ensemble's investigation of the sonic affordances of dancing produced two principal sound-movement paradigms of what I term *visuosonic choreography*. In these modes of working, the boundary is effaced between Forsythe's choreo-scenography and the dancing bodies that populate his stage worlds of moving light (and darkness), sound, and objects. In effect, this dancing renders the performer a constituent part of the expanded scenography of visual and sonic elements in a way that reflects Forsythe's use of set pieces as "instruments." In the 1993 version of *As a Garden in This Setting*, Willems' highly mobilized soundscore is joined by the sounds of large ovular objects that roll across the stage space, "moving, sounding, and responding on their own volition without regard to human presences."[5] In *Eidos:Telos* (1995), wires stretching across the stage were played by a violinist and Dana Caspersen stuffed a huge length or orange cellophane into a light projector, producing an amplified and morphed wall of sound. Of this work, Paul Derksen comments:

> The stage is the place for a multitude of projections and interactions to happen, in which performers and 'environment' change each other in a symbiotic manner. Whereas in the previous part the dancers silently used the information on the monitors, here the electronically generated sounds and images react. Their interaction is realised by Joel Ryan, a media artist aligned to STEIM (the Foundation for Electro Instrumental Music, based in Amsterdam). Movement is transformed into sound, text is projected and spoken at the same time, rhythm is transposed in motion: Forsythe questions the act of perception, one of the through lines in his work, a mystery that has seduced, stupefied and provoked mankind through the centuries.[6]

This third and final part of the volume moves from a general discussion of visuosonic counterpoint to consideration of Forsythe's "breath scores," which include not only breath gestures but also footfall, physical contact, and other sounds produced by bodies in motion, and then to improvisational paradigms in which the movement of dancing prompts fully vocalized sound. These two visuosonic modes reveal a focus on the perceptual propensity to merge sensory information across the senses of vision and audition. By choreographically interrogating this merging, Forsythe deploys the aural channel—the perceptual channel through which textual significance usually reaches us—as a vector for a visceral, performative experience of corporeal significance. The interplay between sound and movement, both of which are visibly produced onstage, subserves Forsythe's broader choreographic strategy of heightening and dividing attention through a transgression of the sensory and physical boundaries that normally define the limits of dancing as a concept. In other words, Forsythe's performative categorical collapse of dance's visual and sonic aspects in his choreo-scenographic processes *re-vises* a perceptual norm that has defined concert dance as a silent art practice with musical accompaniment. In doing so, he opens an arena in which to explore attention to and in performance from an intermodal perspective.

NOTES

1. Paul Kaiser, "Dance Geometry: William Forsythe in Dialogue with Paul Kaiser," 67. During the early 1990s, Forsythe and the Ballett Frankfurt dancers also developed close to 150 distinct movement operations known as the "alphabet" but also referred to as "algorithms," or "modalities," which they employed singly or in combination to translate movement in works from that period. Forsythe, who has used all three terms at various times in his career, has favored the latter term in recent years.
2. Forsythe in Kaiser, "Dance Geometry," 66.
3. Nik Haffner, "Forsythe und die Medien." For a key detailed treatment of Forsythe work with Libeskind, see also Patricia Baudoin and Heidi Gilpin. "Proliferation and Perfect Disorder: William Forsythe and the Architecture of Disappearance."
4. Forsythe, in conversation with the ensemble, March 13, 2008.
5. Chris Salter, "Timbral Architectures, Aurality's Force," 68.
6. Paul Derksen, "Eidos:Telos, Some Images."

BIBLIOGRAPHY

Baudoin, Patricia, and Heidi Gilpin. 1989. Proliferation and Perfect Disorder: William Forsythe and the Architecture of Disappearance. In *Il Disegno che Non Fa il Ritratto: Danza, Architecttura, Notazioni II*, ed. Marinella Guatterini. Reggio Emilia: Teatri di Reggio Emilia. Also published in *Parallax* evening program (1989). Frankfurt am Main: Ballett Frankfurt.

Derksen, Paul. 2001. Eidos:Telos, Some Images. Accessed 24 April. (archived)

Galloway, Stephen. 2021. [Instagram]. January 9. Available at: https://www.instagram.com/p/CJz2vnpHv7B/?igshid=YmMyMTA2M2Y=

Haffner, Nik. 2000. Forsythe und die Medien. *tanzdrama* 511 (2): 30–35. English Version: Forsythe and the Media. www.frankfurt-ballett.de/nikmedia-english.html. Accessed 31 May 2003.

Kaiser, Paul. 1999. Dance Geometry: William Forsythe in Dialogue with Paul Kaiser. *Performance Research* 4 (2): 64–71.

Salter, Chris. 2011. Timbral Architectures, Aurality's Force. In *William Forsythe and the Practice of Choreography: It Starts from Any Point*, ed. Steven Spier, 54–72. Abingdon and New York: Routledge.

CHAPTER 9

Visuosonic Counterpoint: Seeing Music and Hearing Dance

Though various species of insects, arthropods, frogs, birds, and primates exhibit rhythmic and synchronic interactions, humans are virtually the only species capable of synchronizing movements to accompanying sound such as music.[1] The discovery of mirror neurons in primates and evidence that such a system may be present in speech-processing areas of the human brain offers support for the motor theory of speech and speech perception, according to which linguistic comprehension is facilitated through access to one's own embodied experience of the vocal gestures required to produce the sounds heard.[2] These mechanisms may also underlie the coordination of gestures with musical qualities such as rhythm, pitch, and dynamics. Since the early twentieth century, the connection between sonic gestures in music and physical motion has been explored from perspectives including movement theory, music theory, and film theory.[3]

Regarding dance, Daniel Levitin and Anna Tirovalas find an extensional or complementary linkage between dance movements and those required to create music. They further note that "the connection between music and dance can be thought of as an extension of the movements required for vocalizing simply applied to other body regions."[4] However, the relationship of dance to music became a subject of intense experimentation in Western concert dance over the twentieth century. Dance scholar Sally Banes noted that postmodern dancers of the 1960s and 1970s were dancing "with/to/before/on/in/over/after/against/away from/without"

© The Author(s), under exclusive license to Springer Nature Switzerland AG 2023
F. Vass, *William Forsythe's Postdramatic Dance Theater*, Cognitive Studies in Literature and Performance,
https://doi.org/10.1007/978-3-031-26658-4_9

music,[5] and *choreomusical* experimentation continues to be carried forward in the works of many postdramatic dance-makers. It is important to note, though, that the above term, which was likely coined by Paul Hodgins in 1992,[6] implies a limitation that in fact does not exist, given that Western concert dance has come to feature a wide variety of sound-scores and choreomusical relationships, a number of which are mentioned below and discussed in Part 2 of this volume. But how did we arrive at such choreomusical diversity?

A HISTORY OF MOVING WITH [ETC.] MUSIC

Though music continued to be composed for ballets as it had been since the earliest court ballets, two linked trends dramatically changed the face of European concert dance in the early twentieth century. Firstly, choreographers began setting works to music that had not specifically been written for dance. Isadora Duncan's groundbreaking early modern works, set to the music of Chopin, Brahms, Strauss, Beethoven Wagner, and even "La Marseillaise," made a strong impression on the young Michel Fokine, whose work also resonated with her influence through its rejection of the artificiality of ballet's dance/mime division in favor of movement that integrated emotion and narrative. His *Les Sylphides* (originally named *Chopiniana*), developed between 1907 and 1909, is the first ballet to be considered properly "abstract."

Change was also afoot musically in Russia, though, with new approaches to tonality, harmony, rhythm, and meter, as well as the emergence of the lush harmonics of Impressionism and an increased inclusion of dissonance. Formerly bound by the rigid tonal structures, through-going meters, and smooth dynamic shifts characteristic of the Classical, Baroque, and Romantic styles, music began to shimmer and punch, to whisper and hammer, and to overcut and compete with itself. A new choreographic liberty and complexity was catalyzed in particular by the early ballets of Igor Stravinsky (1882–1971), who, as Lincoln Kirstein claimed, "made music, not to serve dance, but to control it."[7] Stravinsky's 1910 *The Firebird*, choreographed by Fokine, evoked a world of iridescent sonority and supernatural power, while *Petrushka* (1911) interjected driving Russian motifs and jarring dissonant chords.

The choreomusical congruency of rhythm and dynamics in Duncan and Fokine's choreographies displays a respectful approach to the music— one necessary, in Duncan's case, to literally keep the show on the road.

However, Vaslav Nijinsky, who was tapped to choreograph by Ballets Russes impresario Serge Diaghilev, presented works in each of the two successive Paris seasons that caused scandal, not just because of the turned-in feet and carnal implications they contained. Set to lush, fluid symphonic poems by Debussy, *L'Après-midi d'un Faune* (1912) and *Jeux* (1913) contrast lush orchestral tone and shifting, ebbing meters with angular, rigid movements that only occasionally reflect the music's structure. The seemingly free-form wash of music in *Faune* belies a complex structure of musical motifs that are traded among the instruments. Against its lack of driving rhythm, Nijinsky set cellular units of movement that run in their own carefully calibrated time. In *Jeux*, livelier movement passages often have little relation to meter but then flow briefly together with the music, before breaking off again into slow, sinuous gestures or friezelike stillnesses.[8]

More so than Fokine, it was Nijinsky's choreographic experimentation that opened new ground for choreomusical relationships. His works assert dance's independence from their accompanying music, as Juliet Bellow has noted.[9] *Faune, Jeux*, and quieter interludes in *Le Sacre du Printemps* (1913) offer up two distinct time registers—one visual and one sonic—which crucially affords interplay between them. Dance and music, rather than being in a "service" relationship in either direction, were instead freed from each other and available as elements of novel and performative contrapuntal structuring. The oeuvre of George Balanchine, who collaborated closely with Stravinsky for over four decades, would follow from the mid-1920s with many highly contrapuntal works to both classical and modern compositions, while Martha Graham and other modern dance choreographers would engage with the psychological potentials of compositions by Schoenberg, Hindemith, Berg, Webern, Milhaud, and others.

In the early 1940s, the sound palette opened up in a new way that would deeply influence choreography. This was the emergence of *musique concrète*, electronic music that was often made from *acousmatic* sounds, a term coined by Pierre Schaeffer for sounds whose sources remain unseen. Composers of *musique concrète* questioned conventional views on the necessity of rhythm and melody by insisting that any sonorous object could be used as an instrument—natural substances, common objects, voices, musical instruments played in unusual ways, and eventually computer-generated sounds. Both Balanchine and Maurice Bejart choreographed to Pierre Henry's 1963 *Variations pour une porte et un soupir*, while Merce Cunningham choreographed his nocturnal *Winterbranch* to

La Monte Young's grating composition *2 Sounds* (1960), which are made by dragging a metal can across a glass pane and scraping a gong with a drumstick. Often arrhythmic and with an abundance of new and sometimes shocking timbres, the new genre challenged the very concept of music, though it was considered by many to be merely noise.

Cunningham, a former Graham dancer who pioneered what came to be called postmodern dance, held that dance and music did not have to reflect each other in any way. Instead, choreomusical relationships could emerge through the simple co-occurrence of sound and movement, which he sometimes instigated by using chance methods to determine which music would accompany which dance piece during performance evenings. His dancers were freed from adherence to determined sonic pulse, moving instead in the natural time necessary to carry out any given movement.[10] As postmodern dance brought this and further assumptions about dance into question—what dance was and wasn't, how and by whom it should be performed and under what conditions, and whether it needed to please or to entertain—further new acoustic possibilities provided fertile ground for experimentation. The repetitive rhythmic patterns of minimalist music informed the works of choreographers from Laura Dean to Anna Teresa De Keersmaeker, while others used minimalist compositions as sonic "washes" underlying contrasting visual dynamics. Throughout this period of choreographic experimentation with more attenuated or differently congruent relationships between dance and music, audiences frequently found their received choreomusical expectations thwarted.

Some early twentieth-century choreographers, however, produced a heightened and highly "illustrative" choreomusical congruency. First developed in 1919 by Americans Ruth St. Denis and Ted Shawn and clearly inflected by Dalcrozian eurhythmics,[11] the goal of *music visualization* was, as St. Denis put it in a 1925 article in her own *Denishawn Magazine*,

> the scientific translation into bodily action of the rhythmic, melodic and harmonious structure of a musical composition, without intention to in any way 'interpret' or reveal any hidden meaning apprehended by the dancer. Each note must have its correlative translation…The rise and fall of the melody should have some answer in the rise and fall of the body above the plane of the stage.[12]

Though these dances did often foreground musical expressivity and emotion, the primary experimental focus was the reflection of music's molar qualities. This could already be found in the pounding, stamping sections of Nijinsky's *Sacre*, which critics—perhaps unsurprisingly—deemed dangerous to both performers and audience.[13]

Negative views of *Sacre*'s rhythmic extremes, though, stand at odds with the pleasure audiences typically derive from close choreomusical congruency. This, though, is itself at odds with more contemporary views of "mickey-mousing," so named due to the deliberately mimetic visuosonic congruence found in cartoons and film. For some, the exaggerated and even "campy" choreomusical synchrony in postmodern choreographer Mark Morris' works is pure pleasure. However, critical response to his early works, and by extension to mickey-mousing, was divided. Inger Damsholt has argued that Morris' musicality, rather than being reactionary or sentimental, constitutes a "choreomusical polemic" that motivates both new choreographic and scholarly thinking.[14] Composer Barbara White instead directly indicates a perceptual effect of mickey-mousing when she suggests that choreographers' and critics' paradoxical responses to mickey-mousing are "less about the resistance to music per se than resistance to the sensations generated by the meeting of music and dance...the loudness and intensity we experience when sound and music join together in glorious excess."[15] Evoking Mickey Mouse as a metaphoric, spectral being that exists only in the negative, White defines choreomusicality in terms of structures which are *avoided* rather than those which are produced. Going further, she casts attitudes toward music-movement synchrony in sexual terms as a "fear of fusing," noting music's seductive influence as an immersive, penetrating percept.[16]

It appears, then, that we have a love-hate relationship with choreomusical congruity. St Denis herself expressed awareness that the public will stand for abstract movement only in small doses,[17] and music visualization choreographies do in fact reveal a non-constant relationship between movement and molar musical qualities, as Stephanie Jordan has pointed out.[18] Choreomusical congruity, though, reflects the type of information we are essentially hardwired to attend to from our earliest age. Infant attention is strongly drawn to anomalous perceptual phenomena, such as objects that appear to violate principles of physics. This reflects an innate cognitive imperative in humans to attempt to infer the structural coherence of complex intersensory events. However, infants' preferential attention to *amodal* stimuli (redundant across multiple senses), such as a toy bouncing in rhythm with a recurring sound, also indicates a preference for information that reflects "real-world" perceptual events.[19]

While amodal percepts ratify our everyday world, complex structured systems of co-occurring visual and sonic events offer themselves perceptually in terms of potential patterns. Eleanor Gibson, who in the 1960s applied James J. Gibson's ecological theory of perception to the study of perceptual development in infants and toddlers, held that the perceptual learning of children, as well as adults, is characterized by a process of increasing ability to differentiate more specified levels of stimulation.[20] Lorraine Bahrick and George Hollich agree, holding that amodal information serves as a "framework" for later perception.[21] In other words, as we mature we progress from being able to perceive global, abstract qualities of information, such as amodality, to being able to discern more refined levels of information about both objects and events. Patterns within events that are complex, but not overly so,[22] offer a challenge that heightens and sustains attention, tapping the brain's innate and culturally inflected tendencies to parse the emergent flow of events into comprehensible occurrences or correct predictions.[23] In between these dual attentional drives—the evolutionary reward of ratified prediction and the provocativeness of novelty—we may find a clue to our fraught relationship with the amodality of strict, mickey-mousing style music visualization. Choreomusical congruency is a perceptual fundamental taken to the extreme, but one that fails to sustain interest over time. It is understandable then that music visualization's novelty wore off quickly, giving way to more complex pairings of music and movement.

And indeed what followed was an extended period of choreographic experimentation fueled by new paradigms in both music and art. As musical complexity evoked increased choreographic complexity, counterpoint emerged as a means to bring the music and dance into a satisfying augmentative relationship—one in which, as Balanchine quipped, audiences could "see the music and hear the dance," but not in a consistently linear manner. Ballet and modern dance works across the mid-twentieth century sustained attention not only through high levels of choreographic and dancerly skill but also through choreomusical intricacy, and the perceptual experimentation of postmodern dance is still quite evident in much contemporary dance that has followed. This includes the choreographic strategy of improvisation, which shifts the dancer's role from choreographic interpreter to real-time co-creator. The free improvisation explored in the 1960s and 1970s largely gave way to more structured improvisations. In much of Forsythe's work, improvisational modalities are developed and refined in rehearsal, but their actual molecular execution is determined by the dancer in the moment of performance. The specifics of choreomusical relation in his choreographies that involve improvisation are likewise emergent, involving not only the dancers but also collaborating live musicians as agents.

(E)MERGE: VISUOSONIC COUNTERPOINT

Counterpoint is described in music theory as involving two distinct and simultaneous vectors—"vertical" or harmonic relationships between components and "horizontal" melodic relationships between lines that are to some degree independent of each other. Anne Holmes, analyzing the structure of Mallarmé's poem "L'Après-Midi d'un Faune" from a musical perspective in order to draw parallels between musical and literary form, points out that

> the listener to musical counterpoint is encouraged to 'listen horizontally,' that is, to hear two or more separate strands individually and, only when the distinctness of each has been registered by the mind, to consider their combined effect vertically.[24]

Similarly, Hilda Hollis, in her analysis of the counterpoint of rhythm and meaning in Gerard Manley Hopkins' poem "The Windhover," notes, "The concept of counterpoint directs us to see contradiction rather than immanent meaning."[25] These views highlight how counterpoint divides attention between perceptual units and differing means of parsing structure. Forsythe's vocal choreography, which I discuss in Chap. 11, enables perceptual dialogue between sonic and visual simultaneities, generating linkages, contrasts, and extrapolations that produce relational structures both within and across the two modalities.

Forsythe and his ensemble began investigating counterpoint dance structure early in the Ballett Frankfurt's second decade. In describing this key choreographic parameter as "one way of providing organization without narration,"[26] Forsythe shows a recognition of the principle of counterpoint, commonly associated almost exclusively with music, as fundamental across further forms of art and design.[27] He is, however, not the only one to hold this extended view. Robert Enggass, who analyzes instances of visual counterpoint in Venetian Barocchetto painting, notes how Tiepolo and other artists of the period, rather than "echoing" Baroque figural arrangements of figures by placing them within Baroque architecture, instead combine them with classical architecture. In doing so, Enggass explains, the work of the Barocchetto period "interweaves the two distinct rhythms (not unlike the use of counterpoint or the combining of two different melodies in a musical composition) so as to achieve an effect that is made up of both."[28] In other words, by combining the diverse aesthetics of the two periods, painters of the Venetian Settecento created sets of contrasts that produce a contrapuntal blend of styles.

The ideas voiced by Enggass above are certainly applicable to the visual aspects of Forsythe's earlier works, which could be said to have effected an inversion of the Barocchetto by framing classical dance form with "Baroque" architectures of extension and complexity. However, while the use of the term *visual counterpoint* provides an indication of the spatio-temporal nature of visual attention that is fully adequate to the perceptual experience of static visual arts such as painting and photography, Forsythe's usage of the term with reference to dance fails to fully capture the dynamic and ephemeral "horizontal" aspect of the perception of dance and other temporally unfolding art forms such as music and literature. Additionally, the monosensory limitations of the concept of *visual counterpoint* downplay the presence of the auditory in art forms such as dance and film.

Is counterpoint actually perceived across different perceptual modalities? In 1929, Russian film pioneer Sergei Eisenstein signaled the importance of contrapuntality between visual image and sound for the development of new techniques of montage by positing spatio-temporal counterpoint as a characteristic occurrence in cinema. Though intermodal, he nonetheless describes it as visual:

> In the moving image (cinema) we have, so to speak, a synthesis of two counterpoints - the spatial counterpoint of graphic art, and the temporal counterpoint of music.
>   Within cinema, and characterizing it, occurs what may be described as: *visual counterpoint.*[29]

In a landmark essay written one year prior in response to the advent of sound film, Eisenstein, together with Vsevolod Pudovkin and Grigori Alexandrov, states that

> ONLY A CONTRAPUNTAL USE of sound in relation to the visual montage piece will afford a new potentiality of montage and perfection.
>   THE FIRST EXPERIMENTAL WORK WITH SOUND MUST BE DIRECTED ALONG THE LINE OF ITS DISTINCT NONSYNCHRONIZATION WITH THE VISUAL IMAGES. And only

such an attack will give the necessary palpability which will later lead to the creation of an ORCHESTRAL COUNTERPOINT of visual and aural images.[30]

The choice of the term *orchestral* to describe the asynchronous structuring of relationships between visual and auditory information indicates the musicality and "polyvocality" perceived by the authors between the two perceptual modalities. Forsythe's description of dance as "a kind of music—maybe a visual music"—similarly reflects perceptual linkages between kinetic events and musical structure.[31] Thus, the term *visuosonic counterpoint* offers a more applicable expression of the relational structures favored by both Forsythe and Eisenstein.

The statement above by Eisenstein and colleagues resonates with White's thinking about image-sound synchrony of the mickey-mousing type. For her, though, the use of the term counterpoint to describe relationships between different sensory streams poses problems, in that

[e]ven in dance, where the phenomenon of live performance and the relatively more abstract use of materials is much more "musical" than the succession of frames in a film, the notion of counterpoint remains awkward. While there may be counterpoint within the dance or within the music, there can be no counterpoint *between* them, because counterpoint presumes voices or bodies interacting in the same plane.[32]

White agrees here with film theorist Michel Chion, who argues that

If there exists something one can call audiovisual counterpoint, it occurs under conditions quite different from musical counterpoint. The latter exclusively uses notes—all the same raw material—while sound and image fall into different sensory categories. If there's any sense at all to the analogy, audiovisual counterpoint implies an "auditory voice" perceived horizontally in tandem with the visual track, a voice that possesses its own formal individuality.

What I wish to show is that films tend to exclude the possibility of such horizontal-contrapuntal dynamics. Quite to the contrary: in the cinema, harmonic and vertical relations...are generally more salient—i.e., the relations between a given sound and what is happening at that moment in the image. So to speak about counterpoint in the cinema is therefore to borrow a notion somewhat wrongheadedly, applying an intellectual speculation rather than a workable concept.[33]

In reducing music to "notes," however, Chion neglects to recognize the wide range of relational possibilities within sound production itself, which include not only temporality but also dynamics, pitch, and timbre. It is precisely the perceptual linkages between these auditory qualities and their visual counterparts—the dimensional correspondences that are highlighted in intermodal perception and manifested in synesthetic metaphor—that underpin intermodal counterpoint and confirm its possibility.

A 2006 paper by composer/musician Allen Fogelsanger and choreographer and cognitive researcher Kathleya Afanador applies research on monomodal and intermodal perception to examine the mechanisms that might underpin the perception of relatedness between dance and its accompanying music.[34] As they emphasize, true multimodal incongruence stands at odds with the cognitive tendency to form perceptual unities out of discrete perceptual events that exhibit coincidental structural elements. Citing research on the "McGurk effect," in which the pairing of the sound of a spoken syllable (e.g., "ba") with a video of a mouth saying a different syllable (e.g., "ga") can lead to the experience of an entirely different syllable being uttered (e.g., "da"),[35] they speculate that this optimizing model of percept combination across the senses underpins a crossmodal "capture" in which sound can influence visual perception and vice versa. This can occur in more abstract representations as well, such as the movement or collision of geometric figures. The authors argue that crossmodal capture through perceptual congruencies may underlie our experience of a fit between sound and movement.

Despite differences in the details, the research above collectively lends support to the concept of visuosonic counterpoint. Both the gestural behavior that automatically accompanies speech and the synesthetic metaphors we derive to describe object and event qualities (onomatopoeic expressions such as "pow" or "bling") demonstrate routine ways in which humans perform and perceive audio-visual correlations. When speaking, we compose and coordinate our actions and our vocalizations in order to enhance communicative clarity and generate varieties of expressive affect. In choreographic structures such as those derived by Forsythe, the visual and sonic elements of communication are raw materials for the production of compositional interplays that performatively merge the senses of vision and audition.

Forsythe's work foregrounds the phenomenological, embodied moment of the experience of dancing over reflective elaboration of narrative or conceptual meaning. One key means by which Forsythe accomplishes this focusing of attention on the moment of performance is by saturating environments with concurrent loci of action and co-occurring sounds. As discussed in Chap. 5, Lehmann holds that the simultaneous presentation of multiplicities of signs causes an inevitable "parcelling of perception"[36] that engenders two responses in the spectator. Through encouragement of a calm but rapid contemplation, simultaneity opens perception to the possibility of connections, relations, and the appearance of clues at any given moment. However, the simultaneity of theatrical events renders the viewer both unable to process the totality of information presented and perceptually overstrained by the effort to take in as much of it as possible. As well, informational saturation in Forsythe's works occurs at both the level of the individual performer and the ensemble, with performers generating complex logical systems of relation across different parts of their own bodies while also moving in complex spatial and temporal relation to other performers. The overstrain that this complexity generates elicits an emotional response driven not by narrative content but instead by the spectator's reaction to the limitations of their own perception.[37]

Choreomusical congruencies are highly evident within Forsythe's "ballet ballets" choreographed to rhythmic music, especially those made for companies other than the Ballett Frankfurt or Forsythe Company. Forsythe seems to revel in the possibilities of inventively reflecting music through movement in works including *New Sleep* (1987 for the San Francisco Ballet), *In the Middle, Somewhat Elevated* (1987 for the Paris Opera Ballet), *the second detail* (1991 for the National Ballet of Canada), *Herman Schmerman* (1992 for the New York City Ballet), and the more recent *Blake Works I* (2016 for the Paris Opera Ballet), *Playlist (Track 1, 2)* (2018 for the English National Ballet) and *(EP)* verison (2019 for Boston Ballet), and *Blake Works II, III, IV, and V: The Barre Project* (2021–2023 for a handpicked ensemble, Boston Ballet, Dance Theatre of Harlem, and Ballet Company of Teatro alla Scala, respectively). *The Vertiginous Thrill of Excatitude*, created for the Ballett Frankfurt in 1996 as one of "Two Ballets in the Manner of the Late Twentieth Century," is an exultant, over-the-top display of choreographic musicality that pays homage to both influential classical choreographer Marius Petipa and to Balanchine's neoclassicism.

In other works or sections of works set to rhythmic music, however, movement interacts with music as a more independent visual "voice" in a contrapuntal intermodal fugue. Based around the idea of ballet as a displaying of and calling attention to different parts of the body, the choreography of Forsythe's chamber work *Trio* (1996) wittily reflects Beethoven's counterpoint through movement that sometimes "sings" notes or phrases of the dominant melody but at other times reflects less prominent counterpointed voices within the string quartet. Watching rehearsals of *Trio*, I noted how Forsythe sang along to the first violin's main melody at the opening of Beethoven's minuet—"Daaaa, da-da-da-da-da"—then added a "boom" that corresponded to a movement accent on a note from the second violin at the end of the phrase.[38] Just as instances of contrapuntal relation emerge fleetingly among the instruments as the minuet continues, instances of visuosonic counterpoint emerge as the dancers move to it.

Forsythe stages a more pronounced and equally wry counterpoint in an early section of *I don't believe in outer space* (2008). Here a performer (Christopher Roman in the work's premiere season) with large balls of gaffer tape down the back of his sweatpants improvises a "butt dance" with his back to the audience, strutting and skimming across the floor and popping his hips to a repeating sample of long bass tones and a quiet snare drum riff. As he moves, dappled twilight picks out and obscures his comically augmented buttocks and footwork. Rehearsing this improvised modality, Forsythe would sing an irregular counterpoint against the smooth bassline and relatively even *rat-a-tat* of the snare ("Um ka, ka, ka ki ka um ka, kakakakaka..."), indicating the contrapuntal rhythm he wished to see across the performer's footwork and backside. Simultaneously, Fabrice Mazliah performs a rhythmically detached "tourist" dance, moving in his own time and oblivious to the music's pulse. Willems' sample loop is overlaid first by the voice of Tilman O'Donnell providing a guttural, irregularly timed recitation of the opening of Gloria Gaynor's pop song "I Will Survive" and then by Dana Caspersen's slow intonation of lines from Cat Stevens' "Wild World." The scene continues to build in complexity as two further dancers enter with different movement dynamics. Thom Willems, playing live in performance, provides each with a "voice" that joins the musical fugue: irregular flute phrases for Roberta Mosca's prancing entrance and twisting, angular movement, and sparse, slapsticky sound effects for Cyril Baldy's skittering attempts to grab balls of gaffer tape littering the stage.

Simultaneity pervades the multiple movement and sound dynamics and loci of voices and action in the works above. Their visuosonic counterpoint permits a reappraisal of Lehmann's evaluation of this key "trait" of postdramatic theatre. When we experience theatrical simultaneity, he notes, "A systematic double-bind arises: we are meant to pay attention to the concrete particular and at the same time perceive the totality."[39] The listening viewer confronted with counterpointed fugues of movement and sound is deliberately made aware of the fragmentary character of perception that everyday conscious experience typically disavows. Faced with an unavoidable apportionment of perception, and in the absence of structuring narrative, viewer-listeners organize their experience through a lossy selective attention to events, generating their experience of the work from whatever presented signs they apprehend. However, as Lehmann explains, this organizing process also "remains an aesthetic of 'meaning in retreat'" since it requires the observer to focus on the individual sub-units of structure as they emerge and to defer reflective thought on meaning to a later time.[40] In this, Lehmann agrees with Holmes and of Hollis, who similarly note counterpoint structuring's encouragement of focus on immediate events and delaying of holistic processing of the larger event.

Other instances of Forsythe movement counterpoints are bewildering in their complexity in and of themselves. The seven-group fugue that opens "Bongo Bongo Nageela" (described in Chap. 5) is a highly rhythmic rendering of its accompanying music (Willems' synthesizer version of a Beethoven *presto*). As the 32 identically clad "schoolgirls" cheekily power through a vast array of moves to a cha-cha beat, the eye flickers over the ensemble, catching a kick here, a slow turn there, flashed underpants or a high-five to a groupmate, or an energetic boogaloo. Forsythe's *One Flat Thing, reproduced* (2000), set to a tense, nonrhythmic soundscore by Willems, is a choreographic reflection of Francis Spufford's description of the technologies of the British Antarctic Expedition as "a baroque machinery."[41] When Forsythe read this phrase, as he comments,

it was a kind of epiphany for me. I thought, 'What would epitomize the Baroque?' For me it's the technique of musical counterpoint. And what would constitute organizational counterpoint that did not depend on music? That struck me as a viable point of departure.[42]

Erin Manning responds to this work by evoking Deleuze's view of the Baroque as an operative function of folding and twisting of cultural influences. In her analysis, *One Flat Thing, reproduced* "is baroque in its emphasis on counterpoint's capacity to create tendencies for aligning and cueing that create folds, not just bodies folding but spacetime folding."[43] This folding of spacetime points squarely to the cognitive function of association and its contingency on memory: while counterpoint can take the form of mimicry, as in the violin line of Beethoven's *presto*, it can also manifest as relational "commentary" on unfolding lines of sound, as in the extrapolations of jazz musicians. This relationality, which we recognize/ re-cognize through the simultaneous feedback of our recollection of percepts, can also be amodal or intermodal.

Forsythe's engagement with visuosonic counterpoint dance structuring subsumes numerous aspects of his *re-viewing* and *re-presentation* of the conventions of classical ballet, including the form's prioritization of verticality, the rotation and codified configuration of limbs, the spatial organization of steps, and the relation of movement to music. However, the improvisational possibilities of differentially producing and coordinating the distinct mechanics, trajectories, and dynamics of simultaneous movement events inhere not only in ballet but in all codified movement forms. In *One Flat Thing, reproduced* and other works, temporal, spatial, and dynamic linkages between movement events take the form of concurrent alignments or "hookups,"[44] or of sequential relations produced by individual bodies or occurring across those of ensemble members. In rehearsal, Forsythe carefully tunes the relations between harmonic and dissonant relational possibilities, optimizing contrapuntal complexity by encouraging translatory variance in referential responses. Performers attend to the form and dynamics of movements and the timing of structures resulting from specific task situations, localizing opportunities for action that, critically, exhibits varying degrees of temporal or formal linkage to other single or multiple events. This variance keeps the attentive search for "traces of connection" active—a search that according to Lehmann "is accompanied by a helpless focusing of perception on the things offered (maybe they will at some moment reveal their secret)."[45] As they move, the performers also take care to afford contrapuntal opportunities to others in the ensemble. Particular emphasis is given to inserting pauses in the flow of action, which not only provides others time to respond but which also creates phrasal or "musical" structure in the flow of events (Forsythe has frequently noted that the critique he most often gives to the ensemble is "Don't forget to stop"). Within the parameters of each improvisational task, the ensemble produces a range of balance between quasi-congruency and more pronounced difference, as well as between immediate and more delayed response—a zone of performance, constrained by tacit and shared knowledge of event perception, within which actions diverge parametrically from their referents while still affording the discernment of structural coherence.

Forsythe has also set choreography to soundscores that layer *vocal choreography* (discussed in Chap. 11) over atmospheric soundscapes including drones (discussed in Chap. 7) or music with irregular rhythms. In these instances, movement counterpoint emerges in relation to both the vocal soundscore layer supplied by performers and the electronic soundscore, which in numerous cases is also played responsively in real time by a composer-musician. In *Heterotopia* (2006), for example, Willems' score of long, soft, trumpet-like tones underscores a scene in which Fabrice Mazliah orates and gesticulates dramatically in a nonce language[46] atop the tables that comprise the set of one of the work's two performance spaces. With his parading gestures, bellowing pseudo-rhetoric, and the occasional blatting raspberry, he "conducts" three women standing on the ground who produce a responsive counterpoint of specifically oblique angles with their arms and upper bodies. The women translate Mazliah's verbal and gestural output into streams of angular, punctuated movement and vertical jumps, which they also set into counterpoint with one another and with different sounds being produced simultaneously by other performers. In a series of scenes in the 2011 work *Sider*, the audiovisuality of counterpoint is partially obscured in line with the work's overarching dramaturgy: the dancers move in relation to recorded scenes from a filmed production of *Hamlet* that only they can hear via earphones.[47] The audience hears and apprehends connections to Willems' irregularly pulsing score, which is also heard by the dancers, and the pulsing light from Spencer Finch's array of tube lighting.

Cognitive semiotician and aesthetics scholar Per Aage Brandt proposes a model of the neuro-semantic economy of meaning construction that departs in important ways from Lehmann's understanding of simultaneity in aesthetic perception. In Brandt's model, which theorizes the production of aesthetic affect, meaning is simultaneously organized on five non-hierarchical strata to which we can attend selectively or simultaneously: the levels of sensation (qualia), perception (objects), apperception (situations), reflection (notions), and affect (emotions). The processes of organizing meaning thus do not constitute linear, integrative "assembly lines" that culminate over and over again at the level of abstract or reflective thinking. Instead, Brandt claims, mental construction is "sloppy," involving overlays of attention that occur in nonstrict orders. Critically for aesthetic perception, this mental economy involves excesses of perceptual material produced at the input levels and remaining unelaborated and unintegrated into higher-order strata. Brandt holds that this unintegrated material, which calls for completion by virtue of its unsubsumed status, is experienced as particularly salient within the aesthetic context.[48] This notion of simultaneous organization of meaning across different levels of cognition complicates Lehmann's view of spectators' search for connections and inability to parse the totality of events. On the other hand, Brandt's emphasis on the salience of input-level information resonates with Holmes' and Hollis' notions of how counterpoint directs focus to the emergent, phenomenal structuring of events.

In Forsythe's works, counterpoint can be either *intra*modal, involving either purely visual or sonic linkages, or *inter*modal, with sonic gestures reflecting rhythmic, dynamic, structural qualities of movements or vice versa. Importantly, our parsing of visuosonic counterpoint involves two separate sensory channels, only one of which—vision—requires overt physical action. Due to the limited spatial scope of the visual apparatus, visual uptake is primarily an active serial process necessitating scopic shifts and the relinquishment of one attentional target in favor of another. Our ears, by contrast, are fundamentally passive and global receivers, favoring "no particular 'point of view.'"[49] Intermodal visual-aural perception runs in parallel, integrating the covert and overt perception of differently sensing systems. Thus, while visuosonic counterpoint does increase the complexity of perceptual information in the performance environment, the constant variance in the merging of the senses evokes procedural transitions and overlaps.

Since both intramodal and intermodal connections between percepts can occur, visuosonic counterpoint thus creates a different kind of "double bind" in which intermodal perceptual uptake competes with the serial process of visual target selection. This simultaneous presence of multiple counterpoint modalities heightens perceptual awareness and contributes to the evocation of what Lehmann, referencing a term used by Freud, delineates as an "evenly hovering attention" (*gleichschwebende Aufmerksamkeit*) that remains open for the potential occurrence of connections from any source or along any dimension.[50] In Forsythe's performance installations *Heterotopia* and *You made me a monster* (2005), in which audiences are able to move around the performance space, attention is scaled up from covert observation into overt action, which renders their performance of perception visible to others. In doing so, these works divide attention yet again, between performer activity and audience activity.

As a performative mode of presentation, Forsythe's contrapuntal choreographic simultaneity differs from the brief scenes of "noisy" perceptual overload discussed in Chap. 8. While chaotic sound and action-scapes assault and overwhelm the senses, the visuosonic musicality of contrapuntal simultaneity partners the ear with the eye, affording connection across the two sensory modes but also increasing the potential for connections to be discerned. The division of attention between atomistic and holistic qualities of visual, sonic, and visuosonic presentation strategically intensifies audience attention, as well as that of the performers—including co-improvising musicians—who, in the case of Forsythe's improvised modalities, face an expanded and emergent field of compositional options. Dancing in partnership with others exponentially broadens the attentional demand on the performers, and by extension on those watching and listening.[51]

Visuosonic counterpoint thus choreographically merges both performer and audience sensing within and across modes, and in doing so invites attention to both choreomusical composition and the performances of perception carried out by performers and those attending. As such, it is both inherently reflexive and performative. The two following chapters detail how this key extension of Forsythe's experimental inquiry into the perceptual economies of dancing *as* music was carried further forward when his dancers became moving producers of sound, contributing their voices and audible actions to the soundscores and choreo-scenographies of his works.

NOTES

1. See Andrea Ravignani, "Rhythm and synchrony in animal movement and communication." For a study of movement synchronization to music observed in a Sulphur-crested cockatoo (*Cacatua gallerita eleanora*), see A.D. Patel et al., "Experimental evidence for synchronization to a musical beat in a nonhuman animal."
2. Vittorio Gallese et al., "Action recognition in the premotor cortex," and Giacomo Rizzolatti et al., "Premotor cortex and the recognition of motor actions"; M. Heiser et al., "The essential role of Broca's area in imitation," S.H Johnson-Frey et al., "Actions or hand-object interactions? Human inferior frontal cortex and action observation," and D.R. Lametti et al., "Mirror neurons and the lateralization of human language." See also Alvin Liberman, "On finding that speech is special," and Alvin Liberman and Ignatius Mattingly, "The motor theory of speech perception revised."

3. See Émile Jaques-Dalcroze, *Rhythm, Music, and Education*; Eduard Sievers, *Ziele und Wege der Schallanalyse*, Gustav Becking, *Der musikalische Rhythmus als Erkenntnisquelle*; Alesander Truslit, *Gestaltung und Bewegung in der Musik*; and Sergei Eisenstein, "A Dialectic Approach to Film Form."

4. Daniel Levitin and Anna Tirovalas, "Current Advances in the Cognitive Neuroscience of Music," 218.

5. Sally Banes, "Dancing [with/to/before/on/in/after/ against/away from/without] Music: Vicissitudes of Collaboration in American Postmodern Choreography."

6. See Stephanie Jordan, "Choreomusical conversations: Facing a double challenge," n.2.

7. Lincoln Kirstein, *Movement and Metaphor: Four Centuries of Ballet*, 194.

8. By contrast, Nijinsky's choreography for *Le Sacre du Printemps* (1913) stamps out Stravinsky's contrasting rhythms, motifs, and dynamics with an urgent choreomusical congruency, underscoring the demand of the sacrifice thematic. The work caused a near riot at its premiere, with the audience at the Théâtre des Champs-Élysée becoming so rowdy that the dancers could not hear score. It probably did not help that the evening opened with Fokine's lilting, poetic *Les Sylphides* (1909), with music by Chopin.

9. Juliet Bellow, "Dance in Debussy's Paris: Re-figuring Art and Music," 55.

10. See Merce Cunningham, "Space, time and dance."

11. See Stephanie Jordan, "Ted Shawn's Music Visualizations."

12. Ruth St. Denis, "Music Visualization." See also Suzanne Shelton, *Ruth St. Denis: A Biography of the Divine Dancer*.

13. See Hanna Järvinen, "Kinesthesia, Synesthesia and Le Sacre du Printemps: Responses to Dance Modernism," 82.

14. Inger Damsholt, "Mark Morris, Mickey Mouse, and the Choreomusical Polemic," 7.

15. Barbara White, "'As if they didn't hear the music,' Or: How I Learned to Stop Worrying and Love Mickey Mouse," 66.

16. Ibid., 68–73. By comparison, Hanna Walsdorf's discussion of mickey-mousing returns to dance performance in cartoons, analyzing Hyacinth Hippo's dainty "divertissement" among a *corps de ballet* of ostriches in Walt Disney's 1940 film *Fantasia*. Using a film analysis model developed by Georg Maas, Walsdorf notes overlaps and common points of reference, as she ties mickey-mousing to Maas' category of connotative semantics. "Minutage und Mickey Mousing. Über das Verhältnis von Ballett- und Filmmusik am Beispiel von Disney's *Fantasia* (1940)."

17. Ruth St. Denis in Cohen, 132.

18. Stephanie Jordan, "Ted Shawn's Music Visualizations," 36, 41.

19. In Elizabeth Spelke's pioneering studies of intermodal perception, infants were presented with video images of two toy animals bouncing at different rates, accompanied by a recorded sound corresponding to the impacts of one of the animals but not the other. The infants tested preferentially looked at the toy whose impacts were in synchrony with the sound rather than the out-of-sync stimulus. "Infants' intermodal perception," and "Perceiving bimodally specified events in infancy."

20. Eleanor Gibson & Anne Pick, *An ecological approach to perceptual learning and development.*

21. Lorraine Bahrick & George Hollich, "Intermodal perception."

22. Advancing from ideas originally espoused by Wilhelm Wundt (1832–1920) about the relationship between stimulus complexity and arousal, Daniel Berlyne developed a theory that hedonic value rises with stimulus novelty, but only up to a point. Too much complexity, according to this model, leads to a precipitous drop in pleasure.

23. See Alain Berthoz, *The Brain's Sense of Movement.*

24. Anne Holmes, "Counterpoint in Mallarmé's '*L'Après-Midi d'un Faune*,'" n.6.

25. Hilda Hollis, "Another Bird? Counterpoint in 'The Windhover'" 441.

26. Quoted in Sulcas, "Kinetic Isometries," 9.

27. Discussion with *Synchronous Objects* team members and the author, 16 May 2007.

28. Robert Enggass, "Visual Counterpoint in Venetian Settecento Painting," 96.

29. Sergei Eisenstein, "A Dialectic Approach to Film Form," 52.

30. "A Statement," signed by Sergei Eisenstein, Vsevolod Pudovkin, and Grigori Alexandrov (1928), in Eisenstein, *Film Form.*

31. Forsythe in conversation with the ensemble, March 13, 2008.

32. Barbara White, "'As If,'" 74.

33. Michel Chion, *Audio-Vision: Sound on Screen*, 36.

34. Allen Fogelsanger and Kathleya Afandour, "Parameters of Perception: Vision, Audition, and Twentieth-Century Music and Dance."

35. Harry McGurk and John MacDonald, "Hearing Lips and Seeing Voices."

36. Hans-Thies Lehmann, *Postdramatic Theatre*, 87.

37. Ibid., 149–151.

38. For a detailed analysis of *Trio*, see Elizabeth Waterhouse, "Choreographic Re-mix. William Forsythe's Trio (1996) and Beethoven's String Quartet No. 15 in a Minor Op. 132."

39. Lehmann, *Postdramatic Theatre*, 88.

40. Lehmann, *Postdramatic Theatre*, 88.

41. Francis Spufford, *I May Be Some Time: Ice and the English Imagination.*

42. Forsythe quoted in Roslyn Sulcas, "Drawing Movement's Connections."

43. Erin Manning, *Always More Than One: Individuation's Dance*, 103.

44. Forsythe's term.
45. Lehmann, *Postdramatic Theatre*, 84.
46. Nonce languages share the phonetic, morphological, rhythmic, tonal, and sometimes semantic characteristics of real languages but are comprehended as either near or complete gibberish. Nonce words are found in Lewis Carroll's poem "Jabberwocky" (e.g., *tulgey*) and in numerous works by James Joyce (e.g., *chelaship, wegebobble*). See Chap. 11 on vocal choreography in this volume.
47. In these scenes, the dancers also respond to stop-and-go commands and other directives from Forsythe that they hear via their earphones. For a detailed analysis of *Sider*, see Freya Vass-Rhee, "Haunted by Hamlet: William Forsythe's *Sider*."
48. Per Aage Brandt, "Form and Meaning in Art."
49. Marshall McLuhan and Quentin Fiore, *The Medium is the Message: An Inventory of Effects*, 111.
50. Lehmann, *Postdramatic Theatre*, 87.
51. Pil Hansen's fine-grained analysis of two scenes from Forsythe's *Whole in the Head* (2010) is informative in this regard.

BIBLIOGRAPHY

Bahrick, L.E., and G. Hollich. 2008. Intermodal Perception. In *Encyclopedia of Infant and Early Childhood Development 2*, ed. M. Haith and J. Benson, 164–176. Amsterdam and London: Elsevier Ltd. and Academic Press.

Banes, Sally. 1994. Dancing [with/to/before/on/in/after/against/away from/ without] Music: Vicissitudes of Collaboration in American Postmodern Choreography. In *Writing Dancing in the Age of Postmodernism*, 310–326. Hannover and London: Wesleyan University Press.

Becking, Gustav. 1928. *Der musikalische Rhythmus als Erkenntnisquelle*. Augsburg: Benno Filser.

Bellow, Juliet. 2012. Dance in Debussy's Paris: Re-figuring Art and Music. In *Debussy's Paris: Art, Music and the Sounds of the City*, ed. Linda Muehlig, 46–61. Northampton, MA: Smith College Museum of Art.

Berlyne, D.E. 1970. Novelty, Complexity, and Hedonic Value. *Perception & Psychophysics* 8 (5): 279–286.

Berthoz, Alain. 2002. *The Brain's Sense of Movement*. Translated by Giselle Weiss. Cambridge, MA: Harvard University Press.

Brandt, Per Aage. 2006. Form and Meaning in Art. In *The Artful Mind: Cognitive Science and the Riddle of Human Creativity*, ed. Mark Turner, 171–188. Oxford: Oxford University Press.

Chion, Michel. 1994. *Audio-Vision: Sound on Screen*. Translated by Claudia Gorbman. New York: Columbia University Press.

Cunningham, Merce. 1952. Space, Time and Dance. *Transformation* 1 (3): 150–151.

Damsholt, Inger. 1993. Mark Morris, Mickey Mouse, and the Choreomusical Polemic. *The Opera Quarterly* 22 (1): 4–21.

Eisenstein, Sergei. 1949. A Dialectic Approach to Film Form. In *Film Form: Essays in Film Theory*, trans. Jay Leyda. New York: Harcourt.

Enggass, Robert. 1982. Visual Counterpoint in Venetian Settecento Painting. *The Art Bulletin* 64 (1): 89–97.

Fogelsanger, Allen, and Kathleya Afanador. 2006. Parameters of Perception: Vision, Audition, and Twentieth-Century Music and Dance. In *Continuing Dance Culture Dialogues: Southwest Borders and Beyond*, Proceedings of the 38th International Conference of the Congress on Research in Dance, 56–65. Congress on Research in Dance.

Gallese, V., L. Fadiga, L. Fogassi, and G. Rizzolatti. 1996. Action Recognition in the Premotor Cortex. *Brain* 119 (2): 593–609.

Gibson, Eleanor, and Anne Pick. 2003. *An Ecological Approach to Perceptual Learning and Development*. New York: Oxford University Press.

Hansen, Pil. 2022. Learning Whole in the Head: Forsythe. In *Performance Generating Systems in Dance: Dramaturgy, Psychology, Performativity*, 51–69. Bristol and Chicago: Intellect.

Heiser, M., M. Iacoboni, F. Maeda, J. Marcus, and J.C. Mazziotta. 2003. The Essential Role of Broca's Area in Imitation. *European Journal of Neuroscience* 17 (5): 1123–1128.

Hollis, Hilda. 2002. Another Bird? Counterpoint in 'The Windhover'. *Victorian Poetry* 40 (4): 433–443.

Holmes, Anne. 2003. Counterpoint in Mallarmé's '*L'Après-Midi d'un Faune*'. *French Studies* 57 (1): 27–37.

Järvinen, Hanna. 2006. Kinesthesia, Synesthesia and *Le Sacre du Printemps*: Responses to Dance Modernism. *The Senses and Society* 1 (1): 71–92.

Johnson-Frey, S.H., F.R. Maloof, R. Newman-Norlund, C. Farrer, S. Inati, and S.T. Grafton. 2003. Actions or Hand-Object Interactions? Human Inferior Frontal Cortex and Action Observation. *Neuron* 39 (6): 1053–1058.

Jordan, Stephanie. 1984. Ted Shawn's Music Visualizations. *Dance Chronicle* 7 (1): 33–49.

———. 2011. Choreomusical Conversations: Facing a Double Challenge. *Dance Research Journal* 43 (1): 43–64.

Kirstein, Lincoln. 1970. *Movement and Metaphor: Four Centuries of Ballet*. New York: Praeger.

Lametti, D.R., and A.A.G. Mattar. 2006. Mirror Neurons and the Lateralization of Human Language. *Journal of Neuroscience* 26 (25): 6666–6667.

Lehmann, Hans-Thies. 2006. *Postdramatic Theatre*. Translated by Karen Jürs-Munby. Abingdon and New York: Routledge. Original version: Lehmann,

Hans-Thies. 1999. *Postdramatisches Theater*. Frankfurt am Main: Verlag der Autoren.

Levitin, Daniel, and Anna Tirovalas. 2009. Current Advances in the Cognitive Neuroscience of Music. In *The Year in Cognitive Neuroscience 2009*, ed. Michael Miller and Alan Kingstone, 211–231. Oxford: Wiley-Blackwell.

Liberman, Alvin. 1982. On Finding That Speech Is Special. *American Psychologist* 37 (1): 148–167.

Liberman, Alvin, and Ignatius Mattingly. 1985. The Motor Theory of Speech Perception Revised. *Cognition* 21 (1): 1–36.

Manning, Erin. 2013. *Always More Than One: Individuation's Dance*. Durham, NC: Duke University Press.

McGurk, Harry, and John MacDonald. 1976. Hearing Lips and Seeing Voices. *Nature* 264: 746–748.

McLuhan, Marshall, and Quentin Fiore. 1967. *The Medium Is the Message: An Inventory of Effects*. New York: Bantam Books.

Patel, A.D., J.R. Iversen, M.R. Bregman, and I. Schulz. 2009. Experimental Evidence for Synchronization to a Musical Beat in a Nonhuman Animal. *Current Biology* 19 (10): 827–830.

Ravignani, A. 2019. Rhythm and Synchrony in Animal Movement and Communication. *Current Zoology* 65 (1): 77–81.

Rizzolatti, G., L. Fadiga, V. Gallese, and L. Fogassi. 1996. Premotor Cortex and the Recognition of Motor Actions. *Cognitive Brain Research* 3 (2): 131–141.

Shelton, Suzanne. 1990. *Ruth St. Denis: A Biography of the Divine Dancer*. Austin: University of Texas Press.

Sievers, Eduard. 1924. *Ziele und Wege der Schallanalyse*. Heidelberg: Carl Winters Universitätsbuchhandlung.

Spelke, Elizabeth. 1979a. Infants' Intermodal Perception of Events. *Cognitive Psychology* 8 (4): 553–560.

———. 1979b. Perceiving Bimodally Specified Events in Infancy. *Developmental Psychology* 15 (6): 626–636.

Spufford, Francis. 1996. *I May Be Some Time: Ice and the English Imagination*. New York: St Martin's Press.

St. Denis, Ruth. 1925. Music Visualization. *The Denishawn Magazine* 1 (3): 1–3. Partially reprinted in *Dance as a Theatre Art*, ed. Selma Jeanne Cohen. Princeton NJ: Princeton Book Company.

Sulcas, Roslyn. 1995. Kinetic Isometries. Interview with William Forsythe. *Dance International* 23: 4–9.

———. 2009. Drawing Movement's Connections. *The New York Times*, 24 March. https://www.nytimes.com/2009/03/29/arts/dance/29sulc.html. Accessed 26 January 2010.

Truslit, Alexander. 1938. *Gestaltung und Bewegung in der Musik: Ein tönendes Buch vom musikalischen Vortrag und seinem bewegungserlebten Gestalten und Hören.* Berlin-Lichterfelde: Chr. Friedrich Vieweg.

Vass-Rhee, Freya. 2019. Haunted by Hamlet: William Forsythe's *Sider.* In *The Oxford Handbook of Shakespeare and Dance,* ed. Lynsey McCulloch and Brandon Shaw, 455–475. Oxford: Oxford University Press.

Walsdorf, Hanna. 2009. Minutage und Mickey Mousing. Über das Verhältnis von Ballett- und Filmmusik am Beispiel von Disney's *Fantasia* (1940). *Kieler Beiträge zur Filmmusikforschung* 3. http://www.filmmusik.uni-kiel.de/beitraege.htm. Accessed 28 October 2009.

Waterhouse, Elizabeth. 2019. Choreographic Re-mix. William Forsythe's *Trio* (1996) and Beethoven's String Quartet No. 15 in a Minor Op. 132. In *Rund um Beethoven. Interpretationsforschung heute,* ed. T. Gartmann and D. Allenbach, 487–504. Schliengen: Argus.

White, Barbara. 2006. 'As If They Didn't Hear the Music,' Or: How I Learned to Stop Worrying and Love Mickey Mouse. *The Opera Quarterly* 22 (1): 65–89.

CHAPTER 10

Breath Scores and Corporeal Sounds: Dance as Symphony

Western concert dance has historically made little sound of its own. Dancers perform behind a sonic fourth wall of music emanating from the orchestra pit or from speakers at the portal and around the auditorium.[1] Onstage sounds are silenced as much as possible; pointe shoes are softened (often inadequately) and technique refined to avoid clatter, especially for the ethereal "white" scenes of Romantic ballet,[2] breath may visibly instigate movement but should itself be inaudible, and dancers mime sonic and vocal gestures, unless stamping or tapping feet, clapping hands, clicking heels, or jingling tambourines sonically mark otherness.[3] Nothing should perturb the image of effortless expression that the accompanying music's sonic purity literally underscores, and neither should the orchestra call attention to itself once the lights go down.[4]

If you have ever been seated in one of the front rows at a dance performance, though, you will certainly have heard the real sounds of dance worlds: feet and bodies contacting the floor, intakes and expulsions of breath, swishes of costumes and slidings of arms and legs, squeaks of rosined shoes, slapping grips or a sudden grunt or gasp due to a nearly missed lift, even occasional *sotto voce* counts, cues, or curses. Rehearsals are even noisier, with choreographers and dancers calling out steps and sections, counting or singing, and feeding back to themselves and each other.

The sounds made by dancing bodies remind us of what traditional Western dance performance and many other dance performance forms

© The Author(s), under exclusive license to Springer Nature Switzerland AG 2023
F. Vass, *William Forsythe's Postdramatic Dance Theater*, Cognitive Studies in Literature and Performance,
https://doi.org/10.1007/978-3-031-26658-4_10

obscure: that dancing bodies are laboring bodies and have never been silent. This chapter focuses on a small set of Forsythe's works in which he has deployed the corporeal sounds dancers make, using breath and action as musicalized soundscape elements. Attending to and experimenting with these sounds and their connections to movement and theatrical spaces offered performative visuosonic potentials to Forsythe, as did the "vocal choreography" I discuss in the subsequent chapter.

INTIMATE SCENOGRAPHIES

As musical conventions, theater architectures, and technologies changed over the twentieth century, sound became an avenue for experimentation not only for playwrights including Chekov, Maeterlinck, Brecht, Beckett, and many others, but also for mid- and late-century choreographers. Acousmatic (recorded) sound expanded the range of aural nuance available in the theater, offering seemingly unlimited possibilities to aggregate and alter live or recorded sounds, including text and ambient noise. Thanks to ever more refined amplification, sounds themselves could also be localized and set into motion in ways that enhanced attention to stage and auditorium space. In essence, sound became a choreographable partner to performers and to the increasingly agile visual space of the stage I have previously highlighted.

In addition to an "independent auditory semiotics," Lehmann signals a further sonic trait of postdramatic theatre that is distinct from visual manifestations: an increased overall musicalization of soundscoring.[5] Though Lehmann notes directors' engagement with electronically manipulated sounds, fragmented soundscores, and overlays of different "sonic worlds," his focus on "musical overdetermination" in postdramatic theatre centers on their inclusion of linguistically diverse spoken text.[6] However, directors and choreo-scenographers have also investigated the potentials of paralinguistic (non-speech) voicings that Klaus Scherer classifies as affect sounds or *affect bursts*.[7] They include unvoiced[8] sounds such as sighs, gasps, sniffs, snorts, clearing the throat, and tutting (dental clicks), as well as voiced nonlexical sounds like laughter, screams, vocal crying, and utterances like *mmm*, *hmm*, *ahh*, or *uhh*. As with language, these nonlexical utterances come to bear meaning through conventional use; meaning is also culture-specific in some cases, such as the relatively louder inhalation present in formal and polite Korean speech.[9] However, the affective valence of affect sounds remains "close to the body" due to their association with automatic or instinctive response states such as startle, surprise, sexual arousal, confusion, nervousness, and boredom or fatigue.

Though breath sounds, as well as pauses, are often overlooked in linguistic analyses, they are a pervasive feature of communication and serve key discursive functions. Steven Connor, whose linguistic-philosophical work has frequently addressed sound and the sounding body, notes,

> The unvoiced air moves between the significant and the senseless. In one sense, it is significance broken in upon by the merely phenomenal, unshaped air. But these occasions of incursion are in fact laced intricately through the fabric of speech. In this sense, voice is suffused by the voiceless.[10]

The duration and intensity of inhalation noises and length of pause, for example, are a factor in speech planning and provide information to listeners about the intended length and loudness of phrases that will follow.[11] Breathing behavior also changes under increased cognitive load and in response to emotional state, relative tension, and perceived coping ability.[12] Unvoiced breath "gestures" can convey meaning on their own without subsequent recourse to words, as anyone who has been the recipient of an isolated, heavy sigh can attest. Indeed, we often turn to these sonically shallow but semantically deep utterances when, as Sappho put it, no speaking is left in us. At such moments, we communicate on a purely embodied level, from our pulmonic-phrenic center.

A number of Forsythe's works contain scenes in which the qualities of breath gestures align with affect bursts described above. In the final moments of *Ricercar* (2003), two dancers' heaving shoulders and chests and spasming inhalations and exhalations evoke sobbing as they slowly walk and then seem to tumble down the stage diagonal to David Morrow's initially strident and then fading piano tones. A duet in *Heterotopia* (2006) is similarly punctuated by interludes in which a woman pants and gasps while her partner waits quietly behind her. *Angoloscuro* (2007), a work whose dramaturgy touches on Freud's theorization of "hysterical" physical symptoms, features exaggerated coughing, snoring, spitting, laughing, crying, and screaming, as well as barking and growling. In one ironic trio, a dancer "plays" the lungs of two other performers and his own, compressing them with his hands as if they were a set of three wheezing musical instruments.

While Forsythe's "ballet ballets" involve mostly set choreography to structurally clear music, his frequent use of soundscores with few easily parsable structural markers, together with his employment of choreo-graphic improvisation, has necessitated the development of innovative strategies for navigating time in performance. Many earlier works relied on "clock time," the use of digital time displays as an aid to navigate musical scores without easily distinguishable features. This system enables dancers to track upcoming soundscore shifts, initiate solos, or meet for "scheduled"[13] events such as duets. In some works, though, deliberate and audible breath sounds are utilized to facilitate temporal navigation. In an interview by Ann Nugent, Stuttgart ballet dancer Ludmilla Bogart recalls ensemble dancers in Forsythe's early work *In Endloser Zeit* (From the Most Distant Time) (1978) relying on breath sounds to coordinate their movements in the absence of music.[14] This likely first example of breath scoring in Forsythe's oeuvre reflects a strat-egy many dancers employ when called on to initiate unison movement in silence.

In the mid-1990s, Forsythe began to produce more works that involved only minimal sound accompaniment. Thom Willems also notes that his compositions became a less dominant factor during this time.[15] Temporal navigation, however, remained a concern. Forsythe choreographed several works in near-silence at this point that involve what he terms "breath scores" as a means to navigate choreographic space and time. The varied nomenclatures that have been applied to the sound palettes of these works (breath score, breath opera, breath song) are all somewhat misleading, as the soundscores include not only deliberate, emphasized breath sounds preceding or accompanying choreographed movements but also corporeal sounds ranging from footfall to slides, falls, or audible contact with the floor or set pieces.[16] Breath scores make it possible for dancers to track each other's progress through choreographic phrases by ear rather than solely by sight or through external sonic accompaniment.

Forsythe began amplifying the breath scores of some works as the result of a chance solution to an attentional problem. On tour in São Paolo in 2003, the Ballett Frankfurt performed two breath-scored pieces (*The Room as It Was* and *N.N.N.N.*) with quiet accompanying musical "fill-ins" that had been created the previous year. Niels Lanz and composer David Morrow recall that the premiere audience, unaccustomed to the extreme quiet of these pieces, made so much noise that the fill-ins were inaudible. For the second performance, Forsythe had the sound team position directional "shotgun" microphones in the front wings to amplify the onstage sounds. Scaling up the performers' breath gestures and the hushed sounds of footfall and limb against limb had the desired result: the second audience was quieter and more attentively focused. Amplification was retained in subsequent performances of these works and also added to *Duo*, in which two performers phase in and out of synchrony and complex counterpoint relations accompanied only by occasional faint, shimmering interpolations and quiet, fleeting baritone zooms by Willems.[17]

In addition to focusing audience attention, amplification of the breath score also enhances the intimacy of performances that are already quite intimate due to minimal or lacking music. The Latin root *intimāre* (to put or bring into, or to make known or make familiar) derives from *intimus*, innermost, and suggests a knowing that transcends everyday acquaintance or experience, while also reflecting the role played by proximity. Dietrich Krüger's comment that the amplification of spoken text in other Forsythe Company works "brings the voice closer" to the audience applies equally if not more to the amplification of the breath score.[18] In the original version of *Duo*,[19] which is performed by a female cast in a relatively narrow downstage space, the amplification of quiet, steady sweeps of breath and feet join with the staging to create a sense of closeness. *Duo*'s proximity, though, is performatively offset by the women's costumes, which reveal their breasts through a sheer layer of black mesh. This "intimate" view of the women, which causes some audience members to react with visible or audible nervousness, gains performative impact from the visuosonically intimate *mise en scène*.[20]

Duo's proximal staging and its audible breath score both align with the enhanced physicality that Lehmann lists as a trait of postdramatic theatre. However, Lehmann warns that such reduced, intimate use of both physical and acoustic space poses a danger to drama's semioticity, complaining that "the physical and physiological proximity (breath, sweat, panting, movement of the musculature, cramp, gaze) masks the mental signification" and counters the distance and abstraction he considers necessary for drama. Under such circumstances, he remarks, "a space of a tense centripetal dynamic develops, in which theatre becomes a moment of *shared energies* instead of transmitted signs."[21] He alludes here to Lyotard's idea of "energetic theatre," which draws impetus from Artaud's visceral presentation of "forces, intensities, present affects."[22] However, his analysis signals a difference that distinguishes postdramatic presentation from Artaud's Theatre of (sensory) Cruelty.[23] Where Artaud's actors "signal through the flames" in transcendent moments of drama, signification in postdramatic theatre is supplanted by "a body of unmeaning gesture (dance, rhythm, grace, strength, kinetic wealth)" in which the body itself—its presence, actions, capacities, and limits—is the subject.[24]

Lehmann discusses audience proximity with reference to Einar Schleef's theatre of stamping, shouting choruses of performers—to which, incidentally, Forsythe paid oblique homage in a scene in *Sider* (2011).[25] Here, Lehmann indicates the visceral effect of others' actions and exertions on spectators, noting how Schleef's audiences experienced "very directly the players' sweat or physical exertion" and felt "the pain and extreme demands on the voice in an awkwardly direct manner."[26] Aligning with Lehmann's observations is a vast body of research detailing the perceptual and neural mechanisms of self-other mappings and the ways that we are able to generate accurate perceptions of others' states, intentions, and emotions through their movements.[27] As well, the idea of *kinesthetic empathy*, which was first posited as *Einfühlung* ("feeling into") by Theodor Lipps in the 1920s, has been elaborated by dance scholars, philosophers, and cognitive neuroscientists, who have brought it into dialogue with the discovery of the mirror neuron system.[28] Schleef's pounding, shouting choruses and *Duo*'s visual and sonic closeness are essentially two sides of the same perceptual coin where the sharing of energy is concerned. But whereas Schleef assaults the aural and visual senses with the presence of the performers, Forsythe's performers in *Duo* insinuate themselves intimately—and for some, even uncomfortably— upon the eyes and ears of their audience. It might be argued that the mediated qualities of the amplified breath score—caused by speaker placement or the characteristic "tinniness" of amplified sound—signal to the audience that the choreographer intends for the mediation to be noticed. However, this is carefully minimized: in addition to reducing amplification effects to a minimum, Forsythe's sound technicians also "place" the sound primarily in speakers flanking the stage, closest to the bodies producing it. The amplified sound closely reflects the sounds produced onstage, with only a subtle increase of level and "surround" effect. Willems' quiet score impinges as if from afar, counterpointing the whispery breath score, and the intimate spell is only broken when the piece ends and silence is replaced by applause.

STOP, LOOK, LISTEN: *THREE ATMOSPHERIC STUDIES* PART 1

There is robust agreement that human perception is visually dominant; greater importance is assigned to information arriving via the eye than to any other sensory mode.[29] But senses function in concert, interacting to optimize apprehension and comprehension of events. In a manner of speaking, dance performances in which performers minimize the sounds they make throw a wrench in the perceptual works by disrupting everyday congruencies of sound and action. This impacts the attentional choreography of gaze and auditory focus, which itself has a complex intermodal dynamic. Just as objects appearing in peripheral vision attract our gaze, the orientation reflex, which develops shortly after birth, also ensures that sounds draw visual attention to their sources.[30] As noted above, Western concert dance audiences anticipate a reduction of onstage noise. Works that are seen as well as heard performatively thwart the expectation of "stage silence" but also afford apprehension of the mores of concert dance. Additionally, highlighting the sounds of dancing foregrounds the physical effort involved—a factor largely obscured in concert dance but which became more of a presentational subject in "Eurocrash" and many later choreographies. Lehmann also recognizes this enhanced physicality as a postdramatic theatre trait.[31]

Forsythe has deployed the sonority of dancing, including breath gestures, as a means of performatively heightening but also complicating audience attention. Part 1 of *Three Atmospheric Studies* (here referred to as *Atmo*) is a case in point (Fig. 10.1). *Atmo* 1 was the first part of the two-part work *Clouds After Cranach*, which premiered in November 2005 and which has occasionally been performed on its own under the title *The First Study*.[32] Approximately 23 minutes long and without musical accompaniment, *Atmo* 1 was partially inspired by the confused action and scattered gazes in press images of conflicts in the Middle East. Forsythe has explained its dramaturgy as being a mother's fragmented, incomplete memory of a marketplace bombing.[33] In *Atmo*'s part 2, it is revealed that her son was accidentally shot and killed by military forces in the ensuing confusion, but trauma has blocked this detail from her memory.[34]

One reviewer described *Atmo* 1 as

a melée, frightening in its desperate urgency, yet at the same time forensically precise. After a time you begin to pick out repeated gestures, defensive twists and feints, and other gestures that seem to tell more of the story: the

Fig. 10.1 The Forsythe Company in *Three Atmospheric Studies* part 1. (Source: photo courtesy of Dominik Mentzos)

sighting of something in the air, a desperate chase, an accidental death. What makes this so compelling is that its chronology is jumbled and all the elements of the story are visible at once, just as any traumatic event becomes compressed and confused in the memory of those who were there.[35]

"This is Composition 1, in which my son was arrested," the barefoot mother figure in a short pink dress matter-of-factly tells the audience at the work's opening, just before the dancers array themselves onstage. After a moment of stillness and connection across the ensemble,[36] the 12 dancers take a swift step toward center stage before one of them launches them into motion with a sudden loud slap to the floor. Cycling through rapid-action sequence fragments and tableaux within the white rectangle of floor space under ominously low-hanging HMI lights, they perform an intricate sequence of set choreography approximately two minutes long.

They then perform it precisely reversed back to its beginning, stepping sharply back and then forward again as a second floor slap sets the sequence repeating at a markedly quicker speed. Halfway through this second run-through, the ensemble splits across two groups, one reversing the sequence while the other continues onward through the choreography. In rehearsal, Forsythe structured *Atmo* 1's variations, solos, duets, and other ensemble passages from the "collisions" that resulted between performers as they moved through the diverged material.

As the dancers move through set group sections interspersed with "scheduled" improvisational solos and passages with others, they slot into the roles of characters in the mother's story, sometimes shifting among character identities and actions. The son figure is accosted again and again at center stage by two other men, sometimes gliding in reverse out of their frozen grasp and into a solo before returning to his position in their tableau. *Atmo* 1's set and improvised passages are both informed by a range of different movement modalities developed within the ensemble's process for this or prior works. Their names, such as "I do to you what you do to me" and "where it is/where it was," reflect themes of oppression, retribution, flashback memories, and other aspects of the experience of conflict.

As with *One Flat Thing, reproduced* (2000), *Atmo* 1 progresses according to a fixed script of visual and sonic cues: an arm flung upward, a heavily stamped landing from a lift, a sharp exhalation, a slap or noisy fall to the floor. Some of the breath score's elements result from relatively quiet and visually unobtrusive gestures that function "locally" as cues for a limited number of dancers, while others with a more "global" effect are larger and louder in scale. As the dancers move through and among the work's shifting, multicentric choreographic structures and changing modalities, it is critical that they attend not only to visual cues but also to the sounds and silences of the breath score unfolding around them, watching and listening for cues that dictate the work's moving synchronies, tempi, and precise, photographic stops. By suggesting in rehearsals that the dancers imagine the breath score's sounds to be shots, bombs, ricocheting projectiles, or the shutter clicks of cameras, Forsythe encouraged a *danced dramaturgy* that is multimodal, linking not only movement but also sounds to meaning.

Atmo 1's sound design also stresses the work's audio-visual dramaturgy. Shortly after the second run-through of the initial group sequence begins, Lanz slowly and slightly increases the volume levels of shotgun microphones positioned in the front wings and pad microphones mounted in the floor, subtly rendering the sounds of the action more audible.[37] Forsythe and Lanz balance volume and EQ levels throughout the rest of the piece relative to the intensity of the performance and the attentiveness of the audience.[38] As the dancers become more fatigued, the breath score's crisp accents are joined by heavier breathing, vocal punctuations of effort, and denser clusters of corporeally produced sounds as the performers dash through blurs of action. *Atmo* 1's finale has the sound and feel of an extended jazz coda: frantic *tutti* sections trade off with a last round of breath-driven, virtuosic solos before a last rushing truncated recap of the opening phrase suddenly leaves the dancers frozen in a tableau. The sound of their ragged breath lingers as the lights go down.

Two recent studies comparing audience reactions to different dance soundtracks provide interesting insight into the effects of dance performed to breath scores of ambient movement sounds. In Matthew Reason et al. (2016), a choreography was performed live to a recorded Bach oboe and violin concerto, an electronic music score, and with only the sounds of the dancers' breath and footfall. While the two music conditions produced no significant difference in qualitatively derived responses, participants identifying as novice dance spectators reported that the dance performed to ambient sounds produced a heightened sense of the performers' physical presence and an increased intimacy and intensity that some found unpleasant. Functional brain imaging data showed processing differences across the dance accompanied by Bach by ambient sounds, as well as greater activation in primary auditory regions of the brain in response to the ambient sounds. The authors interpreted this as evidence of a stronger embodied experience when breath sounds are heard.[39]

A 2020 study by Claire Howlin et al. extended this research by pairing dance only with the sounds of the performers' breath, footfall, and vocalizations, in order to eliminate musical bias. However, one group heard the dance's actual ambient score of breath, humming, counting, and footfall, while another heard it played backward, which disrupted the congruency of the sounds and movements. A control group watched the dance with no soundtrack. Using continuous measures (wristbands measuring physiological responses and tablet devices to capture viewers' reported enjoyment ratings in real time) as well as qualitative data collected *a posteriori*, the authors found that both the congruent and silent conditions were significantly disliked, while responses to the audiovisually incongruent performance were neutral but effectively more enjoyable than the other conditions. A lack of enjoyment in the congruent condition aligns with Reason et al.'s findings that participants dislike the sounds of performers' movement; however, Howlin et al.'s study shows that the discomfort subjects experienced was a result of the sound-movement congruence specifically, rather than due to the movement sounds themselves. In their view, the incongruent condition's disruption of the embodied linkage of sound and movement also disrupted the role that kinesthetic empathy plays in aesthetic evaluation. The study supports research on the role of *aesthetic capture*, in which music has a steering function on attention to specific aspects of dance movement,[40] while also provides evidence for the aesthetic pleasure of crossmodal incongruency, with its inhering instances of unpredictable and nonlinear audio-visual association.

Both of the studies above highlight the unsettling nature of breath score-movement congruency, with the latter one indicating a degree of pleasure attached to incongruent paring of movement and ambient sound. *Atmo* 1's complexity causes both congruency and incongruency to occur; however, the breath score of *Atmo* 1, like its choreography, is structured in a music-like manner that Forsythe has described as "symphonic." Noting the work's overall structure, repeating motifs, and oscillation between solos, counterpointed groups, and full-ensemble fugues, Forsythe also encourages audiences to hear this work's breath score as a musical composition.[41] *N.N.N.N.* (2002), a witty and highly musical *tour de force* for four men,[42] likewise features a "symphonically" structured breath score with only the faintest tonal underscoring by Willems. In this work's breath score, which is the loudest of those described here, the dancers produce not only effortful and audible breath and corporeal gestures but also onomatopoeic vocal sounds like those often heard in rehearsals. The coupling of breath score and choreography generates a descriptive, conversational soundscore that literally *incorporates* rhythm, accents, suspense, and physical humor.

SUSPENSE AND DECEPTION IN *THREE ATMOSPHERIC STUDIES* PART 1

Discussing *Three Atmospheric Studies* in a 2008 interview, Forsythe remarked:

We're only interested in one thing, which is basically the quality of attention. So the performers only have one real directive…and that's to stay in the situation – pay attention to the other person. That's all they have to do. But their larger job is to focus *your* attention...You see things differently. So I'm interested in the nature of attention and of collective attention, and that part of it, more than anything, is what we try to tune.[43]

Whether in structured (task-based) improvisations, free improvisation, or set choreography, variances in execution play a key role in the heightening and sustaining of performer attention, and by extension that of audience members. Like soloists in an orchestra or jazz ensemble, performers of Forsythe's breath-scored works are afforded—and expected to take—liberties in determining their timings, as well as the specific content and tenor of their improvised passages. Essentially, the performers know *what* will happen on a scenic and task-based level, but not the precise details of *how* and *when*. The desired result, rather than repetitive accuracy, is instead choices that heighten the attention of both oneself and other performers each time the works are performed.[44]

Forsythe considers the suspense of not knowing—which in *Three Atmospheric Studies* resonates with the themes of the overall work—to be crucial to the energy of performances and the presence of performers. Choreographic tasks support this, including how dancers aim not to be predictable in their "approach" to anticipated cues. For example, at a point in *Atmo* 1's opening choreographic sequence described above, a dancer (Sang Jijia in the original cast) stumbles noisily out of a kick delivered to the back of his knee as the other dancers freeze in various positions. He walks a swift, wide arc in the sudden silence, slowing down and accentuating his heel strikes. Arriving at a position behind a cluster of dancers on the floor, he drops suddenly with a sharp, arcing floor slap that cues the rest of the ensemble back into action. His marked *rallentando* and *decrescendo* call on the frozen performers, most of whom cannot see him, to track his position by listening carefully to his footfall as they seek to predict the arrival of the slap. Their focus is palpable and contagious.

In effect, *Atmo* 1's breath score, in addition to confounding the categories of noise and music, perceptually snares spectators between the contrasting attentional draws of amodal events, which ratify the connectedness and causal linkages of information across the senses, and the perception of crossmodal connections that potentially offer parsable relational structure. As the dancers run, collide, tangle, and collapse, any visible sonic or gestural cue at one location may motivate or interrupt one or more centers of action elsewhere, prompting those watching and listening to make rapid attentional choices within an environment which, as in many other Forsythe works, complicates attempts at holistic perception through a surfeit of competing loci of focus and sensory information. Variation in both the sonic and the visual "volume" of gestures further enhances this complicating effect. Near the end of the *Atmo* 1, Forsythe renders this performative strategy wryly explicit: a male performer, after traveling downstage center in a tightly contorted solo, suspends himself for a moment and then cues the rest of the ensemble out of a freeze with a noisy, almost melodramatic collapse.

Atmo 1 is motivated by a danced dramaturgy of not only suspense but also deception. The gestural and sonic visuosonic cueing strategy becomes clear at the outset of the piece; once spectator-auditors have discerned it, they anticipate and seek further cue-and-response linkages. Forsythe, however, performatively exploits the cognitive tendency to predict future events based on known regularities and patterns,[45] because not all visual and sonic gestures in *Atmo* 1 are cues—but each one is a *potential* cue. Forsythe is inherently aware of the habituating effects of predictable outcomes and the attentional and emotional effects of inconsistent or deceptive causality. As he occasionally commented on his strategy of maintaining audience engagement, "I give them a little, and then I take it back."

Further, many of *Atmo* 1's gestures and sounds belong to a class of actions that elicit strong attentional responses because they indicate the attention of their producer. Research in embodied communication has focused on ways that gestures of the hands, eyes, face, and other parts of the body are used to direct attention and communicate thought and intention to others.[46] Humans attune from a very early age to these *deictic* behaviors, which are elements of a complex intermodal network of *attention-directing interactions* that serve to first gain the focus of others and then direct it toward a target. These include pointing or directional gestures of the fingers, hands, chin, or other body parts, contact gestures with hands or feet (pats, taps, stamps), directed gaze, and also linguistic or paralinguistic vocal utterances including words like "this" or "look," coos, and gasps. By reflecting our own attentional focus and our intentions for the focus of others, deictic actions and sounds essentially enable and encourage others to "read" our minds—or if we are being deceptive, to misread them.

A scene late in *Atmo* 1 is an anxious study in deictic gestures. The ensemble freezes while Fabrice Mazliah executes an improvised solo of erratic, whirling countertorsions that alternate with passages of swift backward walks that veer between clusters of standing or prone dancers. His transitions into each veering passage are loud and unexpected two-footed stamps, but he sometimes breaks the alternation of whirling steps with retreating steps and further non-transitional stamps. As he moves, he glances nervously around and points his fingers at the floor, into space, or at other frozen dancers, who produce a small-scale counterpoint of occasional movements and gaze shifts. None of Mazliah's stamps or pointing gestures in this approximately 40-second solo are cues, except for a final stamp he delivers at a specified location onstage. The context of cueing via sharp sounds has been firmly established by this point in the work; however, Mazliah's multiple stamps have a dishabituating effect, confounding expectations that they will cue further action. His last stamp, delivered with an ironic "this is a cue" quality, sets the ensemble back into motion and breaks the audience out of the expectant state produced by the solo.

Throughout *Atmo* 1's set choreography sections, the direction of the dancers' gaze is also choreographed into complex deceptive patterns of not only attention but crucially also of *disattention*. Forsythe intended the choreography to reflect the scattered gazes of people in the images that inspired the work: press photos of bombing scenes in the Middle East and paintings of the crucifixion by Lucas Cranach the Elder. Several of Cranach's paintings—which, like *Three Atmospheric Studies*, depict the killing of a son in the Middle East[47]—are packed full of anachronistic crowds of saints, bystanders, children, knights, and horses looking in all directions, while the soldiers in the Associated Press image of a young man being carried from a burning building do the same. Because sonic cues can be discerned without looking, *Atmo* 1's breath score permits the performers' gazes to become potentially deceptive indicators of attention. The strongly focused "fierce" gaze[48] encouraged by Forsythe in this and other works provides visible vectors of attention, along which audiences seek meaning by attempting to establish intention and causality. However, though the dancers' gaze vectors occasionally coalesce on a single locus, they are more often scattered across many different ones, or are occasionally—as the mother figure says when she is finally able to recall her dying son's gaze in *Atmo* 2—"staring into the distance, at nothing."

Tracking across Forsythe's visuosonic choreographies that include breath scores reveals an extended investigation of the potentials of dance's sounds to inform temporal navigation and the creation of atmosphere.

The exploration of synchrony and counterpoint in *Duo, The Room as It Was* and *N.N.N.N.* afforded performative engagement with the intimacy and the humor that the sounds of dancing can evoke, while in *Atmo 1* the inquiry yielded physical dramaturgies reliant on attentional strategies of suspense and deception. Breath scores, like the choreographed gaze, tap our instinctive drive to understand action by perceiving attention, intention, and effort. Forsythe's amplification of dancers' sounds and performance of attention unsettles everyday modes of watching, listening, and understanding dance.

NOTES

1. Typically, stage monitor speakers are also placed onstage out of view of the audience to ensure that dancers hear the soundscape and to eliminate delay from the auditorium speakers.
2. *Ballets blancs* are fantastical scenes in Romantic and Classical ballets featuring supernatural female characters, such as fairies, enchanted girls, or spirits dressed in long or shorter white tutus. Examples include the wilis in act 2 of *Giselle* (1842), the "Kingdom of the Shades" scene in *La Bayadere* (1877), and acts 2 and 4 of *Swan Lake* (1877/1895).
3. Forms such as tap dancing or traditional Spanish dance are obvious exceptions. In these, however, the dancer's body essentially becomes an audio-visual instrument. See Aili Bresnahan's deft analysis of jazz tap dance as dance percussion in "Is Tap Dance a Form of Jazz Percussion?"
4. On orchestral etiquette, see Daniel Wakin, "Cracking the Secret Orchestral Codes."
5. Hans-Thies Lehmann, *Postdramatic Theatre*, 91.
6. Ibid., 92.
7. Scherer notes that affect bursts are both vocally and facially expressive. Here I focus on their sonic aspects. See Klaus Scherer, "Affect Bursts," and M. Schröder, "Experimental study of affect bursts." See also Fernando Poyatos, *Paralanguage: A Linguistic and Interdisciplinary Approach to Interactive Speech and Sounds.*
8. Unvoiced vocal sounds are audible but produced without vibrating the vocal cords. Consonants can be either voiced (as in *d*) or unvoiced (as in *t*), whereas vowels are by definition voiced.
9. B. Winter and S. Grawunder, "The phonetic profile of Korean formal and informal speech registers."
10. Steven Connor, *Beyond Words: Sobs, Hums, Stutters and Other Vocalizations*, 51.

11. A.L Winkworth et al., "Variability and consistency in speech breathing during reading: Lung volumes, speech intensity, and linguistic factors"; Philip Hoole and Wolfram Ziegler, "A comparison of normals' and aphasics' ability to plan respiratory activity in overt and covert speech"; and Susanne Fuchs et al., "Acoustic and respiratory evidence for utterance planning in German."

12. See F.A. Boiten et al., "Emotions and respiratory patterns: review and critical analysis," I. Homma and Y. Masaoka, "Breathing rhythms and emotions," and Mariel Grassmann et al., "Respiratory changes in response to cognitive load: a systematic review."

13. Term used by former Ballett Frankfurt member Jodie Gates. Interview, 12 March 2007.

14. Anne Nugent, "William Forsythe and the Lost Stuttgart Ballets," 24.

15. Interview with Thom Willems, 20 April 2008.

16. Waterhouse more aptly chooses to refer to these as "breathing-movements," noting that they are "a hybrid medium of movement, sound and sensation." *Processing Choreography: Thinking with William Forsythe's* Duo, 163. I have retained Forsythe's usage here.

17. *Duo* has extremely quiet scoring for both live piano and taped synthesizer. For a close description of its musical and breath score and its variances over time, see Waterhouse, *Processing Choreography*, pp. 79–80. For a detailed analysis of synchrony and joint action in this work and its later iterations, see E. Waterhouse et al., "Doing *Duo*–a case study of entrainment in William Forsythe's choreography '*Duo*.'" Willems' score for *Duo* was reused in sections of Forsythe's *Sider* (2011) at a much louder volume.

18. Dietrich Krüger, interview with the author, 2 July 2008.

19. A version of *Duo* developed from 2012 onward and performed by two men in practice clothing came to be known as *Duo2015*. As part of the 2018 program *A Quiet Evening of Dance*, which toured numerous cities worldwide, it was retitled *Dialogue (Duo2015)*.

20. Waterhouse offers salient observations on the impact and interplay of the women's costuming, lighting, and audience proximity on *Duo*'s intimacy, noting the delicate balancing necessary to protect it. As well, she highlights the necessity—and difficulty in some venues—of achieving a "faraway" sound from the live piano that featured in the women's version of *Duo*. See *Processing Choreography*, 78–82.

21. Lehmann, *Postdramatic Theatre*, 150.

22. Jean-François Lyotard, "The Tooth, the Palm," 282, cited in Lehmann, 37.

23. See Antonin Artaud, *The Theater and Its Double*. Artaud's essay "The Theatre of Cruelty" was originally published in 1932 in *La Nouvelle Revue Française*.

24. Lehmann, *Postdramatic Theatre*, 96.

25. Forsythe, telephone discussion with the author, 26 October 2015. See Vass-Rhee, "Haunted by Hamlet."
26. Lehmann, *Postdramatic Theatre*, 97.
27. For overviews of key research, see Günter Knoblich et al., *Human body perception from the inside out: Advances in visual cognition,* and Kerri Johnson and Maggie Shiffrar, eds., *People Watching: Social, Perceptual, and Neurophysiological Studies of Body Perception.*
28. For a review of this literature, see Dee Reynolds et al., "Editorial Introduction: Dance and Neuroscience – New Partnerships."
29. See, for example, F.B. Colavita, "Human sensory dominance"; M.I. Posner et al., "Visual dominance: An information-processing account of its origins and significance"; H.E Egeth and L.C. Sager, "On the locus if visual dominance"; and S. Sinnett et al., "Visual dominance and attention: the Colavita effect revisited."
30. Max Wertheimer, "Psychomotor coordination of auditory and visual space at birth." See also Chaps. 6 and 7 in this volume.
31. Lehmann, *Postdramatic Theatre*, 96. See also Ann Cooper Albright, "Techno Bodies."
32. The second part of the early two-part version of *Three Atmospheric Studies* first produced by Forsythe in 2005 became part 3 of the later version, while the two parts of *Clouds After Cranach*, which premiered in November 2005, became *Three Atmospheric Studies* parts 1 and 2. In 2012, Forsythe commented that part 3, with its specific references to government policies and personalities under George Bush, Jr., was no longer relevant, and parts 1 and 2 were performed for the last time in 2013 as *Clouds After Cranach*. Originally, *Clouds After Cranach*'s two parts (later *Three Atmospheric Studies* parts 1 and 2) were performed on two stages facing each other, with the audience turning around after the first part.
33. Diane Solway, "Is it Dance? Maybe. Political? Sure."
34. Forsythe wrote the mother character's narrative account, which she attempts to have an official character accurately translate into Arabic in part 2 (the second part of *Clouds After Cranach*).
35. Jenny Gilbert, review of *Three Atmospheric Studies.*
36. For this work, Forsythe and the ensemble worked extensively with Budo master practitioner Akira Hino on heightening perception and sensing connection with others. Of this collaboration, Forsythe commented, "Akira Hino has shown me the most significant example of human awareness that I have ever witnessed. He has mastered a degree of perceptual unity so profoundly fundamental, that is almost incomprehensible to our contemporary sensibilities...His influence on our work has been of inestimable value. The source of his work resides in the heart of the most pro-

found aspects of the danced." https://www.hinobudo-kokoro.com/about-1 (accessed 1 July 2017).

37. Pad microphones were typically only deemed necessary in larger venues.

38. As with most of his non "ballet-ballet" works, Forsythe supervised *Three Atmospheric Studies* from the technical booth in the auditorium, communicating directly with the sound and lighting teams and musicians. He refers to this "live direction" as "conducting" performances. See Chap. 3 and interview with Florian Malzacher, "You can be a virtuoso at being sloppy," 65.

39. Matthew Reason et al., "Spectators' aesthetic experience of sound and movement in dance performance: A transdisciplinary investigation."

40. See Allen Fogelsanger and Kathleya Afandor, "Parameters of perception: Vision, audition, and twentieth-century music and dance," and R.W. Mitchell and M.C. Gallaher, "Embodying music: Matching music and dance in memory."

41. William Forsythe in post-performance talk with Steve Valk and Michael Kliën, Dublin, Ireland, 7 April 2008.

42. In 2021, the Netherlands Dance Theater premiered a rework of *N.N.N.N.* with a cast of 12 titled *N.N.N.N.N.N.N.N.N.N.N.N.* (now known as *12 N*). A performance of *N.N.N.N.* by Forsythe Company members can be viewed and heard at https://www.youtube.com/watch?v=45RQLJjD8hY (accessed 20 May 2022).

43. Forsythe, post-performance talk with Steve Valk and Michael Kliën, 7 April 2008.

44. Indeed, Forsythe has always been prone to make changes to sections of works where he detects potential to increase energy onstage. These have frequently involved the aggregation or extension of perceptual tasks but have also taken the form of generating completely new tasks and/or putting new dancers into scenes. See Freya Vass-Rhee, "Schooling an ensemble: The Forsythe Company's Whole in the Head."

45. The idea of predictive processing has its roots in the thinking of Kant and Helmholtz. For reviews, see A. Bubic et al., "Prediction, cognition and the brain," and L.R. Swanson and R. Link, "The predictive processing paradigm has roots in Kant."

46. See, for example, Charles Goodwin, "Gesture as a Resource for the Organization of Mutual Orientation," C.L. Schmidt, "Adult understanding of spontaneous attention-directing events: What does gesture contribute?" Evelyn Z. McClave, "Linguistic functions of head movement in the context of speech," and Sotaro Kita, *Pointing: Where Language, Culture, and Cognition Meet.*

47. Forsythe, post-performance talk with Steve Valk and Michael Kliën, 7 April 2008. Several large-format renderings of the press photos and Cranach

paintings are always displayed in a space between the auditorium and theater foyer when *Three Atmospheric Studies* is performed.
48. Dana Caspersen's term. Interview with the author, 25 March 2003.

BIBLIOGRAPHY

Allbright, Ann Cooper. 1997. Techno Bodies: Muscling with Gender in Contemporary Dance. In *Choreographing Difference: The Body and Identity in Contemporary Dance*, 28–55. Hannover, NH: Wesleyan University Press.

Artaud, Antonin. 1958. *The Theater and Its Double*. Translated by M.C. Richards. New York: Grove Weidenfeld.

Boiten, F.A., N.H. Frijda, and C.J.E. Wientjes. 1994. Emotions and Respiratory Patterns: Review and Critical Analysis. *International Journal of Psychophysiology* 17 (2): 103–128.

Bresnahan, Aili. 2019. Is Tap Dance a Form of Jazz Percussion? *Midwest Studies in Philosophy* 44 (1): 183–194.

Bubic, A., D.Y. Von Cramon, and R.I. Schubotz. 2010. Prediction, Cognition and the Brain. *Frontiers in Human Neuroscience* 4: 25.

Colavita, F.B. 1974. Human Sensory Dominance. *Perception & Psychophysics* 16: 409–412.

Connor, Steven. 2014. *Beyond Words: Sobs, Hums, Stutters and Other Vocalizations*. London: Reaktion.

Egeth, H.E., and L.C. Sager. 1977. On the Locus If Visual Dominance. *Perception & Psychophysics* 22: 77–86.

Fogelsanger, Allen and Kathleya Afanador. 2017. Parameters of Perception: Vision, Audition, and Twentieth-Century Music and Dance. *AVANT. Pismo Awangardy Filozoficzno-Naukowej* 1: 59–73.

Fuchs, Susanne, Caterina Petrone, Jelena Krivokapić, and Philip Hoole. 2013. Acoustic and Respiratory Evidence for Utterance Planning in German. *Journal of Phonetics* 41 (1): 29–47.

Gilbert, Jenny. 2006. Review of *Three Atmospheric Studies*. *The Independent*, 13 October. https://www.independent.co.uk/arts-entertainment/theatre-dance/reviews/three-atmospheric-studies-sadler-s-wells-london-419903.html. Accessed 13 October 2006.

Goodwin, Charles. 1986. Gesture as a Resource for the Organization of Mutual Orientation. *Semiotica* 62 (1–2): 29–49.

Grassmann, Mariel, Elke Vlemincx, Andreas Von Leupoldt, Justin M. Mittelstädt, and Omer Van den Bergh. 2016. Respiratory Changes in Response to Cognitive Load: A Systematic Review. *Neural Plasticity* 2016: 8146809.

Homma, I., and Y. Masaoka. 2008. Breathing Rhythms and Emotions. *Experimental Physiology* 93 (9): 1011–1021.

Hoole, Philip, and Wolfram Ziegler. 1997. A Comparison of Normals' and Aphasics' Ability to Plan Respiratory Activity in Overt and Covert Speech. *Forschungsberichte-Institut für Phonetik und Sprachliche Kommunikation der Universität München* 35: 77–80.

Howlin, Clare, Staci Vicary and Guido Orgs. 2020. Audiovisual Aesthetics of Sound and Movement in Contemporary Dance. *Empirical Studies of the Arts* 38 (2): 191–211.

Johnson, Kerri, and Maggie Shiffrar, eds. 2013. *People Watching: Social, Perceptual, and Neurophysiological Studies of Body Perception.* Oxford: Oxford University Press.

Kita, Sotaro. 2003. *Pointing: Where Language, Culture, and Cognition Meet.* Mahwah: Lawrence Erlbaum Associates.

Knoblich, Günter, Ian Thornton, Marc Grosjean, and Maggie Shiffrar. 2006. *Human Body Perception from the Inside Out: Advances in Visual Cognition.* Oxford: Oxford University Press.

Lehmann, Hans-Thies. 2006. *Postdramatic Theatre.* Translated by Karen Jürs-Munby. Abingdon and New York: Routledge. Original version: Lehmann, Hans-Thies. 1999. *Postdramatisches Theater.* Frankfurt am Main: Verlag der Autoren.

Lyotard, Jean-François. 1977. The Tooth, the Palm. In *Mimesis, Masochism and Mime*, ed. T. Murray, 282–288. Ann Arbor: University of Michigan Press.

Malzacher, Florian. 2010. You Can Be a Virtuoso at Being Sloppy. Interview with William Forsythe. In *Herbst. Theorie zur Praxis*, 62–65. Graz: Steirischer Herbst Festival GmbH.

McClave, Evelyn Z. 2000. Linguistic Functions of Head Movement in the Context of Speech. *Journal of Pragmatics* 32 (7): 855–878.

Mitchell, R.W., and M.C. Gallaher. 2001. Embodying Music: Matching Music and Dance in Memory. *Music Perception* 19 (1): 65–85.

Nugent, Anne. 2006. William Forsythe and the Lost Stuttgart Ballets. *Dance Chronicle* 29 (1): 17–48.

Posner, M.I., M.J. Nissen, and R.M. Klein. 1976. Visual Dominance: An Information-Processing Account of Its Origins and Significance. *Psychological Review* 83 (2): 157–171.

Poyatos, Fernando. 1993. *Paralanguage: A Linguistic and Interdisciplinary Approach to Interactive Speech and Sounds.* Amsterdam: John Benjamins Publishing Company.

Reason, M., C. Jola, R. Kay, D. Reynolds, J.P. Kauppi, M.H. Grobras, J. Tohka, and F.E. Pollick. 2016. Spectators' Aesthetic Experience of Sound and Movement in Dance Performance: A Transdisciplinary Investigation. *Psychology of Aesthetics, Creativity, and the Arts* 10 (1): 42–55.

Reynolds, Dee, Corinne Jola, and Frank Pollick. 2011. Editorial Introduction: Dance and Neuroscience—New Partnerships. *Dance Research: The Journal of the Society for Dance Research* 29 (2): 259–269.

Scherer, Klaus. 1994. Affect Bursts. In *Emotions: Essays on Emotion Theory*, ed. S. Van Goozen, N. Van de Pol, and J. Sergeant, 175–208. New York: Psychology Press.

Schmidt, C.L. 1999. Adult Understanding of Spontaneous Attention-Directing Events: What Does Gesture Contribute? *Ecological Psychology* 11 (2): 139–174.

Schröder, M. 2003. Experimental Study of Affect Bursts. *Speech Communication* 40 (1–2): 99–116.

Sinnett, S., C. Spence, and S. Soto-Faraco. 2007. Visual Dominance and Attention: The Colavita Effect Revisited. *Perception & Psychophysics* 69: 673–686.

Solway, Diane. 2007. Is It Dance? Maybe. Political? Sure. *The New York Times*, 18 February. https://www.nytimes.com/2007/02/18/arts/dance/18solw. html. Accessed 20 March 2008.

Swanson, L.R. 2016. The Predictive Processing Paradigm Has Roots in Kant. *Frontiers in Systems Neuroscience* 10: 79.

Vass-Rhee, Freya. 2018. Schooling an Ensemble: The Forsythe Company's Whole in the Head. *Journal of Dance & Somatic Practices* 10 (2): 219–233.

Wakin, Daniel. 2005. Cracking the Secret Orchestral Codes. *The New York Times*, 13 February. https://www.nytimes.com/2005/02/13/arts/music/cracking-the-secret-orchestral-codes.html. Accessed 4 February 2022.

Waterhouse, Elizabeth. 2022. *Processing Choreography: Thinking with William Forsythe's Duo*. Bielefeld: Transcript Verlag.

Waterhouse, E., R. Watts, and B.E. Bläsing. 2014. Doing *Duo*—A Case Study of Entrainment in William Forsythe's Choreography "*Duo*". *Frontiers in Human Neuroscience* 8: 812.

Wertheimer, M. 1961. Psychomotor Coordination of Auditory and Visual Space at Birth. *Science* 134 (3491): 1692.

Winkworth, A.L., P.J. Davis, E. Ellis, and R.D. Adams. 1994. Variability and Consistency in Speech Breathing During Reading: Lung Volumes, Speech Intensity, and Linguistic Factors. *Journal of Speech, Language, and Hearing Research* 37 (3): 535–556.

Winter, B., and S. Grawunder. 2012. The Phonetic Profile of Korean Formal and Informal Speech Registers. *Journal of Phonetics* 40 (6): 808–815.

CHAPTER 11

Auditory Turn: Vocal Choreography

Forsythe's comments in a 2010 interview with curator and dramaturg Florian Malzacher reflect a holistic perception of scenographic space, music, and language as related architectures:

> Music has the quality of an object for me. It is not a thing I hear, I feel it. And I feel it as structure. The same thing with language. It has the same quality in terms of affect. And you can basically use language as set, context, scenery. It creates the space you are in. It can put you in a relation to cultural history – you can pull these different associations in. What it does: It triangulates you. You put yourself in relation to events that happened, to songs, to films you remember. If you have no relationship to these associations: that's where you are. But if you do, then it puts the dance in context. And the relationship can change during the dance, because the music and the language move in time – if you have a set design: that does not change; I notice it for five seconds and then…But language, as a time based phenomenon, moves with a counterpoint to all the action.[1]

Though language and song are human universals, there are substantial variances across individuals and cultures. Differences between speech and song have been extensively analyzed within the fields of neuroscience, phonetics, and ethnomusicology, but it has proven more valuable to consider the two vocal registers as a pair rather than as a dichotomy.[2] Such a view recognizes that both speech and song share characteristics of

F. Vass, *William Forsythe's Postdramatic Dance Theater*, Cognitive Studies in Literature and Performance, https://doi.org/10.1007/978-3-031-26658-4_11

calculated pitch, timbre, rhythm, and phrasing. Speech also becomes more songlike in specific contexts; examples include ritual or other forms of chanting, "motherese" (the instinctive universal register used when caregivers speak to infants), persuasive or emotional rhetoric, and also theatrical speech. As noted in the introduction, Lehmann indicates an increased musicality in postdramatic theatre speech through the inclusion of polyglossia (multiple languages), diverse accents and pitch registers, electronic voice treatments, and "musical-architectonic constructions" like those found in James Joyce's writings.[3] The postdramatic voice, then, sits squarely at the fluid juncture where distinctions between speech and song become less meaningful.

Forsythe began breaking the sonic fourth wall early in his choreographic career. As Ann Nugent notes, the dancers in the site-specific performance *EVENT 1 2 3*, staged in a highway tunnel in Stuttgart in 1979, "stepped out of their normal performing personae, using not only their bodies quite differently...but also using their voices, speaking and singing."[4] In works commissioned by various companies in 1980, an encyclopedia salesman delivered a glib pitch (*Joyleen Gets Up, Gets Down, Goes Out*), dancers screamed at each other (*Say Bye Bye*) and made vomiting noises (*'Tis a Pity She's a Whore*), while a few years later performers uttered texts written by Forsythe for the works *Gänge (Ein Stück über Ballett)* (1982/1983), *Mental Model* (1983), *Square Deal* (1983), and *France/ Dance* (1983). In *Artifact* and *LDC*, from 1984 and 1985 respectively, syntactic permutations of small sets of words foregrounded the musicality and abstracting cognitive effect that emerges through repetition and variation of phrases.[5] This combinatoric language has a sonic parallel in Forsythe's exploration of "algorithmic" recombination of steps from the formal, abstract ballet codex of geometrically defined positions and steps.

Speech also afforded Forsythe a means to explore the performative dynamics of theatrical attention in several works. Forsythe overtly addresses the high attentional value we as a species place on acts of speaking, which causes us to allocate attention preferentially toward speakers,[6] in the second version of *The Loss of Small Detail*. As described in Chap. 7, Dana Caspersen's whisper into the microphone early in this work is barely audible above the music and her words are not distinguishable, while David Kern's voice, altered into a weird hornlike bass, booms out from the apocalyptic blizzard that closes the work. In *Invisible Film* (1995), virtuosic dancing unfolds around David Morrow, who stands intoning lyrics from funk songs syllable by syllable into a microphone

("Bow!...wow!...wow!...yip...pee!") as a lush Baroque *larghetto* plays. In other work sections, including the cacophonic third part of *Artifact* discussed in Chap. 8, speakers overcut each other while seemingly oblivious dancers move.

Forsythe's vocalizing dancers, however, have frequently received negative responses. Both early and later critics have flagged Forsythe's inclusion of spoken text as too "intellectual"—difficult for audiences and detrimental to the quality of his works.[7] Of *Artifact*, Anna Kisselgoff complains of the performers who speak over Eva Crossman-Hecht's music, recommending "Less screaming, more dancing."[8] Though *Decreation*, which was made 19 years after *Artifact*, has fared somewhat better with regard to its textual content, Debra Craine remarked, "While the dancers speak relentlessly...the choreography bubbles away on the sideline...David Morrow's music barely registers."[9]

Dance performances that include speaking dancers essentially breach categorical norms due to received notions of dance as a non-verbal, mimetic practice. Dancing is described by many, including dancers, choreographers, and dance theorists, as speaking with or through the body, while practitioners acknowledge that dancing is at least in part the translation of ideas verbalized by choreographers into movement.[10] This of course does preclude the co-production of dance and speech, and inclusions of speech by postmodern choreographers—for example, Trisha Brown's *Accumulation with Talking Plus Watermotor* (1979), Simone Forti's danced and spoken improvisations, and Bill T. Jones' *The Breathing Show* (1999)—have been viewed as interrogating the tacit dichotomy between corporeal and verbal communication. The perceived inappropriateness of Forsythe's inclusion of speech seems due to the labeling of his choreographies as *ballets*, which, in Sandra Francis' 1996 study examining how subjects (students at a US university) categorize activities as instances of dance or not, emerged as the most prototypical representation of dance.[11]

Forsythe's interest in the musicality of language resulted in several scenes in works containing pseudo-languages derived by various means. *Heterotopia* (2006), described in greater detail below, featured performers recombining letters into meaningless words that guided both movement and vocal improvisations. In one scene from *The Defenders* (2007), an actor bellows a quote by Blaise Pascal in a manner reminiscent of Ping Chong's "dictator's speech" in Meredith Monk's Quarry (1978), only the text he reads is reversed line by line so that "The sensitivity of men to small matters..." becomes "Fo ytivitisnes eht srettam llams ot nem...."[12] *LDC*

(1983), *Heterotopia*, and *Angoloscuro* (2007) also included dancers speaking nonce languages (utterances that resemble meaningful speech), while in *Sider* (2011), performers were tasked in some scenes with simultaneously "garbling" lines of a film version of *Hamlet* that they heard through earpieces, while preserving the rhythm of the speech.

Pseudo-language is distinct from *heteroglossia*, in which the aim is to produce partially recognizable semantics, as in Charlie Chaplin's famous "schtonk" diatribe in *The Great Dictator* (1940). Sometimes derogatorily referred to as "gibberish," true pseudo-language elides concrete semantic meaning and in the process isolates the sonic communicative qualities of language by eliding the lexical. Pseudo-language taps our innate instinct to decode meaning from utterances; when this is rendered impossible, the receiver is forced to rely on the structure, rhythms, timbre, and prosody (speech melody) of what they hear, along with the speaker's embodied and expressive performance of speech. We experience a similar effect when observing speakers of languages that we do not understand. Pseudo-language also opens an avenue for inadvertent or deliberate interface with literal meaning through the inclusion of sound units present in the receiver's language(s). *Sider*'s garbled renditions of Shakespearean text were intentionally more parsable in some scenes than in others.[13]

Speech and speech-like utterances aside, we are capable of a far greater range of vocalizations. Forsythe's investigation of the possibilities for voice to inform choreography further extended to the musicality of the non-textual voice and manifested in choreographic reflection of movement through fully voiced contrapuntal performance, a visuosonic modality I refer to as *vocal choreography*. In following, I discuss how translation between the kinetic action of dancing and the vocal action of sound performatively heightens and divides attention while deliberately eliding the textual content of speech. In this register, the dancing body blurs the distinction between visual and sonic aspects of scenography by itself becoming a visuosonic aspect of the soundscore.

Amplifying Embodied Experience: *Decreation*

Like many choreographers, teachers, and dancers across different dance forms and cultural geographies, Forsythe generates aural images of his own or others' movement when working with his dancers. In a "sing-through" of the choreography of *One Flat Thing, reproduced* recorded for the project *Synchronous Objects*, Forsythe can be heard illustrating selected movements with an idiosyncratic repertoire of sounds: *"Bah BO, bahhh, ki-ka WUMMM...ya pahhh-um pahhh um, boom...."*[14] Though the exact sounds dancers and choreographers produce to aurally represent movement vary across individuals, they reflect a conventional set of melodic, punctual, and timbral relations to the movements they are intended to represent: describing movements into fixed positions with short, sharply articulated sounds (e.g., *ki-ka*), rising or falling gestures with corresponding tonal arcs (e.g., *DEE-yah*), or strong sweeping movements with relatively long tones (e.g., *WUMM*). These constitute instances of the broader and very common human practice of onomatopoeic reflection, through which vocal sounds (e.g., *pow, zoom, bling*) describe dimensions of object size, attributes, position, movement, or the temporal structure of events.

The ways in which we translate our experiences of the world, including our observations and actions, point to the fundamentally embodied nature of communication.[15] In trials across 25 different languages, the so-called bouba/kiki effect, through which subjects associate roundish shapes or spiky ones with these respective nonce words, was confirmed to be robustly and cross-culturally rooted in crossmodal correspondences between visual properties and speech sounds[16]—which, crucially, we experience through our enacted performance of uttering them. Speakers also unconsciously correlate dimensions of speech prosody (intonational patterns of melody, rhythm, and stress) with hand, head, and postural gestures including iconic movements (e.g., depicting a guitar or an arch), deictic gestures like pointing or chin jerks, and "beat" gestures of the hands or the torso that accompany and add emphasis to speech.[17] In a similar vein, we also make robust dimensional correspondences across percepts from differing sensory modes, such as the relative "brightness" of sounds, "warmth" of colors, or "sharpness" (also called "piquancy") of flavors.[18] These are reflected in the perceptual language of synesthetic metaphor, which Donald Brown holds to be a universal factor in the way that we understand and describe attributes.[19] While specific synesthetic vocabulary perpetuates along embodied and cultural lines, folk tales, literature, and songs are replete with expressions like "dark" voices, "soft" lights, "loud" colors, and "sweet" sounds of musical instruments.[20] The language in which we couch our ideas reflects our sensuous relationship with the world we inhabit, as well as with imagined desirable aspects of that world.

Turning from words to nonlexical sounds, Hinton et al. (1994) describe the use of onomatopoeic vocal sounds to describe perceived aspects of our world and things in it as a form of imitative sound symbolism or aural imagery.[21] Over time, such usages can become broadly conventionalized among speakers of a language; equally, though, they can develop and persist as idiolects within communities defined by practices (such as concert dance) or even be "resident" within individual groups of practitioners. Such symbolic use of vocal sounds typically goes hand in hand with enacted physical imagery and emerges across different practitioner groups through trial-and-error practices that are subconsciously informed by both practice histories and group- or individual-specific innovation. In cross-linguistic investigations of dance teaching practices from the perspective of situated discourse, Leelo Keevallik describes how dance instructors pair up bodily "quoting" and nonlexical vocalizations or use them individually to convey information,[22] while David Kirsh et al. note the way in which choreographer's and collaborating dancers' vocalizations accompany their fully performed or marked movements to convey information about desired or intended movement qualities.[23] Orchestra conductors also commonly sing phrases in rehearsal and embody qualities of sound when communicating about the sound and embodied sensation of music.

Forsythe explored the perceptual linkage of external-visible and internal-audible gestures from a choreographic perspective in several works created with the Ballett Frankfurt in the early 2000s, expanding this experimentation further with the smaller Forsythe Company ensemble. In the process of developing *Decreation* (2003), Forsythe and the dancers returned to earlier investigation of the counter-rotational dynamics and "disfocusing" perceptual effects of extrapolated *épaulement* with which the Ballett Frankfurt company had begun working in 1991 while creating the second version of *The Loss of Small Detail*.[24] From this, they developed a radical, emotionally driven corporeal dramaturgy based on complex, wringing countertorsions of the entire body: limbs, spine, face, and eyes. During the rehearsal process, Forsythe observed that this operation, in addition to productively confounding proprioception, also de-forms and reshapes the vocal apparatus: mouth, trachea, larynx, and diaphragm. He asked the dancers, "What happens now when you exhale?" and observed that the result constituted a sonic rendering of the state of the body—a translation of movement into vocalized sound.[25]

In scenes in *Decreation* involving this modality, one is actually "hearing the dance," to quote Balanchine's famous edict. However, rather than reflecting an externally produced musical composition, the wringing, writhing bodies of the dancers become the loci of both dance movement

and its torqued, allied sound. Motivated by triangular structures of relationship that underpinned the work's dramaturgical sources—an essay and
a book by Anne Carson[26]—Forsythe distributed subtasks of this visual-
aural translation across series of watching, listening, and responding performers in such a manner that movement or sound is only produced in
response to the actions of other performers onstage. At times, dancers'
movements or vocalizations reflect other distant dancers; at others, a video
camera operator onstage projects time-lapsed close-up clips onto a large
screen. In one of *Decreation*'s final scenes, one female performer (Roberta
Mosca) contorting in gouts of twisted movement is watched by another
(Jone San Martin) who, seated with her back to the audience, translates
the action she sees into wrenching guttural sounds. The work's male pro-
tagonist (Richard Siegal) completes the translatory triangle, slowly deci-
phering her sounds into the phrase "This is the deal: you give me everything
and I give you nothing." San Martin then rises and performs an equally
harrowing translatory solo, amplifying and voicing the sensations of her
own movements.[27]

In subsequent works, Forsythe's ensemble continued to elaborate the
linkage of dance movement to vocalization by conceiving of the vocal
apparatus as exquisitely responsive to movement generated virtually anywhere in the body and refracted across its spaces. This system of internal
isometry, says Forsythe, "takes a state of your whole body and connects it
to your throat" such that "the sum of the body is in your windpipe."[28]
Underpinning these processes was Forsythe's recognition/re-cognition of
the vocal apparatus (mouth, nose, and throat, larynx, trachea, and lungs)
as contiguous with the body's dancing exterior rather than divided from it
at the visible surface of the lips. In other words, the dancer's moving body
houses a related movement performance not available to the eye but
potentially available to the ear. The contiguous muscularity of this intermodal *vocal choreography* controverts reifications of inside and outside
boundaries of the body, extending the action of dancing to the body's
sonorous interior and *re-presenting* visibly perceptible dance via the aural
perceptual channel. As with many of Forsythe's improvisatory structures,
this mode of visuosonic composition constitutes an innovative domain of
not only the dancers' physical virtuosity, but also their perceptual virtuosity. It demands a manifold division of attention and action from its performers across the external-internal spaces and temporalities of the body
and across their own and other performers' physical and sonic output.
Likewise for spectator-auditors, this dual output affords a radical and

multiple division of attention across the visual and auditory modes of both production and reception.

READING THE ROOM: SOUNDING SCORES

In 2005, Forsythe coupled this extrapolation of vocal sound from movement with the translation of visual scores into movement, which the ensemble first elaborated in works such as *Limb's Theorem* (1990) and *ALIE/N A (C)TION* (1993). In *You made me a monster*, created ten years after the premature death of Forsythe's wife Tracy-Kai Maier, audience members are asked to add pieces to sculptures of twisted paper skeleton pieces on tables and to trace shadows of the sculptures onto paper. After a short period, two male performers invade the installation's darkening space, lurching and howling erratically as they "read" and respond to the detail of the sculptural objects. The skeleton sculptures provide the performers with daunting amounts of visual structure: not only can they be parsed linearly across the randomly connected pieces, they can also be read across their surfaces or by tunneling one's vision through their depths. Arriving at a stage-like area at one end of the room, the two men and a female performer translate the shadow tracings placed on music stands into movement and sound (Fig. 11.1).[29]

The performers of *You made me a monster*, like those of *Decreation*, translate a state of the body through the vocal apparatus, only in this work it is "bodies" of warped, disordered paper skeleton pieces that represent a body wracked by cancer. These translations find a further parallel in the reading task of *Heterotopia*. Here, nonce words and the forms of letters themselves offer stimulus for not only corporeal translation as found in Forsythe's "universal writing" modality developed with the Ballett Frankfurt in the early 1990s and catalogued in the CD-ROM *Improvisation Technologies: A Tool for the Analytical Dance Eye*;[30] they also prompt translation into sound and interactions between the corporeal and vocal results. An "O," for example, can be shaped or described with any part of the body but also visualized anywhere along the vocal tract from the lips to the lungs, or attempted as a shape of the vocal tract. The O-forming body can in turn voice an "amplified" rendering of its sensed state as it moves.

Forsythe's choreographic engagements with intermodality in these three works, which were made within a few years of each other, constitute a strikingly progressive program of practice as research that moves from an initial

Fig. 11.1 David Kern, Roberta Mosca, and Christopher Roman translate the visual score elements of *You made me a monster* into vocal choreography. (Source: photo courtesy of Julieta Cervantes)

translatory finding to its application using a range of stimuli within different scenographic environments. Beyond this, though, his exploration of vocal choreography is a further extension of his longstanding investigation of theatrical attention. As with *Three Atmospheric Studies* (which was created between *Decreation* and *Heterotopia* and is discussed in Chap. 10), the performers' visual (and visible) focus in all of these works provides vectors for audience members to seek what Lehmann refers to as "traces of connection"[31] among surfeits of visual and sonic information in the space and across the dancers' visual and sonic performances. The intermodality of these and other works clearly demonstrates how the search for linkages, along with performative experience, are rooted in the so-called lower level of sensory perception, the immediate sense perception of environment and action that precedes and underpins "higher" reflective cognition.

Forsythe exploits the scenography of these three works to draw out the perceptual performativity that they afford. *Decreation* features a relatively uncluttered stage, with a large table and a plasma screen upstage plus a few chairs that are moved from place to place, and a "roving" cameraperson whose presence emphasizes the role of vision and perspective. *You made me a monster*, conversely, is performed in a dark and quite oppressive installation space in which the performers lurching between the sculpture tables intrude on the personal space of the clustered audience while their huge, reverberating processed sounds feed back into the room as an overwhelming soundscore. *Heterotopia's* performance in two concurrently played "rooms"—a choice, incidentally, that Forsythe made a few days prior to the premiere[32]—as well as under and between the 56 tables in the "orchestra" room distributes corporeal and vocal choreography between seen and unseen spaces, evoking Foucault's text on heterotopias titled *Des espaces autres* that underpinned the dramaturgy.[33]

In both "reading" of visual and sonic scores and intermodal translation tasks, Forsythe's performers radically divide their attention by simultaneously parsing and translating multiple sources of information into movement and sound. Forsythe instructs performers of *You made me a monster* to "keep your drawing all over your body" by distributing the translation of the score elements across different physical regions.[34] *Heterotopia's* informational sources and improvisational tasks are concatenated and scattered in intricate networks of cause and effect across the installation's spaces, objects, and bodies. In one scene, for example, a dancer on the tabletops in the first room performs a silent improvised solo that visually "directs" a vocal-and-movement trio of performers standing in holes between the tables. Two of these three produce responsive contrapuntal sound while physically translating it into movement of the others' body. The trio's third member uses the overall vocal score to guide his selective danced/vocal reading of selected nonce words. In another hole, an additional dancer performs a "blind" solo in which she tries to avoid moving simultaneously with the third trio member by focusing on his voice and attempting to derive his stops from it.[35] The combined sounds of this front-room scene—four voices linked by differing degrees of agency and counterpoint, the sounds of the performers' movements, and Willems' subtle music—issue from a bowl-shaped speaker in the back room, where they serve as accompaniment for a silent trio of performers there. The physically shifting, counterpointed action and sound, coupled with the audience's liberty to move about and between the performance's spaces, motivate attendees to optimize their visual and auditory perspectives, choosing between the two environments and among the multiple targets of monomodal and intermodal attention simultaneously available at any moment—also including the gazes, postures, vocal and gestural responses, and perambulation of other spectators. The performance of the performers' perception, simultaneously, is a subject of numerous improvisational modalities in the two rooms, where Forsythe encourages them to think of themselves as both conductors and musicians.[36]

Step, Inside

Forsythe's intermodal modalities of breath scores and vocal choreography extend dance beyond the visual surface of performers' bodies into their other/inner spaces, permitting what Roland Barthes refers to as the "grain" of the voice[37] to be translated and re-presented across the senses of vision and audition. Through performative linkages between visible and audible action, the performers' sounds and movements afford comprehension on a level that is literally visceral. In some works, these modalities counterpoint coherent speech, as in *Decreation, Angoloscuro,* and *The Defenders.* In *Heterotopia*, for which the en-voiced body's ability to communicate without language was a dramaturgical focus, coherent speech is circumvented entirely, while breath scores are by definition wordless.

Here, however, as with many other instances within Forsythe's works, the perceptual complexity of the visuosonic choreographies offers only partial, fleeting, and often questionable moments of closure. Discussing postdramatic theatre's reflection of Baudelaire's spiritually inflected theory of *synaesthesia*—the synthesizing confusion or conflation of sensing across modalities—Lehmann explains in a passage worth quoting at length that

> instead of contiguity, as it presents itself in dramatic narration (A is connected to B, B in turn to C, so that they form a line or sequence), one finds disparate heterogeneity, in which any one detail seems to be able to take the place of any other…As in surrealist writing games this circumstance continually leads to the intensified perception of the individual phenomenon and simultaneously to the discovery of surprising *correspondances*. Not coincidentally this term stems from poetry, and it aptly describes the new perception of theatre beyond drama as 'scenic poetry'. The human sensory apparatus does not easily tolerate disconnectedness. When deprived of connections, it seeks out its own, becomes 'active', its imagination going 'wild' – and what then 'occurs to it' are similarities, correlations and correspondences, however far-fetched these may be. The search for traces of

connection is accompanied by a helpless focusing of perception on the things offered (maybe they will at some moment reveal their secret) (...)

Perception always already functions dialogically, in such a way that the senses respond to the offers and demands of the environment, but at the same time also show a disposition first to construct the manifold into a texture of perception, i.e. to constitute a unity. If this is so, then aesthetic forms of practice offer the chance to intensify this synthesizing, corporeal activity of sensory experience precisely by means of *a purposeful impediment*: they call attention to it as a quest, disappointment, retreat and rediscovery. [emphasis mine][38]

Here Lehmann explicitly signals a performativity that calls the attendee's attention to themself as a perceiver of signs which, though not necessarily taking the form of words or symbols are always in the form of sensations. He does so by evoking the sensuous *correspondences* of Charles Baudelaire's eponymous poem, in which forests of symbols voice "confused words" and percepts, echoing across modalities, "sing the ecstasy of the soul and senses."[39] He notes, however, that these correspondences do not form a theatre of completion for contemplation, but instead one that indicates and proposes negotiation with the incomplete, possible, and unsettled processes of theatrical communication. "Purposeful impediment"—whether of vision, audition, or comprehension—results in an intensified performance of perception, which opens avenues for its apprehension as such.

NOTES

1. Forsythe in Florian Malzacher, "You can be a virtuoso at being sloppy," 64.
2. See Fred Cummins, "The Territory Between Speech and Song: A Joint Speech Perspective."
3. Hans-Thies Lehmann, *Postdramatic Theatre*, 92.
4. Ann Nugent, "William Forsythe and the Lost Stuttgart Ballets," 36.
5. See Gerald Siegmund, "The space of memory: William Forsythe's ballets," 128–132.
6. For a review of this literature, including interesting cross-cultural variations, see Federico Rossano, "Gaze in Conversation."
7. See Louise Levene, "If Only They'd Shut Up and Dance." See also Mark Franko, "Splintered encounters: The critical reception to William Forsythe in the United States, 1979–1989."
8. Anna Kisselgoff, "The Sound and the Flurry of William Forsythe."
9. Debra Craine, review of *Decreation*, 16.

10. See Donna Napoli, "Stimuli for initiation: a comparison of dance and (sign) language," 4.

11. Sandra Francis, "Exploring dance as concept: Contributions from cognitive science."

12. These modalities from *Heterotopia* and *The Defenders* also inform *Wirds* (2011) and *Inversion* (2018), two of Forsythe's "choreographic objects." The full catalogue of Forsythe's choreographic objects, including the text of the quote by Pascal (which was also printed with the letters upside down and reversed) can be viewed at https://www.williamforsythe.com.

13. See Freya Vass-Rhee, "Haunted by Hamlet," 10–12.

14. Forsythe's "sing-through" of *One Flat Thing, reproduced* can be accessed by toggling the audio settings of the work's video score at the *Synchronous Objects for One Flat Thing, reproduced* project at www.synchronousobjects. osu.edu/content.html#/fullVideoScore (accessed May 7, 2020).

15. See Raymond Gibbs, Jr., "embodied experience and linguistic meaning" and Gibbs, Jr. et al., "Metaphor is grounded in embodied experience."

16. A. Ćwiek et al., "The bouba/kiki effect is robust across cultures and writing systems."

17. See, for example, U. Hadar et al., "The timing of shifts in head posture during conversation"; F. Quek et al., "Gesture cues for conversational interaction in monocular video"; and David McNeill, *Gesture and Thought*.

18. See, for example, Lawrence Marks, "Bright Sneezes and Dark Coughs, Loud Sunlight and Soft Moonlight"; Lawrence Marks, "Synesthetic perception and poetic metaphor"; Ernst Gombrich, *Meditations on a Hobby Horse and Other Essays on the Theory of Art*; and V.S. Ramachandran, *A Brief Tour of Human Consciousness*. For comprehensive overviews of synesthesia, see Richard Cytowic, *The Man Who Tasted Shapes* and Lawrence Rosenblum, *See What I'm Saying: The Extraordinary Powers of Our Five Senses*, 283–293.

19. See Stephen Pinker, *The Blank Slate: The Modern Denial of Human Nature*. See also M. Werning et al., "The cognitive accessibility of synaesthetic metaphors" and N. Yu, "Synesthetic metaphor: A cognitive perspective."

20. Interestingly, high-dynamic intensities such as loud, hard, and dark tend to bear negative and often specifically masculine connotations, while the inverse qualities of quiet, softness, and light become negative only at their extremes, requiring modifiers as in "sickly sweet" or even distinct terms like "syrupy," "saccharine," or "mushy." When structure or patterning is described, rather than using dichotomized synesthetic descriptors, evaluation shifts almost entirely into a negative, active register: visual patterns may be "calm" but are not typically "quiet" or "soft," while those relatively high in density or complexity, or low in organization, are "busy" or "noisy."

21. See Leanne Hinton et al., *Sound Symbolism*, 3.

22. Leelo Keevallik, "Bodily Quoting in Dance Correction" and Leelo Keevallik, "Vocalizations in dance classes teach body knowledge." See also Jessica Douglah, "BOOM, so it will be like an attack."

23. David Kirsh et al., "Choreographic methods for creating novel, high quality dance."

24. Forsythe's refiguring of the gaze in *épaulement* can be traced further back to the work *Artifact* (1984). See Caspersen, "Decreation," 95–97.

25. *Decreation* post-performance talk, Haus der Berliner Festspiele, Berlin, January 21, 2009.

26. Anne Carson, "Decreation: How Women Like Sappho, Marguerite Porete, and Simone Weil Tell God" and Anne Carson, *The Beauty of the Husband: A Fictional Essay in 29 Tangos*.

27. San Martin performs a similar translation in *Three Atmospheric Studies* part 2.

28. Rehearsal, Frankfurt am Main, August 21, 2006.

29. For an extended discussion of this work, see Freya Vass-Rhee, "Dancing Music," 395–398. *You made me a monster*'s improvisational tasks are also sometimes performed as an installation titled *Monster Partitur*. For this work, a large wooden wall covered with shadow tracings serves as the score.

30. First commercially released in 1999, *Improvisation Technologies* offers a subset of the modalities included in the prototype version, which was developed for use as a learning tool by the Ballett Frankfurt in 1995. A copy of the hard drive version of this prototype is housed at the Deutsches Tanzarchiv in Cologne.

31. Lehmann, *Postdramatisches Theater*, 144.

32. The Zürich Schiffbauhalle had been divided by a floor-to-ceiling screen to create a performance space and a smaller space fitted with a Marley-covered sprung floor and piano for the dancers' daily class. Forsythe staged scenes in both spaces.

33. Michel Foucault, "Des espaces autres" (Of other spaces).

34. Forsythe in rehearsal, Frankfurt am Main, October 10, 2007.

35. As with many of Forsythe's works, the exact parameters of *Heterotopia*'s improvisational tasks have changed over the history of the works' performances. This task series was altered in 2008, two years after the work's premiere.

36. See Freya Vass-Rhee, "Auditory turn," 401–406.

37. Roland Barthes, "The Grain of the Voice," 188.

38. Lehmann, *Postdramatic Theatre*, 84–85.

39. *Nature is a temple in which living pillars*
    Sometimes give voice to confused words;
    Man passes there through forests of symbols
    Which look at him with understanding eyes.

Like prolonged echoes mingling in the distance
In a deep and tenebrous unity,
Vast as the dark of night and as the light of day,
Perfumes, sounds, and colors correspond.

There are perfumes as cool as the flesh of children,
Sweet as oboes, green as meadows
— And others are corrupt, and rich, triumphant,

With power to expand into infinity,
Like amber and incense, musk, benzoin,
That sing the ecstasy of the soul and senses.
—Charles Baudelaire, "Correspondances," Transl. William Aggeler, *The Flowers of Evil* (Fresno, CA: Academy Library Guild, 1954). See https:// fleursdumal.org/poem/103 for original text and other translations.

BIBLIOGRAPHY

Barthes, Roland. 1977. The Grain of the Voice. In *Image, Music, Text*. New York: Hill and Wang.

Carson, Anne. 2002a. Decreation: How Women Like Sappho, Marguerite Porete, and Simone Weil Tell God. *Common Knowledge* 8 (1): 188–201. Reprinted in Carson, Anne. 2005. *Decreation: Poetry, Essays, Opera*. New York: Knopf.

———. 2002b. *The Beauty of the Husband: A Fictional Essay in 29 Tangos*. Toronto: Vintage.

Caspersen, Dana. 2011. Decreation: Fragmentation and Continuity. In *William Forsythe and the Practice of Choreography: It Starts from Any Point*, ed. Steven Spier, 93–100. London and New York: Routledge.

Craine, Debra. 2009. Review of *Decreation*. *The Times*, 28 April.

Cummins, Fred. 2020. The Territory Between Speech and Song: A Joint Speech Perspective. *Music Perception* 37 (4): 347–358.

Ćwiek, A., S. Fuchs, C. Draxler, E.L. Asu, D. Dediu, K. Hiovain, S. Kawahara, S. Koutalidis, M. Krifka, P. Lippus, and G. Lupyan. 2022. The Bouba/Kiki Effect is Robust Across Cultures and Writing Systems. *Philosophical Transactions of the Royal Society B* 377 (1841): 20200390.

Cytowic, Richard. 2003. *The Man Who Tasted Shapes*. Cambridge, MA: MIT Press.

Douglah, Jessica. 2021. "BOOM, So It Will Be Like an Attack." Demonstrating in a Dance Class Through Verbal, Sound and Body Imagery. *Learning, Culture and Social Interaction* 29: 100488.

Forsythe, William, and ZKM Karlsruhe. 1999. *Improvisation Technologies: A Tool for the Analytical Dance Eye*. CD-ROM. Ostfildern: Hatje Cantz Verlag.

Forsythe, W., M. Palazzi, N. Zuniga Shaw, and S. de Lahunta. 2009, January. Synchronous Objects for One Flat Thing, Reproduced. In *Website Installation* or *On Line Resource (2009: Columbus, Ohio)*. The Ohio State University and The Forsythe Company.

Foucault, Michel. 1984. Des espaces autres (Of Other Spaces). Talk Delivered for the Cercle d'études architecturales, 14 March 1967. *Dits et écrits* IV.

Francis, Sandra. 1996. Exploring Dance as Concept: Contributions from Cognitive Science. *Dance Research Journal 28* (1): 51–66.

Franko, Mark. 2011. Splintered Encounters: The Critical Reception to William Forsythe in the United States, 1979–1989. In *William Forsythe and the Practice of Choreography: It Starts from Any Point*, ed. Steven Spier, 38–50. London and New York: Routledge.

Gibbs, R.W., Jr. 2003. Embodied Experience and Linguistic Meaning. *Brain and Language* 84 (1): 1–15.

Gibbs, R.W., Jr., P.L.C. Lima, and E. Francozo. 2004. Metaphor Is Grounded in Embodied Experience. *Journal of Pragmatics* 36 (7): 1189–1210.

Gombrich, Ernst. 1963. *Meditations on a Hobby Horse and Other Essays on the Theory of Art*. London: Phaidon.

Hadar, U., T.J. Steiner, E.C. Grant, and F.C. Rose. 1984. The Timing of Shifts in Head Posture During Conversation. *Human Movement Science* 3: 237–245.

Hinton, Leanne, Johanna Nichols, and John Ohala, eds. 1994. *Sound Symbolism*. Cambridge, UK: Cambridge University Press.

Keevallik, Leelo. 2010. Bodily Quoting in Dance Correction. *Research on Language and Social Interaction* 43 (4): 401–426.

———. 2021. Vocalizations in Dance Classes Teach Body Knowledge. *Linguistics Vanguard 7*: 1–10.

Kirsh, D., D. Muntanyola, R.J. Jao, A. Lew, and M. Sugihara. 2009. Choreographic Methods for Creating Novel, High Quality Dance. In *Proceedings, DESFORM 5th International Workshop on Design, Semantics and Form*, 188–195.

Kisselgoff, Anna. 1987. The Sound and the Flurry of William Forsythe. *The New York Times*, 19 July.

Lehmann, Hans-Thies. 2006. *Postdramatic Theatre*. Translated by Karen-Jürs-Munby. Abingdon and New York: Routledge. Original version: Lehmann, Hans-Thies. 1999. *Postdramatisches Theater*. Frankfurt am Main: Verlag der Autoren.

Levene, Louise. 2001. If Only They'd Shut Up and Dance. *The Sunday Telegraph*, 11 November.

Malzacher, Florian. 2010. "You Can Be a Virtuoso at Being Sloppy." Interview with William Forsythe. In *Herbst. Theorie zur Praxis*, 62–65. Graz: Steirischer Herbst Festival GmbH.

Marks, Lawrence. 1982a. Bright Sneezes and Dark Coughs, Loud Sunlight and Soft Moonlight. *Journal of Experimental Psychology: Human Perception and Performance* 8: 177–193.

————. 1982b. Synesthetic Perception and Poetic Metaphor. *Journal of Experimental Psychology: Human Perception and Performance* 8 (1): 15–23.

McNeill, David. 2005. *Gesture and Thought*. Chicago: Chicago University Press.

Napoli, Donna. 2022. Stimuli for Initiation: A Comparison of Dance and (Sign) Language. *Journal of Cultural Cognitive Science*: 1–17.

Nugent, Ann. 2006. William Forsythe and the Lost Stuttgart Ballets. *Dance Chronicle* 29 (1): 17–48.

Pinker, Stephen. 2002. *The Blank Slate: The Modern Denial of Human Nature*. London and New York: Penguin.

Quek, F., D. McNeill, R. Ansari, X. Ma, R. Bryll, S. Duncan, and K.E. McCullough. 1999. Gesture Cues for Conversational Interaction in Monocular Video. In *ICCV99 Workshop on Recognition, Analysis, and Tracking of Faces and Gestures in Real-Time Systems*, 64–69.

Ramachandran, V.S. 2004. *A Brief Tour of Human Consciousness*. New York: Pi Press.

Rosenblum, Lawrence. 2010. *See What I'm Saying: The Extraordinary Powers of Our Five Senses*, 267–293. New York: W.W. Norton & Company.

Rossano, Federico. 2013. Gaze in Conversation. In *The Handbook of Conversation Analysis*, ed. Jack Sidnell and Tanya Stivers, 308–329. Chichester: Wiley-Blackwell.

Siegmund, Gerald. 2011. The Space of Memory: William Forsythe's Ballets. In *William Forsythe and the Practice of Choreography: It Starts from Any Point*, ed. Steven Spier, 128–138. London and New York: Routledge.

Vass-Rhee, Freya. 2010. Auditory Turn: William Forsythe's Vocal Choreography. *Dance Chronicle* 33 (3): 388–413.

————. 2011. Dancing Music: The Intermodality of The Forsythe Company. In *William Forsythe and the Practice of Choreography: It Starts from Any Point*, ed. Steven Spier, 73–89. London and New York: Routledge.

————. 2019. Haunted by Hamlet: William Forsythe's Sider. In *The Oxford Handbook of Shakespeare and Dance*, ed. Lynsey McCulloch and Brandon Shaw, 455–475. Oxford: Oxford University Press.

Werning, M., J. Fleischhauer, and H. Beseoglu. 2006. The Cognitive Accessibility of Synaesthetic Metaphors. In *Proceedings of the Twenty Eighth Annual Conference of the Cognitive Science Society*, ed. R. Sun and N. Miyake, 2365–2370. Lawrence Erlbaum.

Yu, N. 2003. Synesthetic Metaphor: A Cognitive Perspective. *Journal of Literary Semantics* 32 (1): 19–34.

CHAPTER 12

Epilogue

"Oh, that the senses are so many! Into bliss they bring confusion," writes Goethe to his muse, the actress and dancer Marianne von Willemer. His exclamation is a lover's complaint, describing the disorienting effect (*Verwirrung*, from *irren*, to lose one's way) of her presence on his emotions, and offering a poetic wish: to be deaf when he sees her and blind when he hears her. In response to being overwhelmed by his senses, Goethe reflects on his own perception and proposes a passionate, rather uncanny solution.

It is not surprising that Forsythe chose this poem, which Arnold Schoenberg set to music as a vocal quartet, to be sung at the ending of one of his ballets, the 1992 *ALIE/N A(C)TION*. In the first part of this work, the dancers referred to an "alphabet" of movement modalities they had elaborated in reference to three-dimensional maps they had individually created. Additionally, they also referred to video screens projecting scenes from the movies *Alien* (1979, directed by Ridley Scott) and *Aliens* (1986, directed by James Cameron) and soundtrack sections, from which they extracted raw perceptual information—shapes, vectors, colors, sounds, rhythms, cut structures—to guide their improvisations.[1] It is unlikely, though, that *ALIE/N A(C)TION* will ever be performed again, and the same is unfortunately true of most of the works discussed in this volume. *Enemy in the Figure*, *In the Middle, Somewhat Elevated*, and *the second detail* remain in the repertory of companies worldwide; however, the

© The Author(s), under exclusive license to Springer Nature Switzerland AG 2023
F. Vass, *William Forsythe's Postdramatic Dance Theater*, Cognitive Studies in Literature and Performance,
https://doi.org/10.1007/978-3-031-26658-4_12

full-length works of which they were constituent parts are not being performed.[2] A slightly altered version of *Artifact* entered the repertory of the Boston Ballet in 2017 as *Artifact 2017*, and *New Sleep* remains in the repertory of Ballett Zürich and Les Ballets de Monte Carlo, while a pas de deux from *New Sleep* has a place in *Neue Suite*, a selection of five duets from works created between 1987 and 1999. Other Forsythe "ballet ballets" and one-act works still being performed by ballet and contemporary ensembles include *Herman Schmerman* (1992), *Quintett* (1993), *Of Any If And* (1995), *Approximate Sonata* (1996), *Duo* (1996), *The Vertiginous Thrill of Exactitude* (1996), *Workwithinwork* (1998), *One Flat Thing, reproduced* (date), and *N.N.N.N.* (2002). To date, no works that were created for The Forsythe Company have been staged on other ensembles.

Since the dissolution of The Forsythe Company in 2015, Forsythe has been creating "ballet ballets" as a freelancer, starting the following year with *Blake Works I* for the Ballet de l'Opéra de Paris and continuing with works for the English National Ballet, Boston Ballet, the filmed performance *The Barre Project* created during the COVID pandemic, and further *Blake Works* versions for the Dance Theatre of Harlem and Teatro alla Scala's ballet company. Perhaps predictably, some critics have used this return as an opportunity to dismiss his previous and less obviously balletic work. One five-star review of *Blake Works I* and *Playlist (EP)'s* "tireless flow of bravura steps" describes Forsythe as returning from "a long, not entirely fruitful wander down some of the blind alleys of postmodernist deconstruction and Tanztheater" to resume "injecting new life into familiar classroom steps" and "reimagining and subverting the classical vocabulary."[3] Forsythe has, however, not stopped working in a more experimental vein: *Catalogue (First Edition)*, created for the Dance On Ensemble in 2016, became part of *A Quiet Evening of Dance* (2018) with former Frankfurt dancers and others including Rauf "Rubberlegz" Yasit, while in 2021 he produced an expanded version of *N.N.N.N.* for the Netherlands Dance Theater via Zoom and assisted by veteran Frankfurt dancers on site.

These continual returns to earlier works and approaches, along with the ongoing changes he makes to works in reflection to his own learning and that of the dancers with whom he now works,[4] made a chronological through-line of Forsythe's development as a choreographing cognitive researcher untenable for this volume. Together with the collaborative processes and the distributed and unspoken nature of the knowledge that underpins large portions of his oeuvre, this also explains why many of his works are essentially irreproducible, except as methodologically impoverished, optics-driven renderings that are inert in terms of research.[5]

Essentially, all of Forsythe's works—and indeed all choreographies—are performed manifestations of both distributed constellations of thinking and the results of choreo-cognitive research. There is great variance, though, in their accessibility for re-presentation and for study. Forsythe has created and will continue to leave a deep legacy, but like all legacies it will be incomplete. In joining the canon of Forsythe literature—and in defiance of Bill's quip that "Enough ink has been spilled already" about his work—this book has opened another avenue along which to "step inside" and think about what you think you see.

Aesthetically, postdramatic dance theater joins a trajectory through twentieth-century avant-garde and postmodern dance, continuing a discursive relationship with positivist aesthetics of beauty, coherence, and closure. Forsythe's work interrogates these by highlighting the limits of sensing and attention through the wide range of performative dynamics of visuosonic give-and-take instantiated and brought into comparative dialogue with empirical research in the preceding chapters. As well, Forsythe's unsettling of perception complicates connections of dance's ephemerality to its in-the-moment temporality, as well as considerations of the "even-more-deeply-ephemeral" nature of one-time improvised performances of dance.[6] Movement produced of course occurs even if it is not seen or is only glimpsed due to darkness, dimness, occlusion, or diverted attention, but its ephemerality impacts differently than fully visible movement—which itself is impacted by selective visual focus. The ways that soundscoring and spatiality affect movement perception also further complicate considerations of dance that isolate it from the made worlds in which its performance was intended.

Every Time I Step Inside I Remember What I Never Thought

I recall an after-performance talk in Dresden with a busload of well-to-do dance afficionados on a visit to Dresden, during which they received a tour of the city, a guided visit to the Palucca-Schule, an evening at the Semperoper watching their sumptuous production of *Sleeping Beauty*, and a performance the following evening of Forsythe's cryptic and at times disturbing *Angoloscuro* at the Festspielhaus Hellerau, followed by a fine dinner with me. The wine flowed as I ran through a quick history of twentieth-century dance's inquiry into the art form's potentials, described the importance of the Festspielhaus as a key experimental venue, and gave an overview of Forsythe's work. I then invited discussion of the work they had just seen. *In vino veritas*: an intensely heated debate broke out among the attendees, with some angrily insisting that the work had failed by having been difficult to understand and others maintaining that comprehension was not the point of the evening. In the midst of the fray, one gentleman stood up and pointed a finger at me, declaring "I'd like to know what Mr. Forsythe would think if he knew we were arguing about his work like this!" I smiled and replied, "I think he might be extremely pleased. You didn't argue like this after *Sleeping Beauty*, did you?"

Works that unsettle perception, and thereby *perceptions*, have the ability to evoke reflection not only about the creative mind but also about one's own, provided that the reflection moves beyond "I liked/didn't like it" or "I got/didn't get it" to an engagement with the lived experience of the event. When Forsythe encourages audiences to "just watch," he is actually indicating more: watch the work but watch yourself as well, noting how you see and hear (or don't) and how you think and feel both about performances as well as about your own performance as a thinking, feeling perceiver. It is when sensing and thought leave the realm of the automatic and effortless that they become more easily available to be apprehended and considered as constitutive facets of our selves. Forsythe's oeuvre reveals that his interests in perception, which were present almost from the outset of his choreographic career, have continuously guided his research as he has moved at the advancing edge of ballet practice, as a postdramatic dance and theatre maker, and also as a creator of *choreographic objects*, of which he says:

> A choreographic object is, by nature, open to a full range of unmediated perceptual instigations without having to prioritize any type of recipient. These objects are examples of specific physical circumstances that isolate fundamental classes of motion activation and organization. The objects instigate processes in the body that instrumentalize the body's readiness to provide input for our heuristically driven, predictive faculties, which work incessantly to secure for us a higher probability of preferred physical and mental outcomes. A principal feature of the choreographic object is that the preferred outcome is a form of knowledge production for whoever engages with it, *engendering an acute awareness of the self* within specific action schemata [italics mine].[7]

Forsythe's performance installations, then, are avenues for full-bodied engagement with the performance of perception. As well, though, they offer a philosophy that is firmly grounded within the relationship between individuals and environments, albeit one inflected by the performative intentions underlying the composition of both environments and actions. Tim Ingold, whose work resonates with Gibson's ecological psychology, Bourdieu's theory of practice, and the phenomenologies of Heidegger and Merleau-Ponty, foregrounds that cultural knowledge arises out of dwelling in conditions that engender "the development of specific dispositions and sensibilities that lead people to orient themselves in relation" to its features and to attend to them in particular ways.[8] It would be easy to draw a dichotomy between the "real" world and the made worlds of performance. However, when postdramatic performance worlds are analyzed from the "surface" perspective of sensory perception, interpersonal and intercultural differences, though not entirely absent, are reduced. Attentional behavior will be inflected by neuroatypicality and sensory deficits, but no one can see in pitch darkness or through a wooden wall, and simultaneous action and soundstreams will robustly impact perceptual focus. Performance worlds composed to unsettle attention are constituted of everyday phenomena—light, sound, forms, movement, associations, contrasts—but they disrupt our perceptual habitus, bringing our sensory tendencies and shortcomings into the spotlight of apprehension.

Forsythe's postdramatic dance theater clearly insists on an ecological consideration by imbricating its stage(d) worlds and in some instances suffusing the boundary between the dancer-as-percept and the scenic/sonic environment. Not only interfacing with but becoming part of architectures of light (and dark), space, objects, and sound or its never-total absence, Forsythe's dancers perform the boundary of figure and ground by traversing it and proliferating its manifestations. In doing so, they paradoxically achieve fleeting moments of synthesis with their environment—which in some instances performs a "duet" of its own agile choreography with them—even as they deny perceptual and cognitive synthesis to those attending.

Lehmann unequivocally posits that postdramatic theatre offers an explicit theory of perception. His description of postdramatic theatre's incoherence as a "retreat of synthesis" is grounded in a semiotic view that takes theatrical signs to include "all dimensions of signification, not merely signs that carry determinable information, i.e. signifiers which denote (or unmistakably connote) an identifiable signified, but virtually all elements of the theatre." As he notes,

> For even a striking physicality, a certain style of a gesture or a stage arrangement, simply by dint of the fact that they are present(ed) with a certain emphasis, are received as 'signs' in the sense of a manifestation or gesticulation obviously demanding attention, 'making sense' through the heightening frame of the performance without being 'fixable' conceptionally.[9]

Lehmann, however, opposes Kant's concept of the "aesthetic idea" through which intuitive imaginative faculties are animated but full conceptualization remains unattainable,[10] arguing instead for an active "self-cancellation of meaning" in postdramatic theatre:

> Synthesis is cancelled. It is explicitly combated. Theatre articulates through the mode of its semiosis an implicit *thesis* concerning perception. It may appear surprising to ascribe artistic discourse the ability to have a thesis like a theoretical discourse...Yet this is precisely why it is one of the tasks of hermeneutics to read in the preferred forms and configurations of anaesthetic practice the hypotheses expressed in them, i.e. to take into account and practice a semantics of form. Enclosed within post dramatic theatre is obviously the demand for an open and fragmenting perception in place of the unifying enclosed perception. On the one hand, the abundance of simultaneous signs in this way presents itself like a doubling of reality: it seemingly mimics the chaos of real everyday experience. But part and parcel of this quasi 'Naturalistic' stance is the thesis that an authentic manner in which theatre could testify to life *cannot* come about through imposing an artistic macrostructure that constructs coherence (as is the case in drama).[11]

This is not to say, however, that interpretation takes a holiday. I concur with Lehmann that postdramatic theatre's "de-hierarchization of theatrical means," in which the experience of environment and action within it are brought onto more equal ground with traditionally privileged sign forms such as language, gesture, and narrative, prompts spectators "to process the perceived instantaneously but to postpone the production of meaning (semiosis) and to store the sensory impressions" as their attention hovers,[12] awaiting potential opportunities to "make sense." We are inherent predictors: body and world-readers, memory machines, story-producers, and image-builders, storing information and creating propositions on the fly. Postdramatic theatre makers harness ambiguity to *flirt* with our innate attempts to "get it,"[13] offering fragments of possible meaning that may or may not settle into ideas that we trust ourselves to believe in. Is there an ethos or an ethics in Forsythe's encouragement to "just watch?" Or even a politics?

EVERYTHING WILL BE ALRIGHT

In 2011, Lehmann addressed accusations that postdramatic theatre lacked a political dimension: that it was just "formalistic (Jan Fabre), mere aesthetic and non-committal play (Robert Wilson), or at best lyrical and refined in successful performances (Jan Lauwers) or cheerfully trendy, cool fun (René Pollesch)." He replaced the suggested question "How political is postdramatic theatre?" which he said sounded like a "multiple choice question" with options like "highly political," "somewhat political," and "not very political," with a question he considered more tractable: "*How* is theatre, for example postdramatic theatre, political?" In his article, he invokes the idea of a theatre with a relationship *to* the political, rather than a theatre with political content, arguing that it is neither the negotiation of problems through "appropriate fables," nor the (re)presentation of oppression, nor the staging of a director's personal political beliefs that make a piece of theatre political. He argues that the political can instead only occur "indirectly" in theatre, coming into play "if, and only if, it is in no way translatable or re-translatable into logic, syntax and terminology of political discourse in social reality." The politics that he sees as a theatrical possibility is not one of reproduction of the political, but rather of its interruption—a "caesura."[14] He continues:

> Theater calls – as does every art – for a pragmatically "impossible" justice…In contrast to this narrow-minded, seemingly well-informed pragmatism, whose rationale nonetheless led to the catastrophe, aesthetic practice stands as the exception to the groundlessness of the law, to everything established and especially to that which we ourselves have established, and thus sharpens – and this would be the core of a perceptual politics of theatre – the *sense for the exception*. Not for the better political rule, not for the alleged or perhaps actually better morality, for the best of all possible laws, but instead an eye for that which typically remains the exception, for what has been left behind, for what is not taken up, for what does not come up and therefore represents a claim: historically to memory, currently to deviation.[15]

The exception that interrupts the political is a return to the fundamentals of existence. In a way, this was reflected in some responses to the enforced lockdowns of the pandemic period: a return to essential practices, to finding ways to get things done, to taking time to be a body in a space, to compose and explore one's space, to sense time and fill it with activities that inform and please, to learn to see and listen again, to think and rethink, to pose questions and seek answers. Of his approach to ballet, Forsythe said in a 2003 interview that it is "a geometric, inscriptive art form. We're inscribing geometry. And let's just start there - it's a really basic approach to it, it's very simple, it's not overtly political but it does have philosophical backgrounds."[16] Community, though, is also fundamental, as the pandemic proved. Describing his recent choreographic work with the Netherlands Dance Theater via Zoom, Forsythe reflected long-held concerns by commenting,

> Right now, with the way the world is operating, I'm very curious about self-regulating communities. Dancers are like citizens of a little country. NDT is its own little entity. Politically, socially, and in many other ways. How can we, they, contribute to that community while retaining a sense of self? They are inheriting a very complex world and anything that might help them navigate, I consider much more important to communicate than the X, Y, Zs of a particular choreographed movement.[17]

Is that all there is? Dancing is performance and an active experience, but so is "just watching." Perception is a performance of our senses and our minds—something, as Alva Noë reminds us, that we *do*: "It is a temporally extended process of skilful probing. The world makes itself available to our reach. The experience comprises mind and world."[18] Sometimes that world is an unsettled place, whether real or theatrical. But even then—and perhaps primarily then—we have an opportunity to come to know ourselves and our world better.

NOTES

1. See Dana Caspersen's far more detailed description of her process at "Methodologies: Bill Forsythe and the Ballett Frankfurt." See also Nik Haffner, "Forsythe und die Medien."
2. The full-length *Limb's Theorem* was last performed by the Ballet de l'Opéra de Lyon and the Bayerisches Staatsballett in 2014 and 2015, respectively, while *Impressing the Czar* was last performed by the Semperoper Ballett

Dresden in 2019. *The Loss of Small Detail* was last performed by the Ballett Frankfurt in 1997.

3. Louise Levene, "English National Ballet's William Forsythe evening—a tireless flow of bravura steps."

4. As Forsythe has recently put it,

> I always assume I can do it better: this is because 25 years ago I didn't have the breadth of skills I have now...I'm like a plumber, I'm always looking for the leaks, haha. I find those everywhere, so then I have to reconcile with knowing I could have built it better to begin with, but I guess I didn't, and that's okay! It keeps me relevant in the rehearsal room, haha. If everything was "fixed" I would probably have nothing to say other than "faster", or "slower" which is not my idea of a meaningful life. Most importantly, by revisiting and renovating work I'm able to keep connected to the dancers of each new epoch.

Judith Vrancken, 2021 "In conversation with William Forsythe."

5. See Freya Vass-Rhee, "Distributed dramaturgies: navigating with boundary objects."

6. Aili Bresnahan, review of Graham McFee. For a prescient overview of discussions of dance's ephemerality, see Aili Bresnahan, "The Philosophy of Dance," 8–9.

7. William Forsythe, "Choreographic Objects." See also Emma McCormick-Goodheart, "Beyond Ballet: How Choreographer William Forsythe Helps us to Return to our Bodies."

8. Tim Ingold, *The Perception of the Environment*, 153.

9. Lehmann, *Postdramatic Theatre*, 82.

10. Immanuel Kant, *Critique of the Power of Judgment*, 314, 342.

11. Lehmann, *Postdramatic Theatre*, 82–83.

12. Lehmann, *Postdramatic Theatre*, 86–87.

13. See Eric Eisenberg, "Flirting with meaning."

14. Hans-Thies Lehmann, Wie politisch ist postdramatisches Theater?" 30–35.

15. Hans-Thies Lehmann, Wie politisch ist postdramatisches Theater?" 37–38.

16. Forsythe, interviewed by John Tusa, BBC, Radio 3, February 2, 2003, http://www.bbc.co.uk/radio3/johntusainterview/forsythe_transcript.shtml (accessed March 12, 2003).

17. Judith Vrancken, "In conversation with William Forsythe."

18. Alva Noë, *Action in perception*, 216.

BIBLIOGRAPHY

Bresnahan, Aili. 2013. Review of McFee, Graham. 2011. *The Philosophical Aesthetics of Dance: Identity, Performance, and Understanding. Dance Research Journal* 45 (2): 142–145.

———. 2019. The Philosophy of Dance. *Philosophy Faculty Publications*, 184. https://ecommons.udayton.edu/cgi/viewcontent.cgi?article=1183&context=phl_fac_pub. Accessed 8 August 2022.

Caspersen, Dana. 2007. Methodologies: Bill Forsythe and the Ballett Frankfurt. https://walkerart.org/magazine/methodologies-bill-forsythe-and-the-ballett-frankfurt-by-dana-caspersen. Accessed 5 February 2010.

Eisenberg, Eric. 1998. Flirting with Meaning. *Journal of Language and Social Psychology* 17 (1): 97–108.

Forsythe, William. 2008. Choreographic Objects. In *William Forsythe: Suspense*. Geneva: Jrp Ringier Kunstverlag Ag. https://www.williamforsythe.com/essay.html.

Haffner, Nik. 2000. Forsythe und die Medien. *tanzdrama* 511 (2): 30–35. English version: Forsythe and the media. www.frankfurt-ballett.de/nikmedia-english.html. Accessed 31 May 2003.

Ingold, Tim. 2000. *The Perception of the Environment: Essays on Livelihood, Dwelling and Skill*. London and New York: Routledge.

Kant, Immanuel. 2000. *Critique of the Power of Judgment*. Translated by Eric Matthews and Paul Guyer. Cambridge and New York: Cambridge University Press.

Lehmann, Hans-Thies. 2006. *Postdramatic Theatre*. Translated by Karen-Jürs-Munby. Abingdon and New York: Routledge. Original version: Lehmann, Hans-Thies. 1999. *Postdramatisches Theater*. Frankfurt am Main: Verlag der Autoren.

———. 2011. Wie politisch ist postdramatisches Theater? In *Politisch Theater machen: Neue Artikulationsformen des Politischen in den darstellenden Künsten*, ed. Jan Deck and Angelika Sieburg, 29–40. Bielefeld: transcript Verlag.

Levene, Louise. 2022. English National Ballet's William Forsythe Evening—A Tireless Flow of Bravura Steps. *Financial Times*, 4 April. https://www.ft.com/content/8143018b-75df-491c-8c48-ebbc0b5288e9. Accessed 5 April 2022.

McCormick-Goodheart, Emma. 2019. Beyond Ballet: How Choreographer William Forsythe Helps Us to Return to Our Bodies. *Frieze*, 201. https://www.frieze.com/article/beyond-ballet-how-choreographer-william-forsythe-helps-us-return-our-bodies. Accessed 20 March 2022.

Noë, Alva. 2004. *Action in Perception*. Cambridge, MA: MIT Press.

Tusa, John. 2003. Interview with William Forsythe. *BBC Radio*, 3, 2 February. http://www.bbc.co.uk/radio3/johntusainterview/forsythe_transcript.shtml. Accessed 12 March 2003.

Vass-Rhee, Freya. 2015. Distributed Dramaturgies: Navigating with Boundary Objects. In *Dance Dramaturgy: Modes of Agency, Awareness and Engagement*, ed. Pil Hansen and Darcey Callison, 87–105. Basingstoke: Palgrave Macmillan.

Vrancken, Judith. 2021. In Conversation with William Forsythe. https://www.ndt.nl/en/story/in-conversation-with-william-forsythe/. Accessed 3 December 2021.

Chronological List of Works

This chronology indicates live and recorded music but does not include the extensive array of other soundscore elements found in many Forsythe works. Some of these have been noted in Parts II and III of this volume. For a full catalogue through 2011, see Vass-Rhee (2011).

This catalogue also includes only selected performance installations and does not include Forsythe's film projects. For a comprehensive listing of installation works, see https://www.williamforsythe.com/williamforsythe.html.

Forsythe has at times given choreographic credit to the ensemble or to specific ensemble members. Where applicable, this has been noted. Unless otherwise indicated, all premieres from 1994 to 2004 are by the Ballett Frankfurt at the Oper Frankfurt, and from 2005 to 2013, all premieres are by The Forsythe Company.

1976

Urlicht (pas de deux)
Music: Gustav Mahler, *Symphony No. 2*, 4th Movement
Premiere: 18 November 1976, Noverre Society, Stuttgart

© The Author(s), under exclusive license to Springer Nature
Switzerland AG 2023
F. Vass, *William Forsythe's Postdramatic Dance Theater*, Cognitive
Studies in Literature and Performance,
https://doi.org/10.1007/978-3-031-26658-4

1977

Daphne (Ein Mythos) (one-act ballet)
Music: Antonin Dvořák, *Symphony No. 7 in D minor*, 2nd and 3rd movements
Stage design and costumes: William Forsythe
Premiere: 26 March 1977, Stuttgart Ballet, Stuttgart

Bach Violin Concerto in A Minor (one-act ballet)
Music: Johann Sebastian Bach, *Violin Concerto in A minor*
Premiere: Basel Ballet, Basel

Flore Subsimplici (one-act ballet)
Music: Georg Friedrich Händel, *Concerti Grossi*, op. 6
Stage design and costumes: William Forsythe
Premiere: 8 November 1977, Stuttgart Ballet, Stuttgart

1978

In Endloser Zeit **(From the Most Distant Time)** (one-act ballet)
Music: György Ligeti, *Double Concerto for Flute and Oboe*
Speaker: Gisela Pfeil
Texts: Tang dynasty poems
Stage design and lighting: William Forsythe
Costumes: Arthur Brady
Premiere: 23 February 1978, Stuttgart Ballet, Stuttgart

Traum des Galilei (one-act ballet)
Music: Krzysztof Penderecki, *Symphony No. 1*
Stage design and costumes: William Forsythe
Premiere: 21 May 1978, Stuttgart Ballet, Stuttgart

Aria de la Folía Española (one-act ballet) (also listed as *Folía*)
Music: Hans Werner Henze, *Aria de la Folia Espagñola*
Premiere: July 1978, Stuttgart Ballet, Montepulciano, Italy

1979

Orpheus (two-act ballet)
Music: Hans Werner Henze
Stage design: Axel Manthey
Costumes: Joachim Herzog
Premiere: 17 March 1979, Stuttgart Ballet, Stuttgart

Seite 1—Love Songs—Alte Platten (currently known as *Love Songs*)
(one-act ballet)
Music: Aretha Franklin, Dionne Warwick
Stage design and lighting: William Forsythe
Costumes: Eileen Brady
Premiere: 5 May 1979, Stuttgart Ballet, Munich

EVENT 1 2 3 (performance installation)
Direction: William Forsythe
Choreography: William Forsythe and Ron Thornhill
Concept: Randi Bubat
Music: William Forsythe, Ron Thornhill, and Michael Simon
Costumes: Randi Bubat
Premiere: 25 September 1979, Wagenburg Tunnel, Stuttgarter Internationaler Kunst Kongress

Time Cycle (one-act ballet)
Music: Lukas Foss, *Time Cycle* (song cycle for soprano and orchestra)
Text: W. H. Auden, A. E. Housman, Franz Kafka, and Friedrich Nietzsche
Stage design, lighting, and costumes: Axel Manthey
Premiere: 22 December 1979, Stuttgart Ballet, Stuttgart

1980

Famous Mother's Club (solo for Lynn Seymour)
Music: David Cunningham, "I Want Money"
Premiere: Single Parents' Gala, London Palladium, London

Joyleen Gets Up, Gets Down, Goes Out (one-act ballet)
Music: Boris Blacher, *Blues, Espagnola und Rumba Philharmonica für 12 Solo Cellos*
Stage design: William Forsythe
Costumes: Eileen Brady
Premiere: 22 May 1980, Bavarian State Opera Ballet, Munich

'Tis A Pity She's A Whore (one-act ballet)
Music: Thomas Jahn
Stage design: William Forsythe and Randi Bubat
Lighting: Hans-Joachim Haas
Costumes: Eileen Brady and Randi Bubat
Premiere: Montepulciano, Italy

Say Bye Bye (one-act ballet)
Music: Moises Simons, Lou Harrison and John Cage, Maria Grever, Maurice Ohana, Little Richard, Jürgen Vater
Stage design: Axel Manthey
Lighting: Joop Caboort
Costumes: Eileen Brady, Axel Manthey
Premiere: 26 November 1980, Nederlands Dans Theater, Circustheater, Scheveningen, The Netherlands

1981

Whisper Moon (one-act ballet)
Choreography: William Forsythe and Axel Manthey
Music: William Bolcom, *Whisper Moon*, *Dream Music No. 3*, and *Quintet for Violin, Violoncello, Flute, Clarinet and Piano*
Stage design: Axel Manthey and William Forsythe
Lighting: Hans-Joachim Haas
Premiere: 12 April 1981, Stuttgart Ballet, Stuttgart

Tancred und Clorinda (one-act ballet)
Music: Claudio Monteverdi, *Il combattimento di Tancredi e Clorinda*
Musical Arrangement: Luciano Berio
Text: Torquato Tasso
Lighting: Hans-Joachim Haas
Costumes: William Forsythe
Premiere: 5 May 1981, Stuttgart Ballet, Stuttgart

Die Nacht aus Blei (one-act ballet)
Music: Hans-Jürgen von Bose
Text: Hans Henny Jahnn
Stage design and costumes: Axel Manthey
Premiere: 1 November 1981, Ballet Deutsche Oper, Berlin

1982

Gänge (Ein Stück über Ballett) (Part 1) (one-act ballet)
Music: composition by William Forsythe, Dick Heuff, and Michael Simon
Stage design and lighting: Michael Simon
Costumes: Tom Schenk
Visual direction: William Forsythe and Michael Simon
Premiere: 25 February 1982, Nederlands Dans Theater, The Hague, The Netherlands

1983

Gänge (Ein Stück über Ballett) (full-length version)
Music: Thomas Jahn
Stage design: Michael Simon
Costumes: Randi Bubat, Igolf Thiel, and Tom Schenk
Premiere: 27 February 1983, Frankfurt Ballet, Frankfurt

Mental Model (one-act ballet)
Music: Igor Stravinsky, *Quatre Études pour Orchestre, Four Norwegian Moods*, and *Scherzo à la Russe*
Stage design: William Forsythe
Lighting: William Forsythe and Joop Caboort
Costumes: Stephen Meaha
Premiere: 16 June 1983, Nederlands Dans Theater, The Hague, The Netherlands

Square Deal (one-act ballet)
Music: William Forsythe, Thomas Jahn, and Michael Simon
Stage design, composition, and visual effects: William Forsythe
Lighting: William Forsythe and Jennifer Tipton
Costumes: Douglas Ferguson
Slides: Arthur Brady
Premiere: 2 November 1983, Joffrey Ballet, New York

France/Dance (full-length ballet)
Music: Johann Sebastian Bach, *Art of the Fugue*; composition by Thom Willems
Music collage, stage design, lighting, and costumes: William Forsythe
Objects and images: Cara Perlman
Premiere: 14 December 1983, Ballet de l'Opéra de Paris, Palais Garnier, Paris

1984

Artifact (full-length ballet in four parts)
Music: Eva Crossman-Hecht (parts I and IV); Johann Sebastian Bach, *Chaconne* from *Partita No. 2 in D minor* performed by Nathan Milstein (part II); sound collage by William Forsythe (part III)
Stage design, lighting, costumes, and text: William Forsythe
Premiere: 5 December 1984, Frankfurt

1985

Steptext (one-act ballet)
Music: Johann Sebastian Bach, *Chaconne* from *Partita No. 2 in D minor*
Stage design, lighting, and costumes: William Forsythe
Premiere: 11 January 1985, Aterballetto, Reggio Emilia, Italy

LDC (full-length ballet)
Music: Thom Willems
Stage design: Michael Simon
Lighting: Michael Simon and William Forsythe
Costumes: Benedikt Ramm
Premiere: 1 May 1985, Frankfurt

How To Recognize Greek Art I and II (pas de deux)
Music: music collage by William Forsythe
Premiere: 31 December 1985, Frankfurt

1986

Isabelle's Dance (full-length musical)
Music: Eva Crossman-Hecht
Lyrics: Eva Crossman-Hecht, William Forsythe, Sara Neece, and Stephen Saugey
Stage design and lighting: Michael Simon
Costumes: Férial Simon
Premiere: 3 February 1986, Frankfurt

Pizza Girl (ninety one-minute ballets)
Choreography: Alida Chase, William Forsythe, Stephen Galloway, Timothy Gordon, Dieter Heitkamp, Evan Jones, Amanda Miller, Vivienne Newport, Cara Perlman, Antony Rizzi, Ana Catalina Roman, Iris Tenge, Ron Thornhill, and Berna Uithof
Music: Thom Willems
Stage design: William Forsythe and Cara Perlman
Lighting: William Forsythe
Costumes: William Forsythe and Benedikt Ramm
Painting: Cara Perlman, "Pizza Girl"
Premiere: 27 February 1986, Frankfurt

Skinny (one-act ballet)
Choreography: William Forsythe and Amanda Miller

Music: William Forsythe and Thom Willems
Text, stage design, and lighting: William Forsythe
Costumes: William Forsythe and Amanda Miller
Premiere: 17 April 1986, Frankfurt

Baby Sam (one-act ballet)
Music: Thom Willems, music collage by William Forsythe
Text: William Forsythe
Stage design, lighting, and costumes: William Forsythe
Premiere: 21 May 1986, Bari, Italy

Die Befragung des Robert Scott † (one-act ballet)
Music: Thom Willems
Text, stage design, lighting, and costumes: William Forsythe
Premiere: 29 October 1986, Frankfurt

Big White Baby Dog (one-act ballet)
Music: Thom Willems
Stage design, lighting, and costumes: William Forsythe
Premiere: 10 November 1986, Frankfurt

1987

New Sleep (one-act ballet)
Music: Thom Willems
Stage design, lighting, and costumes: William Forsythe
Premiere: 1 February 1987, San Francisco Ballet, San Francisco

The Loss of Small Detail (version 1) (full-length ballet)
Music: Thom Willems, digital glove played by Amanda Miller
Text: William Forsythe, David Levin, and Patrick Primavesi
Digital gloves: Michel Waisvisz
Stage design and lighting: William Forsythe
Costumes: Benedikt Ramm
Premiere: 4 April 1987, Frankfurt

In the Middle, Somewhat Elevated (one-act ballet)
Music: Thom Willems in collaboration with Leslie Stuck
Stage design, lighting, and costumes: William Forsythe
Premiere: 30 May 1987, Ballet de l'Opéra de Paris, Palais Garnier, Paris

Same Old Story (one-act ballet)
Music: Thom Willems
Text: Nicholas Champion, Kathleen Fitzgerald, and William Forsythe

Stage design, lighting, and costumes: William Forsythe
Premiere: 5 June 1987, Ballett Frankfurt, Hamburg

1988

Impressing the Czar (full-length ballet)
(Part I: *Potemkins Unterschrift*; Part II: *In the Middle, Somewhat Elevated*; Part III: *La Maison de Mezzo-Prezzo*; Part IV: *Bongo Bongo Nageela* and *Mr. Pnut Goes to the Big Top*)
Music: Ludwig van Beethoven, *Opus 131, string quartet no. 14*, fifth movement; Leslie Stuck, Thom Willems, and Eva Crossman-Hecht
Stage design: Michael Simon and William Forsythe
Lighting: William Forsythe and Michael Simon
Costumes: Férial Simon
Text: William Forsythe, Richard Fein, and Kathleen Fitzgerald
Premiere: 10 January 1988, Frankfurt

Behind the China Dogs (one-act ballet)
Music: Leslie Stuck
Lighting: William Forsythe
Costumes: William Forsythe and Barbara Matera
China dogs: Cara Perlman
Premiere: 7 May 1988, New York City Ballet, New York

The Vile Parody of Address (one-act ballet)
Music: Johann Sebastian Bach, *The Well-Tempered Clavier*
Stage design, lighting, and costumes: William Forsythe
Text: William Forsythe
Premiere: 26 November 1988, Frankfurt

1989

Enemy in the Figure (one-act ballet)
Music: Thom Willems
Stage design, lighting, and costumes: William Forsythe
Premiere: 13 May 1989, Frankfurt

Slingerland (Part 1) (one-act ballet)
Music: Gavin Bryars
Stage design and film: Cara Perlman
Lighting and costumes: William Forsythe
Premiere: 25 November 1989, Frankfurt

1990

Limb's Theorem (full-length ballet; incorporates *Enemy in the Figure*)
Music: Thom Willems
Stage design: Michael Simon (parts I and III) and William Forsythe
(part II)
Lighting: William Forsythe and Michael Simon
Costumes: Férial Simon (parts I and III) and William Forsythe (part II)
Premiere: 17 March 1990, Frankfurt

Slingerland (full-length ballet)
Music: Thom Willems; Gavin Bryars, *Sub Rosa*
Stage design, lighting, and costumes: William Forsythe
Objects and images: Cara Perlman
Premieres: 25 June 1990, Ballett Frankfurt, Amsterdam (parts I–III)
and 20 October 1990, Paris (parts I–IV)

1991

the second detail (one-act ballet)
Music: Thom Willems
Stage design and lighting: William Forsythe
Costumes: William Forsythe; "Colombe" dress by Issey Miyake
Premiere: 20 February 1991, National Ballet of Canada, Toronto

Snap. Woven Effort (one-act ballet)
Music: Thom Willems
Text, stage design, and lighting: William Forsythe
Costumes: Gianni Versace
Premiere: 26 October 1991, Frankfurt

Marion/Marion (duet)
Music: Bernard Herman, *Temptation No. 5*
Stage design and lighting: William Forsythe
Costumes: Gianni Versace
Premiere: 8 November 1991, Nederlands Dans Theater III, The
Hague, The Netherlands

The Loss of Small Detail (full-length ballet in two acts; incorporates *the
second detail*)
Music: Thom Willems
Stage design and lighting: William Forsythe
Costumes: William Forsythe and Issey Miyake

Text: William Forsythe, Yukio Mishima (excerpts from *Runaway Horses*), and Jérôme Rothenberg (excerpts from *Technicians of the Sacred*)
Film: Helga Funderl, *Hund im Schnee* and Fiona Léus, *Between Mediums*
Premiere: 21 December 1991, Frankfurt

1992

Herman Schmerman (pas de cinq)
Music: Thom Willems
Stage design: William Forsythe
Lighting: Marc Stanley
Costumes: Gianni Versace
Premiere: 28 May 1992, New York City Ballet, New York

As a Garden in This Setting (one-act ballet)
Music: Thom Willems
Stage design and lighting: William Forsythe
Costumes: Issey Miyake and Naoki Takizawa
Video: Sean Toren
Premiere: 13 June 1992, Frankfurt

Herman Schmerman (pas de deux)
Music: Thom Willems
Stage design and lighting: William Forsythe
Costumes: Gianni Versace
Premiere: 26 September 1992, Frankfurt

ALIE/N A(C)TION (full-length ballet)
Music: Thom Willems; Arnold Schönberg, "O, daß der Sinnen doch so viele sind"
Stage design and lighting: William Forsythe
Costumes: Steven Galloway
Video: Sean Toren
Computer programming: David Kern
Dramaturgical assistance: Steven Valk
Premiere: 19 December 1992, Frankfurt; new version 5 November 1993, Frankfurt

1993

Quintett (one-act ballet)
Choreography: William Forsythe in collaboration with Dana Caspersen, Stephen Galloway, Jacopo Godani, Thomas McManus, and Jone San Martin

Music: Gavin Bryars, *Jesus's Blood Never Failed Me Yet*
Stage design and lighting: William Forsythe
Costumes: Stephen Galloway
Premiere: 9 October 1993, Frankfurt

As a Garden in This Setting (full-length version including *And Through Them Filters, Futile*)
Music: Thom Willems
Stage design and lighting: William Forsythe
Costumes: Issey Miyake and Naoki Takizawa
Dramaturgical assistance: Steven Valk
Premiere: 18 December 1993, Frankfurt

1994

Self Meant To Govern (one-act ballet)
Music: Thom Willems in collaboration with Maxim Franke
Stage design and lighting: William Forsythe
Costumes: Stephen Galloway
Violin: Maxim Franke
Premiere: 2 July 1994, Frankfurt

Pivot House (one-act ballet)
Music: court music of Kraton Surakarta, *Srimpi* (Provisions for Death)
Stage design and lighting: William Forsythe
Costumes: Stephen Galloway
Video: Richard Caon
Premiere: 13 December 1994, Ballett Frankfurt, Reggio Emilia, Italy

1995

Eidos:Telos (full-length ballet in three acts; incorporates *Self Meant to Govern*)
Choreography: William Forsythe in collaboration with the ensemble
Music and DSP processing: Thom Willems in collaboration with Maxim Franke (Part I); Thom Willems in collaboration with Joel Ryan (Parts II and III)
Music assistant: Dirk Haubrich
Stage design and Lighting: William Forsythe
Costumes: Stephen Galloway (Part II) and Naoki Takizawa (Miyake Design Studio)
Texts: Dana Caspersen (monologue, Part II), William Forsythe (additional texts, part II)
Premiere: 28 January 1995, Frankfurt

Firstext (one-act ballet)
Choreography: Dana Caspersen, William Forsythe, and Antony Rizzi
Music: Thom Willems
Stage design and lighting: William Forsythe
Costumes: Naoki Takizawa and Raymond Dragon Design Inc.
Premiere: 27 April 1995, The Royal Ballet, London

Invisible Film (one-act ballet)
Music: Johann Sebastian Bach, *Goldberg Variations*, George Friedrich
Händel, *Concerti Grossi*, Op. 6; Henry Purcell, *Fantazias, In Nomines*
Text: William Forsythe and pop music lyrics
Stage design and lighting: William Forsythe
Costumes: Stephen Galloway
Speaker: David Morrow
Premiere: 27 May 1995, Frankfurt

Of Any If And (one-act ballet)
Music: Thom Willems
Stage design and lighting: William Forsythe
Costumes: Stephen Galloway
Text: Dana Caspersen and William Forsythe
Premiere: 27 May 1995, Frankfurt

The The (one-act ballet)
Choreography: Dana Caspersen and William Forsythe
Music: ambient background noise (recorded)
Stage design and lighting: William Forsythe
Costumes: Stephen Galloway
Premiere: 8 October 1995, Holland Festival, The Hague, The
Netherlands

Four Point Counter (one-act ballet)
Music: Thom Willems
Stage design and lighting: William Forsythe
Costumes: Stephen Galloway
Premiere: 16 November 1995, Nederlands Dans Theater, The Hague,
The Netherlands

1996

Duo (one-act ballet; later performed as *DUO2015*)
Music: Thom Willems
Stage design, lighting, and costumes: William Forsythe
Premiere: 20 January 1996, Frankfurt

Trio (one-act ballet)
Music: Ludwig van Beethoven, *String Quartet No. 15 in A minor*, op. 132, and Alban Berg, *String Quartet*, op 3
Stage design and lighting: William Forsythe
Costumes: Stephen Galloway
Premiere: 20 January 1996, Frankfurt

Approximate Sonata (one-act ballet; later performed as *Approximate Sonata 2016*)
Music: Thom Willems; Tricky, "Pumpkin"
Stage design and lighting: William Forsythe
Costumes: Stephen Galloway
Premiere: 20 January 1996, Frankfurt

The Vertiginous Thrill of Exactitude (one-act ballet)
Music: Franz Schubert, *Symphony No. 9 in C major*, 3rd movement
Stage design and lighting: William Forsythe
Costumes: Stephen Galloway
Premiere: 20 January 1996, Frankfurt

Sleepers Guts (full-length ballet in three parts)
Choreography: William Forsythe in collaboration with the ensemble (Part I); William Forsythe (Part II); Jacopo Godani (Part III)
Music: Thom Willems and Joel Ryan; DSP composition by Joel Ryan and Dirk Haubrich
Music assistant: Chris Salter
Stage design and lighting: William Forsythe
Costumes: Stephen Galloway
Video: Nik Haffner and Bill Seaman
Projection graphics: Mark Goulthorpe
Premiere: 25 October 1996, Frankfurt

Hypothetical Stream (one-act ballet)
Choreography: William Forsythe
Realisation: Mié Coquempot, Vincent Druguet, Dylan Elmore, Anne
Laurent, Judith Perron, Laurence Rondoni, José Valls, Daniel Larrieu
Music: Stuart Dempster, *Standing Waves*
Stage design and lighting: William Forsythe
Costumes: Raymond Dragon, Simon Frearson
Premiere: 15 November 1996, Centre Chorégraphique National de Caen,
Théâtre de Caen, France

1997

Hypothetical Stream II (one-act ballet)
Choreography: William Forsythe, Regina van Berkel, Christine Bürkle,
Ana Catalina Roman, Jone San Martin, Timothy Couchman, Noah
Gelber, Jacopo Godani, Antony Rizzi, and Richard Siegal
Music: Stuart Dempster, *Standing Waves* and Ingram Marshall,
Fog Tropes
Stage design and lighting: William Forsythe
Costumes: Stephen Galloway
Premiere: 14 September 1997, Frankfurt

1998

Small Void (one-act ballet)
Choreography: William Forsythe in collaboration with Stefanie Arndt,
Alan Barnes, Dana Caspersen, Noah Gelber, Anders Hellström, Fabrice
Mazliah, Tamas Moricz, Crystal Pite, Jone San Martin, Richard Siegal,
Pascal Touzeau, and Sjoerd Vreugdenhil
Music: Thom Willems
Stage design and lighting: William Forsythe
Costumes: Stephen Galloway
Premiere: 30 January 1998, Frankfurt

Opus 31 (one-act ballet)
Music: Arnold Schönberg, *Variations for Orchestra*, op. 31
Stage design and lighting: William Forsythe
Costumes: Stephen Galloway
Premiere: 30 January 1998, Frankfurt

Quartetto (one-act ballet)
Music: Thom Willems
Stage design and lighting: William Forsythe
Costumes: Stephen Galloway
Premiere: 8 September 1998, Balletto del Teatro alla Scala, Milan

Quartette (one-act ballet)
Music: Thom Willems
Stage design and lighting: William Forsythe
Costumes: Stephen Galloway
Premiere: 16 October 1998, Frankfurt

Workwithinwork (one-act ballet)
Music: Luciano Berio, *Duetti for two violins*
Stage design and lighting: William Forsythe
Costumes: Stephen Galloway
Premiere: 16 October 1998, Frankfurt

1999

Woundwork 1 (one-act ballet)
Music: Thom Willems
Stage design and lighting: William Forsythe
Costumes: Stephen Galloway
Premiere: 31 March 1999, Ballet de l'Opéra de Paris, Palais Garnier, Paris

Pas./parts (one-act ballet; later performed as *Pas/Parts 2016 and Pas/ Parts 2018*)
Music: Thom Willems
Stage design and lighting: William Forsythe
Costumes: Stephen Galloway
Premiere: 31 March 1999, Ballet de l'Opéra de Paris, Palais Garnier, Paris

Endless House (full-length ballet in two parts)
Part I
Direction: Dana Caspersen
Music: court music of Kraton Surakarta, *Srimpi* (Provisions for Death)
Stage design and lighting: William Forsythe
Text: Charles Manson
Part II
Music: Autopoiesis (Ekkehard Ehlers and Sebastian Meissner) and Thom Willems

Sound Design: Bernhard Klein, Dietrich Krüger, and Niels Lanz
Direction, stage design, and lighting: William Forsythe
Text: Emily Brontë, Dana Caspersen, William Forsythe, and
Charles Manson
Costumes: Stephen Galloway
Dramaturgical assistance: Dana Caspersen and Steven Valk
Premiere: 15 October 1999, Oper Frankfurt (Part 1) and Bockenheimer
Depot (Part 2), Frankfurt

2000

Slingerland Duet (pas de deux)
Music: Gavin Bryars
Lighting and costumes: William Forsythe
Premiere: 13 April 2000, Schauspielhaus Frankfurt

Die Befragung des Robert Scott † (new full-length version)
Music: Thom Willems
Stage design and lighting: William Forsythe
Costumes: Stephen Galloway
Premiere: 2 February 2000, Bockenheimer Depot, Frankfurt

One Flat Thing, reproduced (one-act ballet; part 3 of *Die Befragung
des Robert Scott †*)
Music: Thom Willems
Stage design and lighting: William Forsythe
Costumes: Stephen Galloway
Premiere: 2 February 2000, Bockenheimer Depot, Frankfurt

7 to 10 Passages (one-act ballet)
Music: Thom Willems
Text: William Forsythe and Edgar Allen Poe
Stage design and lighting: William Forsythe
Premiere: 23 February 2000, Frankfurt

Kammer/Kammer (full-length ballet)
Music: Johann Sebastian Bach, Heinrich von Bieber, Georg Philipp
Telemann, Johann Sebastian Bach (arr. Ferruccio Busoni), Thom
Willems, and Lynn Anderson ("Cry")
Stage design, lighting, and costumes: William Forsythe
Film: Martin Schwember, First Touch
Video software 'Image/ine': Tom Demeyer/S.T.E.I.M.

Video design: Philip Bussmann
Live video coordination: Agnieszka Trojak
Camera: Ursula Maurer
Sound design: Joel Ryan
Piano: David Morrow
Text: William Forsythe, Anne Carson, and Douglas A. Martin
Premiere: 8 December 2000, Bockenheimer Depot, Frankfurt

2001

Woolf Phrase (one-act ballet)
Music: Ekkehard Ehlers and Thom Willems
Stage design, lighting, and costumes: William Forsythe
Sound design: Bernhard Klein
Text: William Forsythe and Virginia Woolf
Premiere: 15 March 2001, Frankfurt

Woolf Phrase (full-length version including *Bees of the Invisible*)
Music, part 1: Ekkehard Ehlers and Thom Willems
Part 2: David Morrow, William Forsythe, Richard Siegal (electric guitar), and Alessio Silvestrin (tubular bells)
Stage design, lighting, and costumes: William Forsythe
Piano: David Morrow
Sound design: Bernhard Klein, Dietrich Krüger, and Niels Lanz
Text: William Forsythe and Virginia Woolf
Premiere: 21 September 2001, Frankfurt

2002

The Room As It Was (one-act ballet)
Music: Thom Willems
Stage design and lighting: William Forsythe
Costumes: Stephen Galloway
Premiere: 14 February 2002, Frankfurt

Double/Single (one-act ballet)
Music: Johann Sebastian Bach (violin sonatas and partitas) and Thom Willems
Violin: Nathan Milstein
Stage design, lighting, and costumes: William Forsythe
Premiere: 14 April 2002, Ballett Frankfurt, Amsterdam

33/3 (one-act ballet)
Music: Thom Willems in collaboration with Olivier Sliepen
Saxophone: Olivier Sliepen
Stage design, lighting, and costumes: William Forsythe
Tap consultant: Holly Brubach
Premiere: 11 September 2002, Frankfurt

N.N.N.N. (one-act ballet)
Music: Thom Willems
Stage design, lighting, and costumes: William Forsythe
Premiere: 21 November 2002, Frankfurt

2003

Decreation (full-length ballet)
Music: David Morrow (played live onstage)
Stage design: William Forsythe
Lighting: Jan Walther and William Forsythe
Costumes: Claudia Hill
Video design: Philip Bußmann
Sound design: Niels Lanz and Bernhard Klein
Text: William Forsythe and Anne Carson
Dramaturgy: Rebecca Groves
Premiere: 27 April 2003, Frankfurt

Ricercar (one-act ballet)
Music: David Morrow (variations on Johann Sebastian Bach, *Ricercar a 6* from *The Musical Offering*)
Piano: David Morrow
Stage design, lighting, and costumes: William Forsythe
Premiere: 13 November 2003, Frankfurt

2004

Wear (one-act ballet)
Music: Ryoji Ikeda, *Op. 1* (performed live by Ensemble Modern)
Stage design and lighting: William Forsythe
Costumes: Yasco Otomo
Premiere: 22 January 2004, Bockenheimer Depot, Frankfurt

we live here (full-length ballet)
By and with: Yoko Ando, Cyril Baldy, Francesca Caroti, Dana Caspersen, Mauricio de Oliveira, William Forsythe, Stephen Galloway, Amancio Gonzalez, Rebecca Groves, Thierry Guiderdoni, Ayman Harper, Sang Jijia, David Kern, Dietrich Krüger, Marthe Krummenacher, Brock Labrenz, Vanessa le Mat, Jone San Martin, Fabrice Mazliah, Georg Reischl, Heidi Vierthaler, Jan Walther, Thom Willems, and Ander Zabala
Music: Thom Willems
Premiere: 19 April 2004, Frankfurt

Artifact Suite (one-act ballet)
Music: Johann Sebastian Bach, *Chaconne* from *Partita No. 2 in D minor* performed by Nathan Milstein (part I); Eva Crossman-Hecht (part II)
Stage design, lighting, and costumes: William Forsythe
Premiere: 15 September 2004, Scottish National Ballet, Theater Royal, Glasgow

2005

Three Atmospheric Studies (original version) (full-length ballet in two acts)
Music, part 1: David Morrow
Music, part 2: Thom Willems
Speakers, part 2: David Kern and Dana Caspersen
Text, part 2: William Forsythe, Dana Caspersen, and David Kern
Sound design and synthesis: Dietrich Krüger and Niels Lanz
Voice treatment, DSP programming: Andreas Breitscheid, Oliver Pasquet, and Manuel Poletti in collaboration with the Forum Neues Musiktheater Staatsoper Stuttgart
Stage design and lighting: William Forsythe
Light object, part 1: Spencer Finch
Costumes: Satoru Choko and Dorothee Merg
Premiere: 21 April 2005, Bockenheimer Depot, Frankfurt

You made me a monster (performance installation)
Music: sound design by Dietrich Krüger, Niels Lanz, and Hubert Machnik
DSP voice treatments: Andreas Breitscheid and Manuel Poletti in collaboration with the Forum Neues Musiktheater Staatsoper Stuttgart

Lighting: Michael JIV Wagner
Video: Phillip Bussman
Premiere: 28 May 2005, Teatro Piccolo Arsenale, Venice, Italy

the first detail (one-act ballet; new part 1 version of *The Loss of Small Detail*)
Music: Thom Willems (*woundwork I*)
Stage design and lighting: William Forsythe
Costumes: Issey Miyake
Premiere: 16 June 2005, Staatsschauspiel Dresden, Dresden

Clouds After Cranach (full-length ballet in two acts)
Music, part 2: David Morrow
Speakers, part 2: Amancio Gonzalez, David Kern, and Jone San Martin
Text: William Forsythe
Sound design: Dietrich Krüger/Niels Lanz
Voice treatment, DSP programming: Andreas Breitscheid and Manuel Poletti in collaboration with the Forum Neues Musiktheater, Staatsoper Stuttgart
Stage design, lighting, and costumes: William Forsythe
Premiere: 26 November 2005, Bockenheimer Depot, Frankfurt

2006

Three Atmospheric Studies (full-length ballet in three acts; parts 1 and 2: *Clouds after Cranach*; part 3: *Three Atmospheric Studies* original version part 2)
Music, part 2: David Morrow
Speakers, part 2: Amancio Gonzalez, David Kern, and Jone San Martin
Music, part 3: Thom Willems
Speakers, part 3: Dana Caspersen and David Kern
Text, part 3: William Forsythe, Dana Caspersen, and David Kern
Sound design and synthesis: Dietrich Krüger and Niels Lanz
Voice treatment, DSP programming: Andreas Breitscheid, Oliver Pasquet, and Manuel Poletti in collaboration with the Forum Neues Musiktheater Staatsoper Stuttgart
Stage design and lighting: William Forsythe
Costumes: Satoru Choko and Dorothee Merg
Premiere: 2 February 2006, spielzeiteuropa, Haus der Berliner Festspiele, Berlin

Heterotopia (full-length ballet)
Music: Thom Willems
Sound Design: Dietrich Krüger and Niels Lanz
Costumes: Dorothee Merg
Dramaturgy: Freya Vass-Rhee
Premiere: 25 October 2006, Schiffbau Halle I, Zürich, Switzerland

Rong
Music: pop song collage by William Forsythe
Stage design and lighting: William Forsythe
Costumes: Dorothee Merg and Gianni Versace
Premiere: 22 November 2006, Bockenheimer Depot, Frankfurt

2007

Fivefold (one-act ballet)
Music: David Morrow
Costumes: Dorothee Merg
Premiere: 1 February 2007, Festspielhaus Hellerau, Dresden

Angoloscuro/Camerascura (full-length ballet/performance installation in two parts)
Music: Thom Willems; Anna Tenta and David Kern (water glass harp)
Sound design: Niels Lanz
Stage design and lighting: William Forsythe
Software design: Andeas Breitscheid
Video direction: Philip Bussmann
Video design: Philip Bussmann, William Forsythe, and Dietrich Krüger
Assistant, camera programming: Hubert Machnik
Assistant, stage design, part 1: Susanne Brenner
Costumes: William Forsythe, Dorothee Merg, and Issey Miyake
Fabric design: Mina Perhonen
Dramaturgy: Freya Vass-Rhee
Premiere: 3 May 2007, Bockenheimer Depot, Frankfurt

The Defenders (full-length ballet)
Music: Dietrich Krüger and Thom Willems
Sound: Dietrich Krüger
Stage design: William Forsythe
Lighting: Tanja Rühl

Costumes: Dorothee Merg
Technical realization: Max Schubert
Dramaturgy: Imanuel Schipper and Freya Vass-Rhee
Premiere: 4 November 2007, Schiffbau Halle I, Zürich, Switzerland

Nowhere and Everywhere at the Same Time (performance installation;
full-length version)
Music: Thom Willems
Lighting: William Forsythe
Costumes: Dorothee Merg
Premiere: 16 November 2007, Bockenheimer Depot, Frankfurt

2008

Yes We Can't (full-length ballet)
Music: Dietrich Krüger, Niels Lanz, and David Morrow
Lighting: Ulf Naumann and Tanja Rühl,
Costumes: Dorothee Merg
Production assistance: Thierry Guiderdoni and Freya Vass-Rhee
Production scoring software: David Kern
Premiere: 5 March 2008, Festspielhaus Hellerau, Dresden

I don't believe in outer space (full-length ballet)
Music: Thom Willems
Additional texts: Dana Caspersen, Tilman O'Donnell, and William
Forsythe
Stage design: William Forsythe
Lighting: Tanja Rühl and Ulf Naumann
Costumes: Dorothee Merg
Sound design: Niels Lanz
Graphics: Dietrich Krüger
Dramaturgical assistance: Freya Vass-Rhee
Premiere: 20 November 2008, Bockenheimer Depot, Frankfurt

2009

Angoloscuro (new version) (full-length ballet)
Music: Thom Willems, David Kern (water glasses)
Sound design: Niels Lanz
Stage design and lighting: William Forsythe
Costumes: William Forsythe, Dorothee Merg, and Issey Miyake

Assistant, stage design: Susanne Brenner
Dramaturgical assistance: Freya Vass-Rhee
Premiere: 12 February 2009, Bockenheimer Depot, Frankfurt

Two Part Invention (solo for Noah Gelber)
Music: Thom Willems
Premiere: 9 April 2009, Cullen Theater, Houston, Texas

The Returns (full-length ballet)
Music: Dietrich Krüger, Sebastian Rietz, Thom Willems, David Kern, and Ricky Lee Jones
Stage design: William Forsythe
Lighting: Ulf Naumann and Tanja Rühl
Costumes: William Forsythe, Stephen Galloway, and Dorothee Merg
Piano: David Morrow
Graphic design: Dietrich Krüger
Dramaturgical assistance: Freya Vass-Rhee
Premiere: 24 June 2009, Festspielhaus Hellerau, Dresden

Theatrical Arsenal II (full-length ballet in two acts)
Music: Thom Willems
Texts: William Forsythe
Lighting: Tanja Rühl and Ulf Naumann
Costumes: Stephan Galloway
Sound Design: Niels Lanz
Video: Dietrich Krüger
Speakers: Dana Caspersen, David Kern, David Morrow, Tilman O'Donnell, Parvaneh Scharafali, Freya Vass-Rhee, and Ander Zabala (later version: Dana Caspersen, David Kern, Tilman O'Donnell, and Ander Zabala)
Premiere: 20 November 2009, Bockenheimer Depot, Frankfurt

2010

Yes We Can't (**"Barcelona" version**) (full-length ballet in one act)
Music: David Morrow
Lighting: Ulf Naumann and Tanja Rühl
Costumes: Dorothee Merg
Production assistance: Thierry Guiderdoni and Freya Vass-Rhee
Premiere: 16 April 2010, Mercat de Flors, Barcelona

Whole in the Head (one-act ballet)
Music: Thom Willems
Lighting: Tania Rühl and Ulf Naumann
Costumes: Dorothee Merg
Premiere 18 November 2010, Bockenheimer Depot, Frankfurt

2011

Sider (full-length ballet)
Music: Thom Willems
Lighting: Ulf Naumann, Tanja Rühl
Light object: Spencer Finch
Sound design: Niels Lanz
Dramaturgy/production assistance: Billy Bultheel, Freya Vass-Rhee, and Elizabeth Waterhouse
Premiere 16 June 2011, Festspielhaus Hellerau

Rearray (duet for Sylvie Guillem and Nicholas Le Riche)
Music: David Morrow
Premiere: 5 July 2011, Sadler's Wells, London

Now This When Not That (full-length ballet)
Music: Thom Willems
Sound design: Dietrich Krüger, Niels Lanz
Stage: William Forsythe
Technical execution: Max Schubert
Lighting: Ulf Naumann, Tanja Rühl, and William Forsythe
Costumes: William Forsythe and Dorothee Merg
Premiere: 5 October 2011, Jahrhunderthalle Bochum

2012

Stellentstellen (full-length ballet)
Music: Thom Willems and David Kern
Light: Ulf Naumann, Tanja Rühl
Costumes: William Forsythe and Dorothee Merg
Premiere: 3 February 2012, Bockenheimer Depot, Frankfurt am Main

Study #1 (full-length ballet)
Music Thom Willems
Stage: Dietrich Krüger, Patrick Lauckner, Max Schubert
Lighting: Ulf Naumann, Tanja Rühl

Sound design: Mara Brinker, Dietrich Krüger, Jennifer Weeger
Costumes: Dorothee Merg
Premiere: 14 November 2012, Frankfurt LAB

Neue Suite
Music: Georg Friederich Händel, Johann Sebastian Bach, Luciano Berio, Thom Willems, and Gavin Bryars
Stage design and lighting: William Forsythe
Sound design: Sebastian Rietz
Costumes: William Forsythe and Yumiko Takeshima
Premiere: 25 February 2012, Semperoper Dresden

Study #3 (full-length ballet)
Music: Thom Willems
Stage: William Forsythe
Licht: Ulf Naumann, Tanja Rühl
Costumes: William Forsythe and Dorothee Merg
Dramaturgy: Freya Vass-Rhee
Premiere: 20 April 2012, Teatro Grande, Brescia

2013

Selon (full-length ballet)
Music: Thom Willems
Text: David Kern and Tilman O'Donnell
Stage: William Forsythe
Lighting: Ulf Naumann and Tanja Rühl
Costumes: William Forsythe and Dorothee Merg
Dramaturgy: Freya Vass-Rhee
Assistance: Simón Hanukai
Premiere: 17 May, 2013, Hellerau—Europäisches Zentrum der Künste Dresden

2016

Blake Works I (one-act ballet)
Music: James Blake (from the album *The Colour in Anything*)
Stage: William Forsythe
Lighting: Tanja Rühl and William Forsythe
Costumes: William Forsythe and Dorothee Merg
Premiere: 4 July 2016, Ballet de l'Opéra de Paris, Palais Garnier, Paris

Catalogue (First Edition) (one-act ballet)
Choreography: William Forsythe in collaboration with Jill Johnson,
Brit Rodemund, and Christopher Roman
Lighting: Benjamin Schälike
Sound: Stephan Wöhrmann, Mattef Kuhlmey
Premiere: 7 October 2016, Dance On Ensemble, Theater im Pfalzbau,
Ludwigshafen

2018

Playlist (Track 1, 2) (one-act ballet)
Music: Peven Everett, Lion Babe (Jax Jones remix)
Stage design and costumes: William Forsythe
Lighting: Tanja Rühl
Premiere: 12 April 2018, English National Ballet, Sadler's Wells, London

Pas de Deux Cent Douze
Music: Azealia Banks
Premiere: 27 April 2018, The Shed, New York City

A Quiet Evening of Dance (full-length ballet; incorporates *Catalogue
[Second Edition]* and *Duo* as *Dialogue [DUO2015]*)
Choreography: William Forsythe and Brigel Gjoka, Jill Johnson,
Christopher Roman, Parvaneh Scharafali, Riley Watts, Rauf
"Rubberlegz" Yasit, and Ander Zabala
Music: Morton Feldman and Jean-Philippe Rameau
Light: Tanja Rühl and William Forsythe
Sound design: Niels Lanz
Costumes: Dorothee Merg and William Forsythe
Premiere: 4 October 2018, Sadler's Wells, London

2019

Playlist (EP) (one-act ballet)
Music: Peven Everett, Abra, Lion Babe (Jax Jones remix), Khalid, Barry
White, and Natalie Cole
Stage design and costumes: William Forsythe
Lighting: Tanja Rühl
Premiere: 7 March 2019, Boston Ballet, Boston Opera House

2021

The Barre Project (*Blake Works II*) (performance for film)
Music: James Blake
Production Design: William Forsythe
Light: Brandon Stirling Baker
Costumes: Janie Taylor, Harriet Jung and Reid Bartelme, Tiler Peck
Designs for Body Wrappers, EPTM Los Angeles
Technical direction: Jonny Forance
Director of Photography/Editing: Devin Jamieson
Executive Producers: Jon Arpino, Tiler Peck, Teddy Forance, William Forsythe
Producers: Chris Quazzo, Jordan Richbart
Premiere: 25 March 2021

12 N (premiered as *N.N.N.N.N.N.N.N.N.N.N.N.N.*) (one-act ballet)
Music: Thom Willems
Stage, lighting, and costumes: William Forsythe
Premiere: 3 December 2021, Netherlands Dans Theater, Amare, The Hague, The Netherlands

2022

Blake Works II (The Barre Project) (one-act ballet)
Music: James Blake
Light: Brandon Stirling Baker
Costumes: Janie Taylor, Harriet Jung and Reid Bartelme, Tiler Peck
Premiere: 4 March 2022, New York City Center, New York

Blake Works III (The Barre Project) (one-act ballet)
Music: James Blake
Light: Brandon Stirling Baker
Costumes: Janie Taylor, Harriet Jung and Reid Bartelme, Tiler Peck
Premiere: 5 May 2022, Boston Ballet, Citizens Bank Opera House, Boston

Défilé (one-act ballet)
Music: soundscape by William Forsythe and Mischa Santora
Light: Tanja Rühl
Costumes: William Forsythe
Premiere: 3 November 2022, Boston Ballet, Citizens Bank Opera House, Boston

2023

Blake Works IV (The Barre Project) (one-act-ballet)
Music: James Blake
Light: Brandon Stirling Baker
Costumes: William Forsythe, Katy A. Freeman
Premiere: 20 January 2023, Dance Theatre of Harlem, Penn Live Arts/Annenberg Center, Philadelphia

Blake Works V (The Barre Project) (full-length ballet in three parts: *Prologue, The Barre Project* and *Blake Works I*)
Music: James Blake
Light: Tanja Rühl; for *The Barre Project* based on an original design by Brandon Stirling Baker
Costumes: William Forsythe
Premiere: 10 May, 2023, Ballet Company of Teatro alla Scala, Milan, Italy

INDEX[1]

---

[1] Note: Page numbers followed by 'n' refer to notes.

Printed in the USA
CPSIA information can be obtained
at www.ICGtesting.com
LVHW011657310823
756878LV00006B/173